Lynn Bue

Numerology
OF Astrology
Degrees of the Sun

Publications by
Lynn Buess

Numerology for the New Age

Forever Numerology.

Numerology: Nuances in Relationships

Heart of Numerology

Numerology
OF Astrology
Degrees of the Sun

Lynn Buess, MA, Eds

For more information about special discounts for bulk purchases, please contact Light Technology Publishing Special Sales at 1-800-450-0985 or publishing@LightTechnology.net

ISBN-13: 978-1-62233-011-9
Published and printed in the United States of America by:

PO Box 3540
Flagstaff, AZ 86003
800-450-0985
www.lighttechnology.com

Contents

Preface

My introduction to astrology plunged me into a lifelong metaphysical path of self-awareness and personal growth some fifty-three years ago. I was in high school at the time. I picked up one of the Dell horoscope booklets at the local pharmacy and began to read. As I have recounted candidly many times since, I wondered how that person could tell so many things about me that even friends and relatives did not know. I had not given the author any information nor participated in any form of testing.

The quest to know has never ended, and it has taken me on a vast journey through myriad studies and systems of self-growth. My many previous books will attest to that journey and serve as a reminder of the constant ongoing process the journey truly is. I ended up as a practitioner in many of the alternative arts of consciousness, and I am probably most well known for accomplishments in the field of numerology.

I studied astrology for some time back then, but I never reached the level of a professional practitioner. I have a grasp of astrology basics that has served me often in counseling work over the years. I have always felt that numerology and astrology work hand in hand. Although each stands powerfully on its own, when you combine the two, there is a far greater amount of insight and potential assistance that can be rendered to those who seek the wisdom of these divine arts.

This book is my first attempt to open up the exchange and integration of information that will hopefully be of benefit to practitioners of both studies. It is just an introduction. There is much more that could be said. I have a writing style that is succinct and to the point. These paragraphs are but glimpses of what could be shared. I encourage those who see the value in this book to take the outline, as it is, and develop these concepts more thoroughly and extensively, along with the metaphors and anecdotes, to give them additional breadth and depth for a more expanded human experience.

— Lynn Buess, 2013

Read This before You Start

Even if you only have a basic understanding of astrology, it is very simple for you to obtain an accurate sun degree for yourself using your birth information. You can obtain a free natal chart from multiple astrology sources on the Internet. Just search for the term "free natal horoscope" or "free natal chart," and choose one of the websites from the results. Enter your birth information, and look for the number listed next to your sun sign, such as "Sun, Libra, 22.41." With this information, go to the chapter for your sun sign, "Libra" for the sake of this example, and look up the 22nd degree (22.41).

While you read the descriptions for your sun sign, the question may arise, "How can so much be said about a single degree?" I have studied and taught esoteric cosmology for decades. As a part of that teaching, I have come to believe that the infusion of divine consciousness comes from the Central Sun (or greater Logos). It then transmits through our own solar Logos into the soul at birth. The solar degree marks the point of infusion from the Central Sun. Its angle of degree gives us a clue about the nature of the impulse coming in at the moment of birth.

It is my feeling that the sun degree serves a role of pinpointing just where the soul has the opportunity to make significant strides in personal growth or potentially stumble into a setback. A combination of the numerical value of the degree and the sun sign are blended together to offer insight about the nature of that commitment. Depending on the aspects and other correlations, the struggle is tougher for some than others.

Also, be aware that the closeness of the degree leads to bleed-through, so there is always some influence from the degree on either side, especially when the minutes following the degree are at the high or low range. If toward the low end, the cusp influence leans toward the previous degree. So it follows that if the minutes are toward the high-end, influence leans from the next degree. For example, with 0 degree 24 minutes (0.24) Cancer, you will want to also look closely at 29 degrees Gemini.

The experienced astrologer is aware of the influence of these cusps — that is, the overlaps of influence from the nearby degrees. It has been my perception that by reading the description of the previous degree, you can receive further insight into leftover issues and opportunities to recognize yet other unresolved issues. There are shades of influence that can be gleaned by giving attention to the prior degree. The subsequent, or following, degree can also reveal carried-over karmic residue, and it can particularly reveal additional clues for working through the current indicated karmic challenges of your primary degree.

When dealing with human nature, you have to consider that no matter how pure the cosmic or divine impulse coming in, it is still subject to the influence of the personal ego. Depending on the negativity and strength of the ego, the impulse can be significantly distorted or redirected. There is always a possibility that you could take an almost opposite path as the descriptions provided. Such is the ever-present paradox of human growth and potential. I have tried to carve a kind of middle road by including a little divine impulse and a little ego distortion.

Each chapter can vary to some degree in terms of how the emphasis is placed. When under stress and when the aspects are more negative and challenging, the personality may revert to the karmic tendencies rather than choosing expanded opportunities to move into greater growth and manifestation of light. A clue to probable behavior can be deduced by looking at the degrees and signs of the progressed chart. The coming challenges and opportunities for growth can be thusly charted.

Keep an Open Mind

These descriptions are not intended to be entirely derivative of your behavior. They represent a part of your character makeup. The behavior patterns can become particularly noticeable when progressed aspects trigger a degree or as planets transit a specific degree. If you do not believe in reincarnation and karma, simply substitute the word "subconscious" for "karma," since the karmic descriptions are reflected in the subconscious and therefore have validity by any name.

Having conducted nearly 10,000 or more past-life regressions over the many years of my work, I have witnessed more than enough supportive information for even me to doubt the reality of prior memories. If you cannot accept such a possibility, you might think of the pattern being discussed as having been rooted in the genetic and soul memories of your family predecessors.

Because of my therapeutic background and psychological training, I often tend to delve into subconscious cracks and crevices of consciousness. Some people seem to find this to be negative and threatening. The American

NUMEROLOGY OF ASTROLOGY

population particularly likes to be entertained with flattering and cutesy personality profiles. Such writings have their place, and many writers accentuate such themes. However, I prefer to put emphasis on the areas of consciousness where my professional background and prying Scorpio personality like to go.

I hope to stimulate the reader into further self-exploration and personal growth by stepping on a few unconscious toes, particularly if it helps to bring repressed issues out into the light and enables the resolution of unconscious conflicts. These descriptions are intended to increase awareness and accelerate personal growth by doing just that: bringing hidden issues and latent potential into the light for resolution. As the reader knows, there is always another side to every description. It is the dual nature of humanity and the ongoing wrestling match between the conscious desire to manifest the light and the underlying negative issues that reside within the dark side.

Obviously, these descriptions will not be exactly accurate for everyone since charts are modified by other factors. They are primarily designed for awakened and searching souls who have made a commitment to clear up their lives and live more closely in alignment with cosmic design rather than remain buried in the darkness of subconscious patterns of victimhood and dysfunction.

The descriptions are archetypal in nature, and it may be necessary to tone them down in some cases. Or you may have to modify them a trifle according to other influences in your chart. Placing too much attention on one degree can lead to missing the greater significance of the entire chart. The proper integration of these descriptions is best done by examining the complete chart with a professional astrologer or through personal investigation as a true seeker of light. Using your inner knowledge to uncover these attributes of your own natal chart can bring both revelation and relief.

A note on the notables: Every effort has been made to be as accurate as possible with the information provided in this section. These details have been collected from posted websites and other sources and, as such, depend on the accuracy of these sources. In some instances, rectification charts might be warranted.

ARIES

0 Degree of Aries

If this is your sun sign, you will likely find yourself far ahead of your contemporaries as they falter and doubt. The paradoxical side of this number-sign combination is such that you may find yourself stalled while those around you push ahead with gusto in pursuit of their life interests. Most likely, you are the first on your block to have the latest toy. Or

NOTABLES WITH THIS DEGREE:

William Shatner: Canadian-American actor, musician, singer, director, author

Timothy Dalton: British actor

if you can't get it, you may make it. At best, you do not recognize barriers that other people put in the way of getting what they want out of life.

There is a karmic hint that in another time and setting, you were in a perfect position to take initiative and spark an advancement in culture. Perhaps you were afraid. Perhaps you became power hungry and tried to control everything rather than share. You find yourself wanting to do something bold and different. There is some reticence because you are concerned about rejection and possible humiliation. You are skeptical and cautious. This is the time to know who you are, what you know, and do something with the extraordinary insight that you have been given in this moment.

Your somewhat enigmatic nature makes you intriguing to some and vexing to others. Your air of mystery can be a magnet to attract someone willing to support and invest in a perceived crazy notion. On the other hand, it can be seen as put-offish behavior that can drive away someone with exactly the same intent. Be truthful with yourself about what you have and with others about what you would like to accomplish. Note: this includes the need for discretion and knowing who to trust. You can get excited about a lot of things, and you can get others excited too. Now is a good time to get them excited about something that you have.

1ˢᵗ Degree of Aries

If this is your sun sign, you are impulsive, quick, and always ready to jump into the next adventure at hand. Your willingness to try the new and do the unusual can lead you into paths others fear to tread. This can result in enormous success and accomplishment and potentially a lot of trouble. For you particularly, it is essential to give some attention to the consequences of your actions before blindly plunging into something new. At the same time, you do not want to interfere with that wonderful enthusiasm that so dynamically motivates you. This is a tricky balance to learn. There is less karmic pressure from this combination than some of the others. This leaves you with less unconscious pressure to cope with what comes your way.

NOTABLES WITH THIS DEGREE:

Chico Marx: American comedian

Stephen Sondheim: American composer, lyricist, Broadway producer

Joan Crawford: American actress

Kaiser Wilhelm I: King of Prussia, first German Emperor

You will be found at the forefront of new things, and you are attracted to people who are at the cutting edge of ideas and innovation. You quickly become bored with routine, and you are at your best in situations in which you are constantly challenged to meet changing conditions and parameters. Travel is always on your mind, whether it is in the material world or on other levels of mind and spirit. Your life path will include many options and alterations, but in the end, you will leave knowing that you did not miss a chance.

Your proclivity to try everything can lead you to make choices in which you can become quickly addicted and unable to extract yourself. You can become intoxicated with change and fail to completely learn the experience right in front of you. This can be a quick trip of denial. Your life will be full of adventure and constantly stimulating events. You can get much done in the karmic accumulation of vital experience. For most of you, this indicates the opportunity for travel and mingling with a wide range of people and social variations. You are found at the forefront of pioneering ventures and can become more than interested in events of chance.

NUMEROLOGY OF ASTROLOGY

2nd Degree of Aries

If this is your sun sign, you are charming, changeable, and challenging. This somewhat perplexing combination bestows you a softer touch than the more blunt and direct Aries tendency. At best, you use this tact to successfully weave your way through the many variable human interactions of life. Your diplomatic skills combined with the hard driving Aries personality can lead to opportunities for leadership roles. Your idealism and enthusiasm can be infectious and serve as an inspiration for others who tend to procrastinate about getting started with what they wish to accomplish.

NOTABLES WITH THIS DEGREE:

Wolf Blitzer: American television journalist, author

Werner von Braun: German rocket scientist

Michelle Monaghan: American actress

Steve McQueen: American actor

Alyson Hannigan: American actress

Dane Rudhyar: French astrologer, author, composer

You may have mixed feelings about social norms and arbitrary rules of behavior. You alternately rebel against social regulations and attempt to earn social recognition. There is a karmic hint of having at one time stood up against severe regulations imposed on the society in which you lived. Your rebellious actions may have led to the harm of many people. This leaves you with both guilt and doubt when taking a stand on current events. Nevertheless, you are determined to be a force of change and reformation anywhere you see social incompetence and abuse taking place.

Your impatience with deception and spin doctoring may find you involved in cases of fraud or misrepresentation. You aspire to the highest level of integrity. Although you are realistic about facts, it is difficult to traverse life without the use of a few white lies. At best, you are quick to see how to get a project started and astute in knowing how to address the details in order to prevent the waste of time and resources. This combination suggests a direct and open demeanor and readiness to address issues right up front. You are quick, efficient, and effective at what you do.

3rd Degree of Aries

If this is your sun sign, the traditional Aries qualities of spontaneity and enthusiasm are boosted up a notch. Troubled aspects and houses can put a damper on some of this pizzazz, but when favorable, you blossom and shine like a bright flower in the forest. Your buoyant optimism encourages others less hopeful to carry on through the stressful moments of doubt and despair. You can be brilliantly imaginative in moments of crisis and under the pressure of a deadline. People with this combination are often spokespersons or communicators of some kind. Poor aspects may diminish some of your shining personality.

NOTABLES WITH THIS DEGREE:

Aretha Franklin: American singer, musician

Gloria Steinem: American feminist, journalist, social and political activist

Clyde Barrow: American gangster (Bonnie and Clyde)

Tom Monaghan: American entrepreneur, created Domino's pizza

Elton John: English singer, songwriter, composer, actor

There is a karmic hint that in another life cycle, you may have been part of an incident that brought gloom and doom to your world. You feel guilty for taking away the joy of living from so many people and punish yourself by believing you do not deserve to have happiness or joy any more. Therefore, you often unconsciously sabotage the opportunity to have good things happen. You are once again learning that life can be a joy and that you deserve to share this with all people. You will be drawn to opportunities to clear out subconscious debris and move on with a more positive life pattern.

There is a gregarious presence with this combination that makes you a natural as a host or hostess. You move among people easily and enjoy sharing conversations with friends and strangers alike. You are the artists and talkers of your trade. Sexuality and creativity get much attention from this combination. You would be very effective working with people who have experienced sexual abuse and misuse in childhood. Perhaps this happened to you. Once in touch with your healthy sexual potential, you can direct that force into masterpieces of accomplishment and novel, but practical, contributions to the world.

4th Degree of Aries

If this is your sun sign, you are determined to get ahead and to do well in whatever field you choose. This combination gives staying power to the easily switchable Aries temperament. You go where others may fear to tread and stay longer than others endure. Many of you could be attracted to professions such as engineering, architecture, or mechanically oriented fields. If you find medicine or science interesting, it may well lead you into the examination of the body or related studies. You wonder how things tick and like to take them apart to figure out just how they do.

NOTABLES WITH THIS DEGREE:

Peyton Manning: American professional football player

Howard Cosell: American sports announcer

James Lovell: American astronaut, U.S. Navy captain

Larry Page: American billionaire computer engineer, cofounded Google

Steve Ballmer: American billionaire computer executive, Microsoft CEO

There is the karmic hint of having been careless and incomplete in previous endeavors. Your oversight most likely resulted in the suffering of many others. Perhaps you blame the system of education for the errors. Or perhaps you blame the institution that you represented. You are outspoken about those who act on impulse and without proper preparation. You strive to be thorough and accurate in your work and in your assessment of others. This is a unique combination that gives you imagination along with the staying power to turn your projections into completed projects.

Your curiosity about the human body may take you into the field of biology or anatomy. You want to bring justice to human sexuality, and you may well find yourself speaking out about the topic in your community. There is a deep desire to promote balance and harmony between the sexes. Once you take on a cause, you most likely follow it to the end, whether it is a bitter end or a delightful conclusion to an often-beleaguered effort. You are a little more open and lighthearted than some of your more serious Aries brethren. This makes for some great moments with friends and loved ones.

5th Degree of Aries

If this is your sun sign, you are fiery, fun, free-spirited, and sometimes fickle. It is difficult to keep you contained, as you constantly come up with something different — and sometimes disturbing — compared to the more conservative thinkers of your time. Since you rarely stay within the norms of the status quo, you can serve as a valuable consultant with a twist. Your distance allows you to recognize what does not work so that you can suggest alternatives to bring resolution. You can do this even when your solutions might be considered too extreme or radical to some of those you advise.

NOTABLES WITH THIS DEGREE:

Diana Ross: American singer, actress

Bob Woodward: American investigative journalist, social activist, author

Jennifer Grey: American actress, dancer

Jim Parsons: American actor

There is a karmic hint that in another setting you may have been fearful, repressed, or unable to trust yourself taking any bold steps or initiative. Perhaps you hid your personality and would not speak up when your inner self knew it was time to do so. Maybe you were unconventional and afraid of public reaction. You are now learning to express yourself at the proper time and in the proper place. You are acquiring the skill to react to resistance with a positive approach and to be respectful of others but not intimidated.

Your boundless energy and willingness to take on the seeming impossible attracts others who want to believe and assist you. You have the potential for a great sense of humor, and you may use this in tense situations to disarm opposition and turn skeptics into allies. There will be chances to travel and see many things that most of the population will never get to. You draw from a wide perspective of human experience and social customs that enables you to quickly assess another person's personality and then adjust your style in order to get along with and learn about them. You will have many friends and associates who come from diverse social environments.

6th Degree of Aries

If this is your sun sign, you have a golden heart and wonderful way of going about assisting other people you meet along life's road. It may not always be that easy. We all have our downsides, and you struggle with dysfunctions just like the rest of us. However, once you have taken care to face your issues and break out into the stream of expanded consciousness, your life can be full of extraordinary moments of human encounter. You are fiercely independent, but this allows you to give other people the opportunity to be themselves as well. This creates a comfort zone around you and allows others to be open and comfortable, revealing themselves to you.

There is the karmic hint that in another life experience, you were likely extremely self-centered and inconsiderate to others. Perhaps you were just neglectful, or you may have taken an active role in some form of mistreatment. There is still a part of you that can turn off and be indifferent, but you are learning to take responsibility and see others as important as your own self. The acceptance of this past pattern can make it easier for you to look into the heart of another person and know just what it is you can do to be of service or render some form of healing.

You have an openness and childlike candor that allows for great fun, humor, and camaraderie among friends. You are clever about seeing alternative ways of getting things done and love to improvise on the spot and pull off tasks that others thought to be impossible. Many of you will be active in service organizations and community-oriented programs that empower those who are less fortunate. You are always looking for rainbows over the horizon and bring cheer to the concerned.

NOTABLES WITH THIS DEGREE:

Vicki Lawrence: American television actress, comedienne

Maxim Gorky: Russian writer, founder of Socialist Realism literary method, political activist, playwright

Quentin Tarantino: American actor, director, screenwriter

Mariah Carey: American singer, songwriter, record producer, actress

Gloria Swanson: American actress, singer, dancer

7th Degree of Aries

If this is your sun sign, you are studious, sagacious, and somewhat more serious than many of your Aries contemporaries. The best of this combination mixes Aries excitement and enthusiasm with an analytical overtone that can result in breakthroughs of thinking and the exploration of how previously uninvestigated theories or inventions might have a place in present society. Your penchant for research and analysis may take you into arcane and rarefied realms of intellectual and speculative thought. Spiritual and metaphysical speculation comes easily to many of you with this combination.

There is a kind of tension between the obvious, rational explanation of things and the impulse to forage out into frontiers of behavior that is not always socially accepted. You seek control. You get caught in impulsiveness that can place you in awkward and embarrassing moments. There is a karmic hint of having been stuck in a rigid belief system in another time and place. You were not able to flex with obvious new information and were likely threatened by the demand for a change of thinking. Perhaps your resistance resulted in the delay and development of reforms and revisions that could have spared the population a lot of anguish.

You rail vociferously against those who control and impede the flow of information. Freedom is important to you, and you want the same for everyone. While other Aries personalities may go on a hunch and a prayer, you have crafted a very clever plan that you believe will lead to your desired goals. You have the mental tools to follow through on instincts and are able to develop your impulses into tangible demonstrations of success. Thus, it is likely that many of you will rise to a recognized level of success in the circle of interest that you have chosen.

NOTABLES WITH THIS DEGREE:

Stacy Ferguson, "Fergie": American singer, songwriter, actress, fashion designer

Reba McEntire: American country music singer, songwriter, actress

Vince Vaughn: American actor, screenwriter, director, producer

Kevin Loughery: American professional basketball player, coach

Kenneth Arnold: American pilot, UFO-event celebrity

8th Degree of Aries

If this is your sun sign, you are quick, cagey, and like to be on top. Aries personalities frequently appear to have a childlike innocence that can be most beguiling. With this combination, such an apparently naïve appearance often masks a strongly assertive, even aggressive, core behavior. You are not inclined to accept things the way they are, and you constantly turn over stones in search of new things and new ways to do things. Your flair for promotion may attract you to some form of marketing or promotional work. This combination lends itself to management and leadership potential, and when you find the right spot, you can rise to the top of the organization in a hurry.

NOTABLES WITH THIS DEGREE:

Sam Walton: American business magnate, founder of Wal-Mart

Lady Gaga: American singer, songwriter, record producer, fashion designer, activist

Eugene McCarthy: American politician, poet, U.S. congressperson

Dave Greenfield: English rock musician

John Tyler: American president, senator, judge

There is a karmic hint or an old pattern of greed and perhaps the arrogance of having had power. You can become a bit pompous when under pressure. Perhaps you feel an almost compulsive need to give back something to others. Perhaps at some time in your previous soul journey, you took life and property at will. You could be attracted to some form of philanthropy or service-oriented type of business. Your go-getter attitude does not leave much room for those who are lazy and indifferent about what they do.

When you let your hair down, you can be dazzling, dynamic, and full of fun. There is a mischievous side to your nature that can be most playful and at times silly. Unfortunately, you are not likely to show this side to others very frequently. Your serious side does not have much time for the seemingly frivolous and foolhardy. Your aggressive and direct manner of approaching things can be intimidating to many, but in the end, you attract the doers of the world who gather around you to help make your dreams become accomplishments.

9ᵗʰ Degree of Aries

If this is your sun sign, you may reach high for perfection and come down perplexed. The idealism of Aries is accentuated by this combination, but at the same time, there is a troublesome duality of differences. The nine vibration emphasizes the collective we. The Aries personality says "me." On one level, this sets up a heightened conflict between the personality ego and the aspiration of the soul. This is a time of testing to see if you hold on to the ego or if you take a leap of trust and become more in touch with your enlightened self.

NOTABLES WITH THIS DEGREE:

Eric Clapton: English singer, guitarist, composer

Warren Beatty: American actor, producer, director, screenwriter

Gabrielle Drake: British actress

Amy Sedaris: American actress, comedienne, author

Jerry Lucas: American professional basketball player, memory education spokesperson

The karmic hint suggests another sequence of soul travel in which you reached a time of transition wherein you could step into a higher level of evolution. Perhaps you held onto a relationship or some other attachment. Perhaps you feared the unknown and chose not to take the step of transition. Perhaps some lingering guilt of past transgressions made you feel unworthy to take the step. This can be one of those "dark night of the soul" lifetimes. It is not easy to let go of ego and take the step toward immortality. You are at the threshold of a grand awakening.

You are idealistic and look for the best within others and from the world around you. A downside of this combination is that you can live in an illusionary world of wonderfulness and fail to see the abuse and misleading behavior right at your doorstep. All in all, you are a breath of fresh air to many weary and downtrodden souls. Your passion and enthusiasm for life are an inspiration to many. Your imagination and creative mind work overtime. You have a high potential for inventiveness and originality that may lead to a refreshing contribution to all.

10th Degree of Aries

If this is your sun sign, you are frequently found around change and new things that are getting started. Your infectious enthusiasm is contagious, and you are a marvel at inspiring other people to get started with things that are new and ever changing. This combination fits the quintessential archetype for Aries daring and dash. You plunge into the unknown like a voyager of old, and then you are off again on a new tangent before anyone can catch their breath. It can be difficult for you to stick with some things long enough to grasp the full benefit of what is happening.

There is a karmic hint that in another time and setting you were a part in reformation or realigning the direction of a large population of people. Perhaps there is pride or ego attached to the need for recognition and applause for daring and drama in the quest of introducing innovation to society. Perhaps you have manipulated facts and figures to justify your cause or belief. You will find yourself in situations that require strict accenting of your suppositions and verification of claims. It is important to be sure that those who give you information are not attached to an agenda that would cause them to feed you false information.

There is a certain charm and almost naïve quality about most of you that make you adorable and easily liked. Your openness and willingness to learn make it comfortable for people to share their personal ideas and beliefs with ease. This makes it easier for you to extract needed information and move on to the next step in the puzzle of your cosmic quest. You are a traveler in time and unlimited by space. You take many people through the portal of the unknowing and allow them to taste a of glimpse of becoming all knowing.

NOTABLES WITH THIS DEGREE:

Herb Alpert: American musician, orchestra leader

Maximilian I: Holy Roman Emperor, patron of the arts and sciences

Celine Dion: Canadian pop singer, actress, entrepreneur

René Descartes: French philosopher, mathematician, scientist, author

Otto von Bimarck: prince of Bismarck, duke of Lauenburg, statesman

11ᵗʰ Degree of Aries

If this is your sun sign, you are charming, capable, and clever at coping your way through the dysfunctional web of society's games. You may go through a landslide of emotional issues before settling into a more conventional life mode. The combination of the Aries drive and the energetic eleven vibration increases the chance that you will be active at some point in your life as a public figure. This could be leading the PTA in your hometown or dancing on the stage of life in front of thousands. You have a kind of wholesome persona that captures people's trust and makes it easy for them to like you.

You may not find it so easy to make choices in life and could find yourself the center of speculation and even controversy for some of the decisions you make. You may find yourself at odds with social opinion during this lifetime. There is a karmic hint of having flaunted social norms and standards in another time and situation of soul experience. You may have been punished or shamed for personal activity that was contradictory to the status quo of that era. Even in this present reality, you struggle between personal choices and the public perception of the behavior that your choose.

You are idealistic and would like to be able to please all you meet. However, this can get you into some tight places, as there are those who will call you wishy-washy and perhaps even forked tongued. You will learn with time that you cannot please everyone. You will also learn to do what is true to you and pleases the best part of you. The best results can come from just being yourself rather than trying to perform all of the time. You set your standards pretty high, and there is deep gratification when you reach them.

NOTABLES WITH THIS DEGREE:

Hans Christian Andersen: Danish author, poet, children's entertainer

Magdalena Maleeva: Bulgarian tennis professional, environmental activist

Jane Adams: American actress

Al Gore: American vice president, social activist, philanthropist

Abraham Maslow: American psychologist, pioneered humanistic psychology

12th Degree of Aries

If this is your sun sign, you might just be more hesitant to take a step into change that seems matter of fact to many of your Aries family members. You can become more deliberate and cautious rather than quick and fearless at the forefront of the next possibility. You sometimes almost seem ashamed to have things go well for you. This can be a great antidote for the Aries' occasional impulsiveness. It can also be a serious detriment to your personal growth if it turns into a neurotic fear. When you are in balance with the self, you can be a good advisor or counselor for others, as you mix daring and restraint with understanding and an impeccable sense of timing.

NOTABLES WITH THIS DEGREE:

Sergei Rachmaninoff: Russian composer, conductor, pianist

Rodney King: American, victim of police brutality

Debbie Reynolds: American actress, singer, dancer

Walter Chrysler: American automobile pioneer

There is the karmic hint that during another soul episode, you may have had to forfeit a passionate personal dream because of the needs and demands of someone else's authority. You may hold resentment because of the loss of opportunity that meant so much to you. Perhaps your wants were ignored for the betterment of the collective good. Perhaps your life was considered worth less than that of someone you disrespected and possibly despised. Perhaps you gave up something for all, and then the entire matter turned out senseless and it failed. You may resent having been placed into the mess when you truly believed the whole matter would not succeed. You seek to find a balance within that enables you to recognize the most appropriate decision and then go forth and do what you must do without attachment to results.

There is a tendency under stress to take on a roll of acting in order to get your point across more effectively. Your awareness is in touch with such a wide panorama of human experience that you can alternately play on the sympathy of the crowd and then turn brazenly aggressive with a pronounced ego and peacock-like display of personal pride. You prey on the worried and wronged memories within the collective consciousness. You enjoy bringing hidden weaknesses in people to light. At best, you offer direction for each soul to find its own source of strength and purpose.

13th Degree of Aries

If this is your sun sign, you are transfixed on the issues of life and the consequences of dying. To be caught in this huge existential dichotomy can have many resultant variables of reaction and behavior. You may feel overwhelmed and give up trying to grasp the dilemma. You may take escapist routes to get away from the issues. You may delve deeply into the meaning of life and death and the ramifications of how you treat living. Whatever path you take, you will most likely find yourself observing and then, in some way, disseminating to others what you have learned.

There is a karmic hint that in a previous life sequence you were involved in the death or destruction of a large group of people, such as a state or tribe. There is leftover guilt from having seen the loss of life and property of so many people that you personally knew. You are quick to spot the process of deterioration within a government or society, and you may find yourself speaking out in protest of misuse of public funds or resources. You know that when the family and clan unit breaks down, a society is weakened and ripe to be overthrown or succumb to internal collapse. You find yourself particularly sensitive to moral breakdown among those who lead.

You are energetic and quick to get started when you become interested in something. Your innovation places you close to pioneers of progress as well as wherever invention and imagination flourish. You are funny and frank about life and its harsh realities. You are trusted as an advisor because you will call an ace an ace when another person may waver, knowing that your inquisitors want to hear another answer. Many of you will flourish in the arts and areas of imagination and entertainment.

NOTABLES WITH THIS DEGREE:

Eddie Murphy: American actor, writer, singer, director, comedian

Dick Sutphen: American New Age author, spokesperson

Doris Chase Doane: American astrologer, author

Émile Zola: French author known for naturalist and romantic style

Mistinguette: French singer, actress, one of the highest-paid female entertainers of her time

14th Degree of Aries

If this is your sun sign, you are adventurous, admired, and able to transcend the everyday routines of life. You have an almost cosmic view of life and see things in a greater perspective than most. Your expanded vision makes you a good planner and in some cases a futurist. Those who are more intellectual and abstract in approaching tasks often appreciate your nuts-and-bolts approach to theoretical matters. This is not to say that you are without keen mental skills. In the end, you love to take on challenges, particularly those that can mend conflicts and improve the human condition.

NOTABLES WITH THIS DEGREE:

Maya Angelou: American author, poet

Marlon Brando: American actor

Andrei Tarkovsky: Russian-Soviet writer, filmmaker, opera director

Isoroku Yamamoto: Japanese admiral, fleet commander

Aki Kaurismäki: Finnish screenwriter, director

There is a karmic hint of having been part of incidents in which many suffered and went through the pangs of chaos and loss of possessions, perhaps life itself. You strive to be benign and of benefit to all. You would like to be an idealist, but you could be thrown into a world that requires you to deal with the harsh realities of life. More than likely, you find yourself taking part in peace movements and programs of social empowerment. There is the feeling of having a destiny, and you are driven to get things right within your soul.

Many of you will be fortunate to travel and be introduced to a variety of class and culture. On your list will be a desire to see ancient sites of power and transcendental cultural achievements. You enjoy being around people who are at the forefront of their chosen professions or life quests. There is a healing quality about your presence, and you are a welcomed friend and comrade among those with whom you associate. Many of you are attracted to the paranormal and transcendental philosophies that seek to better grasp the role of humanity in the whole cosmic scheme of things.

15th Degree of Aries

If this is your sun sign, there is an enigma that follows you that is not easy to detect, nor is it easy to discover. You like to see yourself as radiating the ever-present Aries torch of optimism and idealistic delight. However, there lurks the oft-troubling presence of that nagging element of the dark side that has not yet been comfortably integrated into your outer personality. If you continue to run from it, your life and works will remain troubled and incomplete. If you work with it and integrate that hidden side of the self, you will blossom into a penetrating and observant purveyor of human growth and potential.

There is the karmic clue of having trampled a few toes and stomped on some hopeful hearts in an earlier life sojourn. Perhaps you were a proud leader, unwilling to let go of your position for the coming of a new messianic personality. Perhaps you were in a position of control over many souls, and the ego was attached to self-aggrandizement rather than improving the conditions of humanity as a New Age approached. You seek to find the balance between giving and dominating. As your awareness expands, you will have the opportunity to assist in the awakening of many sleeping souls.

You have a street-smart sense about dealing with the psychology of others. This native insight accompanied by ancient learned skills enables you to see deeply into the needs of other people and help them to find their own truth. You can be caring and concerned about others, but you may not be comfortable with outward displays of affection and direct physical contact. You are active and accomplished at getting things done and can inspire and lead once you have found your heart committed to a soul purpose.

NOTABLES WITH THIS DEGREE:

Ram Dass: American spiritual teacher, self-growth spokesperson, author

Bette Davis: American actress

Maggie Nalbandian: American astrologer, educator

Colin Powell: American statesman, four-star U.S. Army general

Kitty Kelley: American investigative journalist, bestselling autobiography author

16th Degree of Aries

If this is your sun sign, you contemplate the many complexities and quandaries of your daily existence. You are attracted to more than your share of paradoxes and unexplained phenomena. Others are amazed at the way you can adapt your relationships to fit patterns unmanageable to most conventional souls. There is a strong inclination toward religious and spiritual investigation. If inclined toward the sciences, you will be at the fringe of belief and speculation. Your color and animated personality easily attracts attention, and your enthusiasm inspires others to question and investigate the deeper realities.

NOTABLES WITH THIS DEGREE:

Francis Ford Coppola: American movie producer, known for The Godfather

Jackie Chan: Chinese actor, comedian, director, producer, martial art expert

Russell Crowe: Australian actor, producer, musician

Gheorghe Zamfir: Romanian master pan flute musician

Guillaume Depardieu: French actor

Your life will most likely not follow the usual flux and flow of social living. You are attracted to the unconventional and look for alternatives while others do everything possible to maintain the status quo. You are fascinated by the mystical and cosmological consequences of Earth life. Your life will be blessed by encounters with the most unusual and fascinating personalities. There is a karmic suggestion of exposure to some powerful cosmic truths in another time and sequence of events. You apparently were not able to comprehend or follow your inspiration to its fullest extent. You now pursue this deep longing and desire to get to the bottom of the mystery of life.

You exhibit a certain dash of drama and flair as you go about the daily events of your life. This combination tends to attract a wide range of experience and the most unexpected variety of encounters through life. You may not fit into the traditional mode of conventional thought and action. The Aries tendency for starting something new and different is benefited by its numerical characteristics. This inspires invention and breaking out from the normal way of looking at how things are done. You may be drawn to the creative inspiration of music or dance. If so, you will establish haunting and unusual rifts of expression and design.

17th Degree of Aries

If this is your sun sign, your notorious spirit of enthusiasm and hopefulness for the future may be considerably more noticeable with this number and sign combination. Your naiveté quotient may also perch perilously higher than other members of the Aries clan and, more than likely, considerably higher than most of the population. The upside is that you inspire and encourage others when there is worry and despair. This get-started attitude is most desirable when trying to get things going. Your encouragement helps take others over the hurdles of life that might otherwise baffle and block them with hesitation and fear.

NOTABLES WITH THIS DEGREE:

Elizabeth Clare Prophet: American author, minister, spokesperson of religious new thought

James Garner: American actor

Gino Severini: Italian artist, leader of the futurist movement

Ravi Shankar: Indian sitar player, composer

When you fall from your heights of hope, you may tumble a long way. There is the karmic clue that in another life progression, you may have led others with great hope and promise right into a situation that turned into a dreaded nightmare of dire consequences and misfortune. Perhaps you were duped by someone in authority or with whom you had deep trust. Perhaps you knew what the possible outcome might be but pushed ahead instead because of some personal agenda that you put ahead of the consideration for others. You can be very cautious about taking a big step forward, but when you are sure, you move with an awe-inspiring attitude. It is essential to hone the skills of trust and recognition of inspiration that come from your highest self.

At best, you blend a mix of mental preparedness with just enough moxie to make your way through the wily wickets and webs that life has a way of putting in front of us. You enjoy some of the sophistication and refinements of success, but you are less likely to let it go to your head than some of the other signs of the zodiac. If you pout and perform childishly when you do not get your way, you know that you are not living up to the full adult potential of this combination. Most likely, you will meet setbacks with your usual gusto and take on the hurdles like a real champion.

18th Degree of Aries

If this is your sun sign, you may find your-self more cautious and less willing to trust the moment than many of your Aries contempo-raries. Those who know you might recognize an uncharacteristic restraint in your outlook on the things that are to come. When stress takes over, your impulsive Aries nature can run you up against some pretty troubled and powerful opposition. You may find yourself stepping on some well-placed toes in the area where you live. You are keen to recognize misuse of power and are inclined to speak out readily on recognition of such behavior.

There is the karmic hint of having partici-pated in some unseemly power struggles in another place and sequence of your soul jour-ney. Perhaps you were emotionally attached to a position or place of prominence. Perhaps you did not want others to recognize the ruse

NOTABLES WITH THIS DEGREE:

Catherine Grant: American astrologer, author, lecturer

Betty Ford: First Lady of the United States, humanitarian, founder of substance abuse and treatment clinic

Mary Pickford: Canadian actress, producer, humanitarian, cofounder of United Artists Studio and the Academy of Motion Picture Arts and Sciences

John Havlicek: American professional basketball player

that you implemented to emotionally manipulate and control the population around you. Perhaps you fear your own motives if you are once again (in this life) promoted to such a position in which you could affect the lives of many people. Once you find the source of your distrust within yourself, you can emerge into a dynamic and convincing promoter of positive change.

You can see far into the future of humanity and your own destiny. These glimpses of fate can be troubling when you are uncertain about what to do in the present moment. Many of you will attract the material possessions needed to help you bring about the changes in the world you believe are important to make. If you do not have the necessary resources, you can be quite adept at gaining the support of someone who does have the needed material assets required to finance the bare essentials for initiating programs that are to alter the course of human awareness.

19th Degree of Aries

If this is your sun sign, you are far-searching, idealistic, and always curious about what will come around the next corner. It may take you some time to find your course in life, but once focused, you have the energy and means to get things done. There is a type of social maturity often associated with this combination that, at its best, lets you move about with an air of near aristocratic charm and polished grace. You can be ambitious, and at times, this can take you into grandiose and over-the-top realms.

You are curious about the entire range of human experience and may find yourself pushing the limits of social beliefs or norms. You may rigidly defend and uphold the law, but once on the other side, you will test and try legal statutes to the limit. There is a karmic hint at having been an active part of the breakdown of society in another time and place. You wish to have what you want to have, but you can be taunting and teasing toward others who hold on to their own values and personal areas of interest. It is not easy to recognize when it is time for a group to let go of outworn codes and ethics to embrace what may be better for all.

This is a combination of great pioneers, both of physical and limitless boundaries of the inner consciousness. The drive for perfection attracts you to invention and consideration of utopian societies, along with other studies that take humanity's dreams and wishes to the furthest projections. Some of the most inspirational artists come from this combination. More often than not, there is both an abstract, artistic side and a part of the artist that wants to see results in human transformation as a result of the renderings given.

20ᵗʰ Degree of Aries

If this is your sun sign, you may become recognized for your uncharacteristic Aries displays of tact, deliberation, and willingness to take time for discernment. In many situations, this can be a true blessing that allows you to avoid the impulsiveness and direct bluntness that is known to get outspoken Aries into the discomfort zone with many people on numerous occasions. It need not distract from your expression of self and verve for the dynamic, nor take away any of your individualistic assets. In fact, when understood and applied, this tempering twosome can allow you to be even more accepted and successful at your chosen pursuit.

NOTABLES WITH THIS DEGREE:

Omar Sharif: Egyptian actor

Linda Goodman: American author, astrologer

Joan Quigley: American astrologer, speaker

John Madden: American football coach, football player, sports commentator

Don Meredith: American professional football player, sports commentator, actor

There is a karmic hint that in another soul sequence you could have been bombastic, overbearing, and harsh. Perhaps you pushed your views and behavior on others without regard for their reaction or response. Perhaps you simply believed that what you knew and what you had learned to do was universally best for all and proceeded to convert or destroy those who did not agree. You are learning to be assertive at the right moment when you know that those you wish to inform are ready to hear what you have to say and willing to respond to what you suggest. Then you can inspire and lead with just the right message and method.

You can be most charming and attuned to the one you choose or the audience around you. You have done many things, learning a lot about the nature of life and the many different and divergent ways that humanity lives and believes. Your unique sense of humor and style of presentation add a quality of entertainment to what could be otherwise uninteresting. You can tap into a touch of the divine and get a glimpse of the expanded realms of experience that await the enlightened soul on Earth.

21st Degree of Aries

If this is your sun sign, you are entertaining, chatty, and occasionally cantankerous. If poorly aspected, the cantankerous part may get you into trouble from time to time because of your outspoken and judgmental attitude. With harmonious aspects, this combination indicates superb communications skills and likely contact with the public. You may write, speak, or act in some form, and it is very likely that people will listen. There is distinctness in whatever road you take, and you will be noticed in any crowd for your individualistic style and manner. You capture attention where you go and leave an imprint where you have been.

The karmic hint suggests an underlying arrogance left over from other times and events. It is easy for you to think that what you say and do is the primal archetype that everyone should also believe or accept to be true. You want to be careful not to overstep your reach, or there could be massive backlash against your behavior or opinion. More often, those with this combination are observant about a wide variety of life topics without really delving into much of anything in a serious or thorough manner. You are impatient and do not like to waste valuable time sidetracked by detail and in-depth analysis.

NOTABLES WITH THIS DEGREE:

Tom Clancy: American author

Swami Narayanananda: Indian author, spiritual teacher

Ann Miller: American actress, singer, dancer

David Letterman: American television comedian, talk show host, producer

Coralie Trinh Thi: French pornography actress, director, writer

You are more likely to act out what you feel rather than acknowledge it to yourself and others in a forthright manner. Nevertheless, you are sought after for your storytelling and anecdotal acumen. Some people may become turned off because of your idiosyncrasies and bizarre mannerisms. Your interests may be wide and varied, and you are one who watches unfolding news events with curiosity and delight. At best, the Aries innocence and youthful charm touches the hearts and lives of those with whom you interact through life's course of events.

22nd Degree of Aries

If this is your sun sign, you are charged, challenging, and sometimes cherubic on your way to getting the most out of life. You have set a high standard for that which you know you must do. Something feels left undone, and you are bound and determined to get whatever that is finalized before this sojourn has transpired. There is a reclusive and distrusting part of your personality that wants to avoid people and the perplexities of this dysfunctional world. However, the Aries influence offsets some of that with an optimistic outlook that keeps you motivated to get things done.

NOTABLES WITH THIS DEGREE:

Annie Hershey: American author, astrologer

Thomas Jefferson: American president, diplomat

Michael Otto: German billionaire, head of German Otto Group

Shannen Doherty: American actress, producer, author, director

Howard Sasportas: astrologer, author, editor

There is a karmic hint that in another life sequence you were likely misled and taken off your life course. Or perhaps you were so harsh and focused on what you needed to get done that you overlooked the human side and the needs of those who were also a part of your work. They might have turned against you or became passive-aggressive in an attempt to purposely deter you from your objective. A loss of trust and of leadership led to disappointment and probable failure. You are more cautious now. You are respectful of other people's needs and acknowledge the importance of their roles in getting things accomplished.

You take pride in getting things done well and are able to attract people around you who are similarly talented and willing to put in the needed hard work to reach a high standard of success. Your Aries personality helps to lighten what can sometimes be a most serious and uncompromising characteristic in your personality. For the most part, you are learned and diverse in the skills needed to get things done in the modern world. It is not so easy for you to take time off for pleasure or socializing. You may benefit from having a partner or mate who can assist you in exploring the more fun side of living.

23rd Degree of Aries

If this is your sun sign, you are wild, wily, and wonderfully aware. You take in life like a child with wide-open eyes of wonderment. There is very little that does not interest you, and you scurry through things in a frenzy to experience it all. The down side of this pattern is the likelihood of overdoing things and excessive indulgence. You can become easily addicted to substances or certain life fetishes. It helps to be surrounded by good friends who provide positive feedback and let you know when they see you out of control or in denial.

There is the likelihood of some abuse and suffering in your life that may very well have started at an early age. This combination heavily suggests the likelihood of dysfunctional addictive behavior by your parents when you were young. There is the karmic hint of having gone to extreme excess and out-of-control behavior in other times and places. It is easy for you to live on the edge and think nothing about it, even though those around you show concern and worry. If this is the case, you will have to expend much effort to keep yourself under control. On the other hand, there are those of you who experience much fear when it comes to trying new things or taking bold steps of initiative.

Your daring makes you a crowd pleaser and great companion to be around, especially when you are on a roll. Your humor and flair for fun keep people at ease and amiable. You can have so many pots over the fire that you may not have time to give each one of them the proper amount of time and attention. It may not be easy for you to slow down and discipline yourself when just that very thing might be best for your health and well-being. Travel, turf, and fun in the sun are a natural part of your life.

NOTABLES WITH THIS DEGREE:

Gary Kasparov: Russian chess champion

Julie Christie: English actress, early pop icon

Erich von Daniken: Swiss author who pioneered texts about extraterrestrial contact with Earth

Ivy Goldstein-Jacobson: Australian astrologer, publisher

Al Green: American gospel and soul singer

24th Degree of Aries

If this is your sun sign, you may be one of the more timid Aries personalities. That is, until you get backed into a corner. Once that happens, the Aries fire comes out and the tenacity of this combination becomes evident. Your sensitivity to image and public persona can get in the way of allowing you to just be yourself and do your own thing. There is a need to serve others, and it is easy to put other people's needs ahead of your own. You are caring in a kind of detached manner. You show affection by what you do for people rather than by direct display to the person.

A lot of Aries burn bright and fade fast, but with this number-sign combination, you have the kind of stubborn streak that gives you the strength to stay with an issue until it is done. It is important to you to get things done right, and you may overextend yourself in that effort. This combination may find you active in charity or philanthropic ventures that allow you to display your generosity to the world. This suggests a karmic pattern of believing you once got something that was undeserved, so you must sacrifice yourself now to be seen as a good and deserving person.

You can be the glue that keeps the group or organization stuck together. Your attention to detail is of enormous benefit when finalizing a project. Appearance of propriety is important to you, and you go out of your way to cultivate a positive public persona. This knack can help get you into places that can be most revealing and interesting in their revelations about human behavior. Your Aries idealism is tempered a bit by this pair of numbers, and you could turn bitter or cynical about life rather rapidly when exposed to issues of the dark side.

25th Degree of Aries

If this is your sun sign, there is a noticeable distance and mental detachment that puts a little of a damper on the usual impetuous, fast-acting Aries personality. This combination can be perplexing and vexing to the Aries or perhaps a blessing in disguise. It encourages a little more thoughtful restraint before acting, which can save the Aries person from impulsively reacting to something and becoming embarrassed. You may become an expert of sorts to people who suffer from obsessive-compulsive behaviors. Many of you learn how to analyze your impulses quickly and are thus able to discover rapid solutions to direct your impulses into the most productive and successful direction. The downside is the possible development of a sort of arrogance about your ability to make repeatedly quick and accurate decisions.

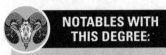

NOTABLES WITH THIS DEGREE:

Emma Watson: English actress, model

Josiane Balasko: French actress, writer, director

Jimmy Osmond: American singer, actor, business executive

Susan Ward: American actress, model

Seth Rogen: Canadian actor, director, producer, screenwriter, comedian

There is a karmic hint of having been flagrantly indifferent to public opinion in another time and setting that resulted in decisions that brought loss to many people. Your haughtiness and condescending attitude resulted in divisiveness among residents and a weakening of the culture. You are torn between not giving a damn what others think and desperately wanting to be acknowledged for your acumen and brilliant solutions to life events. You have the potential to shine brilliantly in what you choose to do.

You are characteristically a risk taker and attract people around you who like to live in the fast lane. Some may find you cold, calculating, and uncaring toward others. Underneath the bruised and battered ego is a person who just wants to do well and strives for a sense of accomplishment. You have many interests and a diverse set of life skills. Once you focus those skills, you are likely to achieve your desired level of achievement.

26th Degree of Aries

If this is your sun sign, you will find yourself in many situations having to do with culture, class, and social mores. You are ambitious and clever in the way that you gain social favor. You may find yourself taking the lead in a reform movement or attempt to get better conditions for those less fortunate. There is an old saying in regard to speaking softly and carrying a big stick. The saying fits your number-sign combination quite well. Many of you will be attracted to the healing arts or positions of service to others. Your fiery idealism can land you in situations of confrontation with strong-willed opposition. This could be parents in an early age or those with strong differing views you encounter later in life.

NOTABLES WITH THIS DEGREE:

George Adamski: Polish-born American, UFO contactee and spokesperson

Margarethe II: queen regent of Denmark

Dusty Springfield: English pop singer, song stylist, record producer

Selena: American singer, songwriter, fashion designer, entrepreneur

This combination adds a little more sensitivity toward others than more-individualized Aries have been known to possess. There is a karmic suggestion of having been harshly outspoken in an earlier time. This may have caused you to be severely punished or reprimanded publicly for your actions. You are a little less impulsive and more calculated in your response to others. There is also a nurturing quality that may surprise those who are familiar with Aries proclivity toward self-centeredness. Your parenting skills can shine under pressure, and you are good at encouraging self-confidence in your offspring.

You are interested in sociology and the dynamics of group behavior. You are curious as to how someone maintains self-identity amid the pressures and demands of social convention. You are attracted to philosophies of society and different plans for humankind to evolve and grow through mutual harmony and cooperation. There is a fear that you must give up personal identity in order to be accepted among the masses. In the end, you will find solace in the art of helping others to be secure within the self amid the mores of social living.

27th Degree of Aries

If this is your sun sign, you are a curious creature who is caught in the social tempest of turbulent times. There is a part of you that wants to be right at the center of the social activity taking place in your location. If you are not in it, you would like to be molding social attitudes in some manner. You are curious but cautious. You are capable of being candidly outspoken in your observations of society. Your position may take on a somewhat biased and personal tone rather than a detached and observational one.

There is the karmic hint that you have previously been an arch critic and revisionist of malprudence by social and government leaders. That also suggests that at some point in your evolution, you were participating in the same. You are still outspoken but desperately seek to encourage a world of openness and forthrightness in the administration of public office. Whatever position you hold, you strive to maintain fairness and openness toward those who are influenced by you. You maintain a high standard of idealism, and it may be difficult for anything or anyone (including yourself) to meet the standards that you set.

You have an air of refinement and sensitivity to people and events that makes you appreciated and noticed by many. You likely show talent in art or entertainment that gives you a cathartic outlet for your rich and often intense pace of life. You relish utopian dreams and thoughts, envisioning a world that truly works in harmony and peacefulness among all. Some may say you are ahead of your times and that you are impractical and hopelessly optimistic in your perceptions and wishes for human development. Such doubting only stirs your conviction to investigate and search for the right combination of circumstances that make it possible for a utopia to come true.

NOTABLES WITH THIS DEGREE:

Charlie Chaplin: English comedian, actor, director

David Tennant: Scottish actor

Nikita Krushchev: Russian political party leader, First Secretary of the Communist Party

J. P. Morgan: American business mogul, financier, philanthropist

28th Degree of Aries

If this is your sun sign, you are likely to weave a more diplomatic web through life than many of your Aries family members. You are learning the subtlety of power and enjoy engaging in the power game. Play it well, and it could bring you some fame. This combination softens, or perhaps more accurately disguises, the usual direct Aries frontal assault. You probably still possess the Aries appearance of innocence. Others are taken in by the appearance before realizing just how capable you are of using your cleverness to get your way.

There is a karmic hint that in another time and life sequence you may have thrived at using inside information or possibly your own advanced intelligence to mislead and manipulate others for less-than-honorable

NOTABLES WITH THIS DEGREE:

Maria Sharapova: Russian professional tennis player, model

Hayley Mills: English actress, consciousness seeker

Nadine de Rothschild: French author and actress, widow of Edmund Rothschild

Conan O'Brien: American comedian, television talk show host

causes. The combination of being in a position of power and being overcome with ego-driven needs could have aroused within you merciless and abusive behavior. You find yourself often mired in the muck of lies and deceit when trying to honestly represent yourself and those with whom you associate. You strive through improved communication methods and ethically based philosophy to resolve conflict and contention among people and institutions alike.

You most likely pay more attention to detail, image, and appearance than other Aries. This can work well to your advantage in the way you prepare yourself and then move quickly with that Aries flash of spontaneity. You keenly appreciate those who are astute and uncannily aware of the subtleties of their profession or craft. You are found busily engaged in a variety of group activities that introduce you to multiple facets of human culture. You most likely enjoy exploring the nature of speech and the way it can be used to persuade, placate, pacify, and predispose.

29th Degree of Aries

If this is your sun sign, you may be one of the more subtle and sensitive members of the Aries family. This combination often softens some of the blatantly assertive Aries characteristics. This can sometimes be a blessing when trying to get along with others or trying to convince people to support you in a specific belief or cause that you espouse. You can otherwise overpower people or appear threatening to many with your characteristic directness. You are more attuned to what other people think and want rather than just focused on yourself, as can happen often with the individualistic Aries personality.

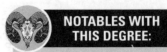

There is a karmic suggestion that in other times and settings, you were out of touch with most people and with the issues of the day. Your fierce sense of ideology may have more than once put you into the doghouse with the social leadership of another era. Perhaps you were so highly idealistic that you could not tolerate any flaws in those who presented themselves as leaders. Perhaps you set such high standards that you could not find anyone who could meet your expectations. You are a visionary and see far ahead of most of the masses. It will take some patience and diplomacy on your part to plant the seeds of change you see coming. You do have the opportunity, however, to witness some of those most-cherished dreams starting to materialize in the mundane dimensions of consciousness.

You are gifted with intuitive clarity that can inspire and encourage many a weary and troubled soul. As you balance out your own unresolved negative emotional issues, your power of persuasion and ability to communicate will improve substantially to the point you can be a lightbearer to a large number of searching souls.

TAURUS

0 Degree of Taurus

If this is your sun sign, you can be endlessly confused about your life and what you want to do, or you can be extremely certain of what you want to do and let nothing get in your way. Strangely enough, both of these can be true. This number-sign combination can be difficult to assess, since there are so many options available. The paradox is that in many cases, you do not feel that there are any options, and you must do a certain thing.

NOTABLES WITH THIS DEGREE:

Adolph Hitler: German politician, Nazi leader

Joan Miro: Spanish painter, sculptor, ceramicist

James McAvoy: Scottish actor

Compounding the uncertainty is the Taurus tendency toward stubbornness and adherence to a given course of action even when factors make it obvious that it may not be going as intended.

There is a little bit less karmic pressure with this number-sign combination than some of the others. That leaves you with more choices in the things you do and achieve. People will never know what to expect from you next, and many times, you don't even know what you will do next. Even for the grounded Taurus, this combination can be a little spacey and far-out. At best, you are ahead of the pack and foresee things that can be done before others ask for them. At worst, you are escapist and fanciful to a fault. You talk about following rules and regulations but enjoy testing them when it is to your personal advantage. You will be a little quicker than some of your Taurus contemporaries when it comes to getting involved in new relationships. There is a short fuse to this Taurus's loyalty when feeling rejected or mistreated.

This combination gives a little zing to the usual staid Taurus temperament. Your broad range of interests and experiences allow you to spin comical and engaging tales. You are blessed with foresight and the necessary follow-through to take a good thing all the way to final closure. Your flair for good taste is accompanied with a slightly offbeat taste. People find your thoroughness and eye for quality very attractive attributes.

1ˢᵗ Degree of Taurus

If this is your sun sign, you are more willing than many of your Taurus contemporaries to move and make changes in accordance with the moment rather than clinging to old habits and prior social programming. This flexible attribute, along with your traditional tenacity and staying power, can make a formidable combination for getting this done quickly yet

thoroughly. You are candid and capable of frank confrontation when dealing with others. This is particularly true when deadlines and prearranged agreements are on the line. Your no-nonsense manner is respected by most but, at times, causes others to put up strong resistance against you.

There is the karmic suggestion that in another setting, you were overbearing and tyrannical. Your steadfast rules and rigidity resulted in stagnation for not only yourself but many other lives as well. You can still fall back to unreasonable stubbornness when placed under stress and extreme uncertainty. You are learning to make decisions that are not based on fear but a more complete confidence of matters as they are in the moment. You have the capacity to inspire people to get things started and then maintain constant forms of motivation until the necessary work is completed.

For the most part, you are thorough and conscientious about what you believe and espouse. This causes people to trust you and gives weight to what you have to say. This thoroughness and attention to essentials puts many of you in a position to be successful at whatever you choose to do. While usually not pretentious, you enjoy being surrounded with items of quality and good taste. You are interested in life and will be found sharing your knowledge in a manner that assists others who are less fortunate. Your loyalty and perseverance in getting the right thing done endears you to all who know you.

2ⁿᵈ Degree of Taurus

If this is your sun sign, you are determined, tenacious, and constantly curious about the social nature of humanity. You ponder the psychology of the crowd and seek to find more effective ways to bring about efficiency in social institutions and the administration of social programs. This number-sign combination blends the tenacity of Taurus with the tact of the 2 that can make you a formidable negotiator and stubborn leader in times of crisis. You enjoy the spoils of victory and the fine things that accomplishment brings into your life. If you are not careful, the indulgence of power can put additional weight on your body as well as your soul.

NOTABLES WITH THIS DEGREE:

Jack Nicholson: American actor, director, producer, screenwriter

Eddie Albert: American actor, social and environmental activist

Yehudi Menuhin: American conductor, accomplished violinist

Vladimir Lenin: Russian political theorist, creator of the Soviet Communist Party

There is the karmic suggestion of past indulgences and misrepresentation of public image. You have believed yourself to be the maker of social legislation rather than the subject of such regulations. Your previous disregard for human values weighs heavily on your shoulders. You are learning to bring about the freedom and evolution of human learning rather than the plundering of human resources. Once you have let go of ego and find connection to your source, there is an abundance of living beyond your wildest expectations.

This combination adds a lot of charm to personal and social engagements. You can be most entertaining with your stories and exploits of life. You are a good host and love to provide your guests with the latest and greatest. Your down-to-earth approach to life provides a lot of common sense and also the ability to anticipate what the next step will be. You are a good provider and make a delightful companion, filling the days and nights with great anecdotal yarns and lovely surroundings.

3rd Degree of Taurus

If this is your sun sign, your feelings dig deep down into the soil of the earth and the souls of humanity. At best, you are connected to the full spectrum of human emotions, and through this, you can connect to any or all planetary life forms. You have a keen aesthetic appreciation and are attracted to performing or expressing yourself though the arts. If not an artist, you most likely implement an artistic touch in your calling. This combination yields many inventors, because you have the knack of turning things from the imagination into something that actually functions in reality.

Your earthy savvy regarding the way people react and behave toward you can make you a natural leader or a predator who manipulates the weak and cons the weary. The karmic pattern suggests you may have done either or both in other times and places. You feel the impulse to touch the hearts of people, and in turn, you allow them to experience a special place in their own hearts that may have been closed down. For some, there can be an almost compulsive need to give, but most of you operate from a genuine understanding of what other people really need. You may preach or teach, but in some manner, you will reach the hearts of many souls.

The earthiness and sense of connectedness to the body give many of you a smoldering sensuality that stirs the libido and creative juices. Because of your entertaining ways and good-natured presence, people like to have you at their social gatherings and as their friends. In times of crisis, you seem to have a sixth sense about what to do, and unlike many panicky contemporaries, you calmly and collectedly administer appropriate advice and assurance to the nervous and needy.

NOTABLES WITH THIS DEGREE:

Shirley MacLaine: American actress, singer, dancer, activist, author, New Age teacher

Barbra Streisand: American actress, singer, songwriter, director, political activist, producer

Willem de Kooning: Dutch-American abstract expressionist artist

Marcus Aurelius: Roman emperor and stoic philosopher

4th Degree of Taurus

If this is your sun sign, you are dogged and determined, and you struggle with details. This number-sign combination adds rigidity and stubbornness to a Taurus disposition that is already inclined to be so. Once on a course, it is really hard to persuade you to change direction, even when logic and facts support the position that it would be best for you to do so. There is a ruggedness and hardiness that gives you tough skin and the ability to stay with a project or plan under the most stressful of conditions. You appreciate things done well and encourage discipline and detail in your preparation for success. It is not easy for you to lighten up and be playful or carefree, but when you do, you are a delight to everyone around you.

NOTABLES WITH THIS DEGREE:

Daniel Logan: American psychic, author, speaker

Richard S. Fuld Jr.: American investment banker, Lehman Brothers CEO

Oliver Cromwell: English military and political leader

There is a karmic hint that you have had control over many people in another time and setting. You are enamored with having things under your control and still long to be heard and admired by the throngs. There is the likelihood of a simultaneous persecution complex that causes you to sabotage your best efforts and punish yourself by denying the very success that you want. You listen to others and then completely disregard what they have said.

The lighter side of your disposition can be most interesting and attractive. You have accumulated a lot of information, and you love to present your observations within a trusted circle of friends or associates. Loyalty is important to you, and you can be generous with those you determine to be steadfast to your beliefs and actions. This blind loyalty can sometimes cause you to place excessive value on someone who may not be terribly skilled for the assigned task. You tend to accumulate garnishments and trophies that reflect your desire for success and recognition from others.

5th Degree of Taurus

If this is your sun sign, there is a lighter and more personable manner that offsets some of the tough and stubborn traits associated with the Taurus personality. This number-sign combination stimulates an easy-to-get-along-with quality, and for many of you, it can manifest in the form of a beguiling and seductive nature. There is a karmic suggestion of previous strict rigidity or dogmatic attachment to some particular belief system. You are learning to overcome prejudice and judgment toward others. You will be placed in situations of constantly having to face issues with the very racial, religious, or social types of people you may dislike the most.

NOTABLES WITH THIS DEGREE:

Jack Schwarz: Dutch author, minister, pioneer in holistic health

Renée Zellweger: American actress, singer, dancer, producer

Michele Ferrero: Italian billionaire confectioner

Al Pacino: American actor, director

Jess Stearn: American journalist, author

You can be very set in your ways, but once convinced of the need for change, you are determined to do the new thing to the best of your ability. You are a little more flighty than many of your Taurus brethren. Your curiosity and imagination take you on a trek into many subjects and wild experiences. However, once you zero in on a particular interest, your Taurus instincts kick in, and you will follow that interest to its ultimate conclusion. You may be a little more fickle in relationships than many Taurus personalities because of your search for variation and something different.

You are a little more casual about appearance. You are willing to explore the underworld of subcultures and counter belief systems. You may even end up following a more unorthodox religious or spiritual regime. You have a metaphysical leaning toward uncovering the hidden truths of life and implementing them into your lifestyle. You are a little less concerned with appearances than most of your Taurus clan, but once settled in, you do enjoy the finer comforts of living as much as anyone — if not more.

6th Degree of Taurus

If this is your sun sign, you can be caring, conservative, cautious, and cold. You are doggedly determined to do good deeds and to accumulate credit for the service you render to others. Most likely, few work harder than you when it comes to getting things done. Your reputation precedes you because of your consistent loyalty and willingness to render assistance to those in need. Friends appreciate your trust, and enemies know to stay clear because you do not tolerate those who lie and prey on others. You want to check every now and then to determine that you have not slipped into codependent compulsivity rather than dogged loyalty. It is, admittedly, not so easy to do this when attached strongly to someone.

NOTABLES WITH THIS DEGREE:

Ulysses S. Grant: American president, Civil War general

Coretta Scott King: American social activist, civil-rights leader, widow of Martin Luther King Jr.

Anouk Aimée: French actress

Rudolf Hess: German Nazi Party deputy and administrator

There is the karmic hint of having been overbearing and oblivious to boundaries in previous relationships of time and experience. Perhaps you felt like you owned someone and it was your duty and fate to determine that person's life direction. Maybe you were hopelessly insecure and let yourself cling fearfully to another to the point of strangling that person's efforts and avoiding any effort on your own part. You simply might not have taken into account anyone's interests or needs but your own. You realize that it is important for you at this time to be fully considerate of those around you and of your own healthy state of being. You seek a balance in your actions and deeds that allows you to be of benefit to yourself and to those with whom you have contact.

You have an air of quality and inherent good taste that results in gaining the respect and attention of others. You have weight when it comes to influencing the decisions of the group. You take the responsibility for this influence seriously and seek to serve with fairness and compassion.

7th Degree of Taurus

If this is your sun sign, you are a puzzle of external delight and internal quandaries. It is not easy to fathom your depth of interest in life and keen scrutiny of the events you encounter. Since you do not externalize feelings easily in private, you may choose to find a public outlet to express your sentiments. You may be blessed with the good things of life and wonder why. You may look at the way the world turns and wonder how it does it. There is almost a feeling of guilt associated with being successful. Your philosophical nature leans toward the practical rather than the obscure and metaphysical.

NOTABLES WITH THIS DEGREE:

Penélope Cruz: Spanish actress, model, singer, dancer

Saddam Hussein: president of Iraq, political activist

Jay Leno: American television talk show host, comedian

Ann-Margret: Swedish-American actress, singer, dancer

Those with this number-sign combination share a rather dramatic flair in their presence and social image. Although you can be gregarious and open, in your private world, you are inclined to prefer privacy and a somewhat reclusive lifestyle that can include dark and dangerous aspirations. This gives you time to brood on your many inner thoughts and questions that interest you. You like to dig into things and solve the mystery of how things work. The karmic suggestion is of one who might have been a kind of court jester who witnessed behind-the-scenes events but had to walk on eggshells in how you revealed things.

While the Taurus personality is known for its stubbornness and rigidity, this combination adds a mental toughness to the stubbornness. You can become impersonal and detached from others. At some point in your life, you could be drawn into the political arena since you have strong sentiments toward certain issues. Your get frustrated with inept leaders and those who fail to take responsibility with respect. This may not be on a huge national scale; perhaps it is in the local setting where you dwell. Whenever you do get involved in a cause, you stay with the issues right to the end. You are particularly troubled by matters of fraud and misuse of public trust.

8ᵗʰ Degree of Taurus

If this is your sun sign, you ponder the perils of power and seek to place yourself near the podium of practical progress. You want to have a voice in the events that shape your life and those who are significant to you. Traditional Taurus tenacity combined with potential for power of the number 8 make for a very determined and capable personality. You are quite capable of surrounding yourself with the things of luxury and taste. Once you have a goal clearly in sight, there is very little that you will let get in your way before accomplishing it.

NOTABLES WITH THIS DEGREE:

Uma Thurman: American actress, model

Terry Pratchett: English author of science-fiction and comic fantasy novels

James Monroe: American president, lawyer

Jerry Seinfeld: American actor, comedian, writer

Hirohito: Japanese emperor

There is a karmic clue that both power and control are past issues that will return to confront you throughout your life. There is the suggestion of previously having had a lavish lifestyle as a result of the power and position you attained. Perhaps you were indifferent to those who were sacrificed for your gains. Perhaps you feel superior to those who have little and are addicted to having control over the lives and times of the masses. You will have an opportunity in this lifetime to inform and awaken the mass consciousness and make it possible for more people to have prosperity and personal empowerment.

There is a tendency with this combination to use people for your own ends rather than sharing and being with them. Your emotional detachment allows you to plunge your way through questionable and sometimes controversial behavior with complete indifference to the reaction of society around you. During times of personal growth and inner awakening, you become fascinated with empowering others and providing education and information that frees the soul and releases the spirit. You can be a great leader or one who is caught in the ego gratification of spreading disinformation and disruption of cosmological law.

9th Degree of Taurus

If this is your sun sign, you have a kind of special aura about you that is not as evident in some born under your sign. Some of your Taurus contemporaries may find you to be a little impractical and off the wall. You definitely do not fit the typical Taurus mold. The upside of this combination is the ability to have far-reaching dreams and the practicality to make them come true. The downside is that you can get quickly discouraged with imperfection and give up on something before really giving it a chance to succeed.

You may have felt compelled to live up to someone else's dream or rebel against the intentions someone else might have had for you. There is the karmic suggestion of having been criticized or rejected by others concerning a wonderful plan you proposed that would have brought much benefit and good things to many people. You feel the sting of rejection and, at times, will sabotage your best efforts just to get back at those who expect too much from you. You fluctuate repeatedly between crosscurrents of your own ambition and the role destiny and society seem to expect of you.

There is a refined quality with this number-sign combination that puts a polish on the often direct and less-delicate Taurus personality. It gives a gracefulness to the body and provides a great mixture of the tough Taurus strength with rare athletic or artistic talent. Your ability to be with the down-to-earth types as well as those who operate right at the edge of reality makes you a sought-after companion and associate. You will meet some very talented and prosperous people as you pass through the different stages of your most unusual life experience.

NOTABLES WITH THIS DEGREE:

David Icke: English reporter, conspiracy investigator

Andre Agassi: American professional tennis player and spokesperson

Johnny Miller: American accomplished professional golfer, sports announcer

Paul Adelstein: American actor

António Guterres: Portuguese politician, international Socialist leader

10th Degree of Taurus

If this is your sun sign, there is an extra little zing to your step and zip in your thoughts. You are quicker to take initiative and, more often than not, get things done sooner than most of your Taurus contemporaries. There is a willingness to try something different and take risks that are not so common with the more deliberate Taurus personality. The combination of get-go and get-done can be a grand asset to have as you plod your way through life. Once you are off to a good start, you know how to follow through with thoroughness and the necessary attention to detail that makes for the most acceptable result.

NOTABLES WITH THIS DEGREE:

J. Allen Hynek: American astronomer, ufologist

Anandamoyi Ma: Indian saint, mystic, spiritual leader

David Koch: American billionaire business mogul, political activist, philanthropist

Carl Friedrich Gauss: German mathematician, scientist

Glenn Ford: Canadian-born American actor

There is the karmic hint that, in a previous experience of soul, you may have been given the opportunity to get something special done but did not apply yourself or take full advantage of that moment. Perhaps you were simply lazy and did not want to put in the necessary effort to complete the opportunity. Maybe you feared the consequences and public reaction since your task was of an unconventional nature and not fully understood at the time. You are learning how important it is to do the best you can with the talent you have been given.

You present a *bon vivant* flair for life that makes you an interesting companion and associate. There are many of you that excel at athletic events and physically demanding activities. You are strong of body, mind, and soul. You look at something with the idea of how it might be improved or altered in such a way as to serve a special capacity that no one had previously considered. There is a willingness to try something new and take on an adventure that attracts you to people who are ahead of the curve and able to alter the course of the world.

11ᵗʰ Degree of Taurus

If this is your sun sign, your imagination spreads out in wonder and childlike delight in its quest to grasp the meaning of events that take place in your life. You desire to walk among the stars and mists of space but find yourself landlocked and laden with issues on this Earth plane. The cosmic child in you becomes befuddled with all of the limitations and restrictions that seem to inhibit the natural inclination of humans to live. Many of you will struggle with abuse and issues of abandonment because there is a part of you that just does not seem to belong anywhere. On the other hand, you are a different person when you do find a comfortable niche with people you enjoy and trust. You come to life with dazzling skills of entertainment and wit.

NOTABLES WITH THIS DEGREE:

David Beckham: soccer professional and spokesperson

Catherine the Great: Russian Empress

Pierre Teilhard de Chardin: Jesuit-trained French cosmologist and philosopher

Louis IX: king of France

You may find yourself growing up in a household with differing belief sets from much of the society around you. You may stand out as different in school and other social events. Perhaps your parents were at odds with many of the social customs of the day. There is a karmic hint that in another setting, you were endowed with quite extraordinary attributes that amazed and, to some extent, frightened others. Perhaps society turned against you or ridiculed you for your differences, causing you to lose self-confidence and esteem. You struggle to believe in your worth and fear reprisal from society for whatever you do.

You will have an opportunity to develop unique talents and can have much impact on your work if you trust your inner strength and ability that God has given to you. It will require much confidence and endurance to make the journey back into the light of communication and healthy exchange with others.

12th Degree of Taurus

If this is your sun sign, you have many potential talents and tantalizing opportunities to make your way through life. While things may not come to you easily in the early years, you still have time to get a lot out of life. There is a lot of push to be novel and ingenious in your endeavors. It seems like so many obstacles can get in your way, but once you see your path clearly, you are dedicated and persevering. Your communication skills can get you far along the path of success if you hone them and watch the trends closely. Some of you will use your inside knowledge to maneuver and manipulate with great flourish.

NOTABLES WITH THIS DEGREE:

Bing Crosby: actor, singer

William Shakespeare: English poet, playwright, preeminent dramatist

James Brown: American singer, songwriter, bandleader, record producer

Manfred von Richthofen: German fighter ace of WW I

Perhaps you may feel like you have something to prove to the world. This may indicate a sort of inferiority complex. The resulting behavior can be seen in the need to overexert yourself while achieving your desired feats of accomplishment. You can easily become dogmatic and blind in your adherence to policies that serve your personal needs and beliefs. There is the karmic hint of having taken from and used others in previous times and settings. You know how to exploit the foibles of the collective consciousness, and you can benefit or badger the masses. Your quest to control can get you into some potentially fanatical courses of action.

On the lighter side of your personality, you can be most charming and dashing in your social interactions. The Taurus touch of good taste is certainly not hampered by this combination, and you are inclined to like those things that suggest luxury and a taste for the finer things of life. You can be most philanthropic when things have gone well, and you are not above polishing your social image with well-placed gifts and donations.

13th Degree of Taurus

If this is your sun sign, you may sweep an industrious path of prodigious productivity before your soul rests itself in the grave. And this might just be the point. Many of you speculate — and some of you know — that part of consciousness is eternal and continues its journey after depositing the body in the soil. You live life to its fullest and give more attention than many to the nature of death and the beyond. This may take the form of a religious belief or perhaps metaphysical theorizing. Whatever path you choose to take, your realization of continuity contributes to your strategy for making the most out of life while you are here.

NOTABLES WITH THIS DEGREE:

Thomas Huxley: English biologist, advocate of Charles Darwin's theory of evolution

Audrey Hepburn: British actress, dancer, humanitarian

Karl Marx: German author, revolutionary socialist, political activist

Your faith in the beyond will be tested many times by those who doubt and ridicule. There is a karmic hint that in another life setting, you introduced or were part of a movement that taught of other worlds and kingdoms beyond. Perhaps you lost your life in the defense of your beliefs. Perhaps others around you perished because they were persuaded to believe and follow you. You are passionate about your spirituality and, at the same time, cautious in the way you present your position to other people. The time will come once again during this cycle when your beliefs will be shared by many and you become part of a community that aspires to live by the ideals inspired by your beliefs.

You have a kind of nuts-and-bolts attitude toward life and the process of maneuvering your way through the maze of material earning. The paradox of this combination is that very often, those who have it frequently have a built-in indifference to grasping for the material. However, many of you will find that material acquisitions come to you readily and easily. You will accomplish many things and encounter some most unusual people and events during this time around.

14ᵗʰ Degree of Taurus

If this is your sun sign, you are likely much less serious than many of your Taurus contemporaries. You can be wild, wily, and willing to get yourself into any number of situations. Your brash and cavalier approach to life can land you into the middle of meaningful moments as well as situations reflecting the madness of the modern world. You feign yourself as independent and in charge of your life while easily compromised by situations of glamour and opportunity. It is most likely that whatever course you choose, it is not going to be conventional. Even if you try to appear conventional in order to fit in, your private life will reveal a much different diversity of unusual penchants.

NOTABLES WITH THIS DEGREE:

Søren Kierkegaard: philosopher, theologian

Brian Williams: American television newscaster, anchor and managing editor of *NBC Nightly News*

Orson Welles: American director, producer, actor

Stewart Granger: English actor

There is the karmic hint of previous stints through life out of control, subject to indulgent and addictive behavior. You may spoof the very weaknesses that plague your own personal life while appearing to be above such habits. You struggle to maintain a healthy balance and search for a way of life that can bring solace to troubled souls. Many of you stay extremely active and busy in order not to feel the deeper angst and inner conflict of restless souls. You will find yourself among many people, and travel will be an important part of your life scenario.

Your naturally gregarious personality attracts attention to you, and you will find yourself surrounded by admirers and people who feed off of your exuberance. Many of you are attracted to some form of charity or volunteer work that lends assistance to the disabled or those suffering from serious health problems. You find physical exercise a great relief for stress and may well be involved in some athletic league since competition comes naturally to you.

15th Degree of Taurus

If this is your sun sign, this combination may actually add to the common perception of a Taurus being dogged and stubbornly determined to do what must get done. You may be a gifted speaker with a touch of social magnetism. This allows you to pursue positions of influence and sway. You are willing to take risks, and that makes you an admirable administrator when things go well. However, when things go wrong and you have overreached, your silver tongue may not be able to deflect judgment by others. There is a bold and daring attitude that goes with this personality. At best, it is chivalrous and noble.

NOTABLES WITH THIS DEGREE:

Tony Blair: British prime minister

Sigmund Freud: Austrian neurologist, founded psychoanalysis

George Clooney: American actor, director, producer

Vladimir Lisin: Russian steel tycoon

Eva Perón: First Lady of Argentina, vice presidential candidate

You could very well become caught up in the politics of personal want and excessive needs. There are many undercurrents associated with this number-sign combination, one of the most prominent has to do with power and its execution. The trophies of luxury that come with power are a potent intoxicant, along with the machinations of administration. It can be most tempting to sell out your position when under the pressure of those who would manipulate the strings of power behind the scenes. You can be seduced by the promise of yet further control and decision-making authority over those you believe to be of lesser worth. There is the karmic suggestion of having been lax in self-control and being compromised by overindulgence and extravagance.

Your down-to-earth common sense can get you far in this world. You do enjoy the better things of life and envy those who have them. It is not above you to take shortcuts or less-than-noble paths to get your share of the good life. At best, you generously shower your friends and loved ones with tasteful and luxurious items of adornment and personal use. You are ardent and loyal once you trust those close to you. Trust is a big issue with this combination, and you will spend a good deal of time looking over your shoulder.

16th Degree of Taurus

If this is your sun sign, you can be set in your ways like most of your other Taurus family members. You do not like to have routines disturbed, and you prefer regularity rather than happenstance. However, when upheaval or calamity occurs, you quickly rise to the occasion and provide simple and efficient strategies to meet the crisis. This knack for quick solutions can help you in daily tasks of a more mundane and less dramatic nature. You just seem to grasp the puzzle of efficiency pretty easily. Your prankster spirit comes out more easily than other Taurus combinations. When this fun and playful side of your personality lights up, people around you especially enjoy and appreciate your presence.

NOTABLES WITH THIS DEGREE:

Marvin Mitchelson: American celebrity lawyer, jetsetter, pioneered the concept of palimony

Ferdinand Magellan: Portuguese-born explorer commissioned by Spain to find the "Spice Islands"

Pyotr Ilyich Tchaikovsky: Russian composer, musical innovator

Johannes Brahms: German composer of the romantic period

You worry about the unexpected and distrust the whims of the gods and of the cosmos. There is a karmic suggestion that in another time and situation, you were in a position of power that was based on faith and belief in your deity or deities. When events did not go your way, you lost faith and became distrusting and cynical. You have flirted with agnosticism and atheism many times and still wrestle with the place and role of a God in our universe. You have learned to rely only on yourself and are prepared to confront any situation thrown your way. Deep down, you long to know your creator and to understand more completely the nature of divine laws. You will come closer to this quest as your life unfolds.

Many good things come your way and some may think of your life as blessed and fortunate. Like many of your Taurus brethren, you enjoy the good things of life and are willing to earn them through dedication and applying the necessary effort. At the same time, you understand the transitory nature of having material possessions and balance out your life with spiritual values and eternal rewards.

17th Degree of Taurus

If this is your sun sign, you can be motivated more quickly to get started than many of your Taurus brethren. There is an air of optimism that goes with this number-sign combination that enables you to see challenges as a refreshing opportunity rather than a potentially arduous task. Subsequently, you take on opportunities that many others might pass on. This can place you in the position to perform some truly outstanding tasks that are a pleasant challenge and may result in directing much applause your way. A more traditionally stubborn Taurus would likely pass up such opportunity because of the risk factors and low percentage of success.

NOTABLES WITH THIS DEGREE:

Dana Haynes: Canadian astrologer, numerologist, author, talk show host

Sir David Attenborough: English broadcaster, director

Socrates: Greek philosopher, heavily influenced Western philosophy

Ricky Nelson: American actor, singer, early teen idol

Mike Wallace: American television journalist

Kate Smith: American singer, entertainer, philanthropist

There is the karmic hint of having been overly optimistic in other life settings. Perhaps you overreached and failed. Perhaps your ego got caught up in challenges of pride, and you wanted to prove something or outperform an enemy or opponent. You are learning to develop the staying power necessary to properly complete challenges that are presented to you. Your sense of organization and ability to manage time and energy are assets that work in your favor. Oftentimes you win accolades because you are able to finish ahead of schedule with excellent results.

You do like things of quality and find yourself surrounded by items of good taste and refinement. You are not likely to flaunt the vulgar and gaudy signs of wealth and status as many pretentious people do. When not active, you like time for mental stimulation. Those who do not know you well are likely to miss the fact that you are an ardent seeker of truth and like to dig deeply into thought-provoking theories of mind, matter, and human madness. All is not serious with you, however, as your playful side does come out when you are relaxed, content, and know you have done things thoroughly and well.

18ᵗʰ Degree of Taurus

If this is your sun sign, you are strong, determined, and committed to the path you have chosen to follow. This combination finds many people who are attracted to administration and roles of leadership in some capacity. You take on responsibility and feel committed to following through until you get satisfactory results. You have a broad range of interests with an inclination toward the sciences and the technical side of matters. Your grasp of history helps in making sense of the current events taking place in the world around you. Your efficient manner of dealing with matters makes you respected and appreciated for your competence.

NOTABLES WITH THIS DEGREE:

Harry S. Truman: American president

John Fredriksen: Norwegian-born Cypriot, billionaire shipping business executive

Kathryn Kuhlman: American faith healer, Pentecostal preacher

Sir J. M. Barrie: Scottish novelist, dramatist

People with this combination are often found in positions of leadership and situations that require tough decisions. Your independent nature and strong will often attract strong opposition and resistance from those who oppose your policies. You can be misled or drawn into compromises that run against your personal moral standards. There is a karmic hint that in another place and setting, you misused a position of power and authority. You may have fallen victim to deception and vulnerability of pride and ego. You will be placed in situations in which you can be easily compromised or tempted to give in to someone else's agenda.

You have an extensive knowledge base and are savvy about the world. Your inclination is toward inventiveness and discovering improvement to technology or the simple tasks of daily living. Many of you have unique talents and entertainment potential. You are a kind of personal detachment that turns off the more emotionally sensitive types, but as a whole, you are considered a loyal and supportive friend or associate. Whatever your interest or pursuit, you usually get things done efficiently and properly. This trait results in getting you admiration from many people.

19ᵗʰ Degree of Taurus

If this is your sun sign, you are curious, cautious, and concerned about the nature of humanity and its development. There is an introspective quality to this number-sign combination that makes you curious about human nature, but you tend to project your issues onto the universe rather than see them as your own. This combination lends itself to detached observation and scrutiny. You are not as easy to approach on a simple, open, emotional level. Idealistic and utopian in your perspective of life, you can be prone to deep discouragement and despair over the dark side of human nature and humanity's inability to recognize it.

NOTABLES WITH THIS DEGREE:

Jean Houston: American human potential and new thought author, speaker

John Wilkes Booth: American actor, Abraham Lincoln's assassin

William Lilly: English astrologer, occultist

Wayne Dyer: author, lecturer, self-help educator

There is the karmic hint of having used your knowledge or wisdom in another time and place in such a way as to purposely confuse or mislead people into believing your way in order to gain personal power and perhaps political or social gain. You created great doubt and confusion about their spiritual nature and psychological makeup. Currently, you want so much to better understand human nature and assist in the process of healing human behavior. Many teachers, counselors, ministers, and medical personnel are found with this combination.

You feel as if you are destined to get something notable accomplished in this lifetime. While other people seem to be able to take more time for recreation, play, and entertainment, you have a dogged notion that there just isn't time for such misspent time. While at times envious of these people, you are critical that they overlook the need to deal with life rather than escape reality by such lighthearted and nondirectional activities. When you try to do so, there is some guilt, and when you are overburdened with work, you wish you had the disposition for play.

20th Degree of Taurus

If this is your sun sign, you have been given a demeanor and personality that lends itself to the world of mediation and negotiating. You are able to stand amid interpersonal strife and group conflicts while deftly maintaining ongoing dialogue even when both opposing parties have refused to communicate with each other. It is not easy for others to readily see how fixed and determined you can be because you deftly present a persona that puts them at ease. You are tidy, tedious, and at times tricky about maintaining the proper décor and appearance.

You will find yourself frequently in the position of mediating between diverse and often confrontational forces. The Taurus

presence gives you stability and the tenacity to stick with issues that would often exhaust others with less durability. There is a karmic hint of having been deceptive and purposely misleading to others in another time and place. Perhaps it gave you influence or money or revenge. Now you find yourself in positions where you are privy to private information, and you are asked to tell a story that is different from what you know to be happening. You would like to see a world of openness and straightforward truth, but you will more likely become mired in the murky world of spin and sociopolitical dodge ball, whether that is in your business, community, church, or public service affairs.

You like to be among activity and present where discourse and discussion are paramount. Your engaging manner and grasp of the facts and issues at hand serve you well. You are calm in times of crisis and critical in times of calm. Your ability to collect facts and information and summarize events makes you a valuable asset when planning and preparation are taking place. You may find your best skills when you are a part of large organizations or institutions.

21ˢᵗ Degree of Taurus

If this is your sun sign, you can be glib, candid, and condescending in your attitude toward life. This is a combination with the powerful desire for self-expression, so it will be difficult to keep you from getting your ideas to others. Your communication skills can take you far in media, entertainment, politics, or other areas of life in which relating to others is a prime asset. At best, you uplift, inspire, and awaken with your words. Disrupting aspects suggest a karmic pattern of disappointment and betrayal that can leave you with the taste for satire and perhaps cynicism.

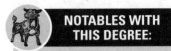

NOTABLES WITH THIS DEGREE:

George Carlin: American comedian, author, social critic

Florence Nightingale: British pioneer of modern nursing, accomplished statistician

Raoul Felder: American divorce lawyer

Burt Bacharach: American singer, songwriter, pianist, composer

You spend a lot of your time wrestling with an inner struggle to integrate the masculine and feminine sides of self. You may find the social roles of man and woman confusing and out of harmony. There is the suggestion of a karmic pattern of having spent other lifetimes uncomfortable with the sexuality of your physical body. Even now, you are often ill at ease with what is the proper behavior in a given social context. As you find inner integration, your physical performances can be beautiful, breathtaking, and beyond the range of previous human achievement in your chosen area of preference.

You are conscious of your position in society and thrive on being able to present an image of prosperity and a higher standard of living. At best, this gives a decorative taste to your home and manner of dress. You may be an adviser for others about how to select and savor the more valuable and finer things of life. With adverse aspects, you are willing to cut corners and even cheat to be able to present such an image. Fun and merriment follow you through life, and you are blessed with interesting and diverse friends and associates.

22nd Degree of Taurus

If this is your sun sign, you are determined to find your destiny and get something done that has been bothering your soul for a long time. You are focused, decisive, and dedicated to whatever you choose to get done, knowing it is something very important to your soul journey. Your relationship with money is most interesting in that you may never seem to have a lot, but you manage to receive just what you need to get by on your own terms. While you are deeply interested in life's many philosophical questions, you are not one to spend much time contemplating them. Rather, you prefer to get something done.

NOTABLES WITH THIS DEGREE:

Stevie Wonder: American singer, songwriter, record producer

Jim Jones: American religious extremist, cult leader

Ritchie Valens: American short-lived pioneer of rock n roll

Pope Innocent XIII: Catholic Pope, known for issues with the Jesuits

Perhaps you are too serious. There is the karmic hint that in another sequential soul lesson you may have frivolously squandered the opportunity to be more accomplished. Perhaps you took divinely given gifts for granted. Perhaps you tarried too long with the temptations of flesh and sensual dalliance. Perhaps you rebelled against an assignment that was given to you by one in authority. There is something left unaccomplished, and you sense emptiness within your soul where that piece of the puzzle should now fit. Your commitment to inner focus will bring you to the place you so longingly seek.

The people with this number-sign combination are not free from the struggles of all mortals, but their journey will be embellished with experiences on all levels of consciousness. This makes the effort more than worth it when you get to the end of a cycle and appreciate all that you have achieved. You are blessed with good people around you and make contact with some very enlightened and accomplished leaders in your community. While others marvel at the paranormal and seek to investigate its mysteries, you live it on an almost daily basis.

23rd Degree of Taurus

If this is your sun sign, this can be a life full of fun and many chances. You are prone to take more risks and explore life with more zeal than most of your Taurus family members (and a large portion of the human population). It's probably a good thing that your traditionally reserved Taurus personality puts some restraints on that go-for-all potential of this number-sign combination. You coast through many assorted life adventures on the way to accumulating a treasure chest of observations about life and the human predicament. Now what to do with all that wealth of accumulated cognition. Perhaps the question has occurred to you more than once.

NOTABLES WITH THIS DEGREE:

Deborah Houlding: English astrologer, author

Otto Klemperer: German conductor and composer

George Lucas: American screenwriter, movie producer, director

David Byrne: Scottish-born, American musician, songwriter

There is a karmic hint that in a past excursion on this rock, you became enamored with sensuous sidetracks of living and lost track of your destined path. Perhaps a naïve experiment into excess led to addictive behavior. Perhaps you used excessive behavior in protest against divine authority. You have all of the tools to reconnect to your highest purpose and ground your feet on Earth as you become a living example of higher purpose fulfilled. You are learning to enjoy the richness of the input that comes from the senses while opening your extrasensory channels to funnel the higher light into this material world.

Because of your openness to living, people find you to be a joyful companion and valued associate. Your graciousness and inclination to laughter add to your many fine personality traits. Most of you demonstrate the traditional Taurus touch for fine quality and tastefulness in your décor and dress. You most likely do it, however, with a distinctly different touch of the quirky and uncommon. Travel opportunities come frequently, and for those of you with a transcendental twist, there are equal opportunities to travel into multiple dimensions of the spheres.

24th Degree of Taurus

If this is your sun sign, you can be more emotionally sensitive to people and experiences around you than many of your other Taurus combinations. Loyalty is an important issue with you and can be taken to a fault if you are not careful. This is a combination that indicates an elevated possibility of codependency in your family past and present. You are observant of the social climate and may produce observations on the world to be shared with other people. Many with this number-sign combination will choose work that is closely connected to the community, rendering aid to those whose struggle with life is much greater than most.

There is a karmic hint of having previously had your personal life thrown about because of social unrest and upheaval. Perhaps you have resentment toward those who tore apart the fabric of a culture you loved. Maybe you harbor anger toward those who would unscrupulously and ruthlessly pillage a society just for personal glory and selfish ends. You may be at odds with those who mismanage their public responsibility, and many of you are found where reform and reorganization flourishes. You are most comfortable within the influence of a relatively healthy and inspired congregation of similar souls.

For the most part, you are into comfort, cleanliness, and a somewhat noticeably cautious way of life. Family is important to you, and you seek the structure of mental, emotional, and physical well-being for yourself and your kindred. An archetypal example of this number-sign combination might be the mom who gives her children a glass of milk every day, which is symbolic of emotional nurturing. You like to think of the entirety of humanity as your extended family, and you would like to see the world blossoming with goodness of heart and well-being for its many inhabitants.

NOTABLES WITH THIS DEGREE:

Jeff Jawer: American astrologer, author, speaker

Mark Zuckerberg: American billionaire computer programmer, Internet business executive, cofounder of Facebook

Pierce Brosnan: British actor, producer, active environmentalist

Swami Muktananda: Hindu guru, Yoga and religious innovator

25th Degree of Taurus

If this is your sun sign, you may find your-self being thought of as daring and willing to dance with jeopardy more readily than many of your Taurus kin. The combination of dar-ing boldness and deliberate care can work in your favor once these two paradoxical parts of your personality become integrated and understood. After methodical preparation, you are ready to leap into action at the right time with the right solution. On the negative side, you may find yourself squandering away talent and time in wasted stages of indul-gence and, sometimes, addictive waste. You do know how to live life to the fullest, and when you do this in the positive vein, you are blessed beyond belief.

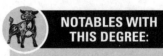

NOTABLES WITH THIS DEGREE:

Marshall Applewhite: American sect leader who founded Heaven's Gate, music teacher

Billy Martin: American professional baseball manager

Laura Pausini: Italian pop singer, songwriter

Janet Jackson: American singer, songwriter, actress, dancer, record producer

There is a karmic hint of having had trouble in other times and settings with the timing of your decisions. You have pushed when you should have pulled. You have waited when you should have gone. You do not like to be wrong and have likely made decisions that have upset the lives of others around you. There is a time for risk taking, and your time may have come. However, the lesson you are learning is to differentiate between compulsive ego reactions in order to respond to your highest self. Your life may be somewhat unconven-tional compared to the norms of society around you. There will come a time when your apparent unconventional knowledge can be useful in saving many.

You may not take the road most traveled, coming to conclusions different from others who have gotten there. This combination is often associated with people who are caught in the middle of changing social trends. You see hope while others panic. You understand a greater purpose when others see chaos. Just when things get bad, you are capable of standing up and performing to your best level. Your ability to mingle among many diverse communities of people will be a true asset throughout your life.

NUMEROLOGY OF ASTROLOGY

26th Degree of Taurus

If this is your sun sign, you will most likely experience a most curious relationship with society, particularly with the institutions of the masses. Your life is interwoven with society in such a way that there is little time left for contemplation or private moments of circumspection. Your strong will and capacity for perseverance make you a formidable personality once you have focused on your intent and purpose. Your street-sense psychology is usually right on, and this lets you do well in the negotiations and games of commerce.

There is the karmic hint that in another time and setting, you were likely angry at society and its rules. This could have turned into a destructive antisocial pattern of living. Perhaps you were unjustly tried by the laws and rules of society. Perhaps you were restricted by parents with extremely rigid moral and ethical codes of family behavior backed by harsh (even cruel) punishment. The conflicting messages became confusing and created intense emotional conflict within. You project that onto the outer world. You are learning to forgive and release deeply seated memories from your past. As you do, you become a prominent figure in the role of social reform and progressive transformation.

You are quite capable of acquiring things of splendor and prosperity around you. At best, you attract a similar circle of accomplished friends and associates. Together you are capable of achieving considerable impact on your culture. You are valued for your loyalty and commitment to those you trust. There is little that you would not do for them if called on for assistance. Your clever, candid, and often comical observations both entertain and educate because of the deeper meanings you inject into your storytelling and sharing with others. This makes you a popular guest or sought-after associate.

NOTABLES WITH THIS DEGREE:

Tony Parker: French professional basketball player

Katherine Spencer Young: American astrologer, lecturer, author

Richard Scruggs: trial and tobacco lawyer

Dennis Hopper: actor, producer, artist

27ᵗʰ Degree of Taurus

If this is your sun sign, you possess a down-to-earth determination along with an almost heavenly inspired outlook toward living. At best, you keep one foot firmly footed on Earth while part of you pines for lofty leaps into the stratosphere of higher worlds. You probably chose this number-sign combination in order to have some kind of footing on the ground. The karmic suggestion is that in another life stream, you invested a lot of time and energy constructing theoretical models of life and human evolution. While entertaining — and in some cases, convincing — time would prove them to be impractical and unsubstantiated. You sought to please the powers of the day rather than firmly validate the truth.

You find yourself torn between the dichotomy of social thought and the scientific, religious, and philosophical dogma of the day. You seek to find balance and peace within yourself by living in harmony with cosmic and natural laws. When you find it, you become a threat to those who preach the orderliness of present communal power structure. You have sold out before to gain temporal power and the temptation still remains within your consciousness. Will you be able to hold on to the inner truth from above and apply it to your everyday living? If so, you will have found a recipe for living that many will want to know.

There will be many challenges for you with authority figures and the institutions of spin. You are easily attracted to the fringe elements of society and want to be careful that you do not go so far out in your affiliations that you become essentially ineffective. Your inspirational nature can reach many people, and you have a chance to be an active participant in a transformational change in planetary awareness.

NOTABLES WITH THIS DEGREE:

Pope John Paul II: Catholic Pope, known for anticommunist stance

Tina Fey: American television actress, writer, comedienne

Nicholas II: last Czar of Russia

Helena Noguerra: Belgian singer, actress, television presenter

Ho Chí Minh: Vietnam president, revolutionary, diplomat

28th Degree of Taurus

If this is your sun sign, you are more of a go-getter than many of your Taurus contemporaries. At best, this combination puts together the impulse of the one to get things done along with the patience and precision of the tedious Taurus. When in harmony, you get inspired and thoroughly pull off the complete package. This number-sign combination lends a keen eye for detail and organizational tendencies that allows you to capture the spirit and mood of the culture around you. Whatever you do, it is done with flair of grace and a flourish of freshness that can be a winning recipe for success.

NOTABLES WITH THIS DEGREE:

Malcolm X: African-American Muslim leader, civil-rights activist

Mustafa Kemal Atatürk: Turkish military officer, revolutionary diplomat, writer

James "Jimmy" Stewart: American actor

Paul Hirst: British sociologist, political theorist

When at odds, you are in a constant state of tension between the go-go push of this numerical energy and the plodding part of the Taurus personality. There is a karmic hint that in another time and setting, you were at odds with convention and essential social dexterity. You may have flaunted your differences and ridiculed the norm. There is a tendency to feel socially superior to many and disregard the sensitivities of other people. If this happens, you flaunt rather than inspire, ridicule rather than refine.

You trek your way among many cultures and classes of people. In the process, you absorb the best of each culture, incorporating it into your comprehensive and creative lifestyle. This allows you to diplomatically mingle amid many diverse subcultures and levels of human society. You have the knack to bring out the best in others, and when you do this, you can reach a pinnacle of success and recognition. Your complex and well-developed perception of life allows you to be entertaining and educational at the same time without appearing to pontificate. At best, this is a number-sign combination of class, culture, and an uncanny grasp on life.

29th Degree of Taurus

If this is your sun sign, you have an additional touch of taste, tact, and refinement than might be seen in other Taurus personalities. You will often get what you want, but those from whom you get it from will probably not feel like they have gotten run over by a bull. This number-sign combination does not eliminate the Taurus tendency toward stubbornness, but it does make you more subtle and less confronting in your tenacity. You see

NOTABLES WITH THIS DEGREE:

Peter Hurkos: Dutch psychic, paranormal performer

Cher: American actress, singer, songwriter, and entertainer

alternative ways to get things done in simple and economical terms. There is an exciting potential for producing highly intuitive and novel solutions with very practical and affordable technologies.

There is a karmic clue that in another soul sequence, you might have made a bad prediction that resulted in disruption to those around you. Or perhaps you were a seer who saw something bad coming and were blamed for causing that event to happen. Perhaps you were a sort of prophet who spoke of radical changes in the behavior of the people. You may have upset those who were in control of the population. There may be a fear of trusting your intuition or getting strange ideas in your head. You are learning once again to discern and to trust what is the truth and figuring out how to apply that inner knowing in an effective manner under the circumstances of the times in which you live.

You are not afraid to rattle the nerves of the socially complacent. When necessary, you are capable of being quite charming and disarming in order to get your way. In those moments, you use the conventional behavior of the times, even if silently mocking some of them. There is a part of you that wants to see the best of humanity and social living exist peacefully. You are saddened by abuse and the harm that many in society inflict on others.

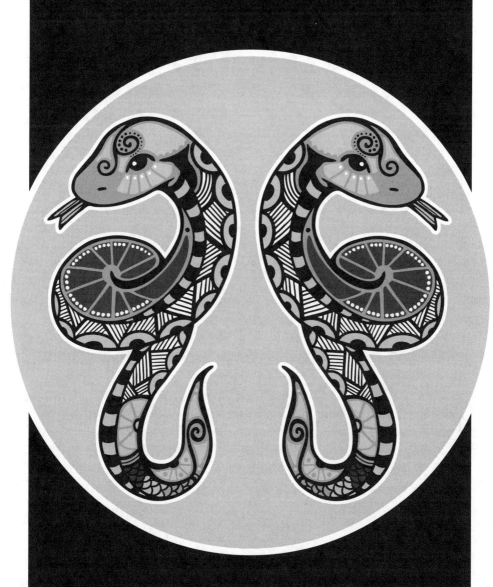

GEMINI

0 Degree of Gemini

If this is your sun sign, you may find your-self in the position to alter the fate of nations. On the other hand, you could become the world's best couch potato and end up doing nothing with your life. This is a number-sign combination of paradox and pause. You may not get as much inspiration from the universe as other people seem to receive about their lives. It can take you longer to figure out your fate than most people, and that can become exasperating to some of you. There can be so much frustration for a few of you that you just give in and give up.

You find yourself constantly challenged with paradox and ambiguity. Just when you have made up your mind, circumstances change. Just when you make a decision, oth-ers oppose you or abandon you. You have a good mental grasp of things and are, in most cases, conceptually competent. However,

NOTABLES WITH THIS DEGREE:

Paul Brenner: American holistic physician, speaker

Leonardo Del Vecchio: Italian billionaire, eyeglass designer and manufacturer

Charles Aznavour: Armenian-French singer, songwriter, actor

Wilhelm Richard Wagner: German composer, conductor, music theorist, essayist

Arthur Conan Doyle: Scottish mystery and science-fiction author, novelist, poet

when you finally believe in something, you fail to act on your belief. Once you decide to take action, it may be too late, and an opportunity has been missed.

There is a karmic hint that in another time and setting, you had the oppor-tunity to make a grand leap in consciousness. Perhaps you were fearful of the change, so you grasped to ego needs and neurotic insecurity. You are once again at the crossroads of change. You might take a large leap along with many others, or you could get caught in the constipation of mass consciousness and miss an evolutionary moment of growth. Life has put you just where you need to be, and you have been blessed with many tools of personality that allow you to accomplish much in this life journey. Now is the time to face your reticence and go after what you know to be your inner calling.

1ˢᵗ Degree of Gemini

If this is your sun sign, you are quick, quiz-zical, and quite likely to bring surprise and sometimes astonishment to others. It is not easy to place you under any classification because you will most likely go out of your way to make sure that you do not fit. You are at your best in an environment of rapid change in which unanticipated challenges constantly arise to be solved. You mix and mingle amid assorted subcultures and groups of people with unorthodox or sometimes bizarre inter-ests. Your imagination is an unlimited source of unconventional ideas. Some of your most far-out thoughts can be turned into useful products or procedures.

NOTABLES WITH THIS DEGREE:

Marcia Moore: American astrologer, author, speaker

Cyril Fagan: Irish astrologer, author

Kylie Minogue: Australian singer, songwriter, actress

Gayatri Devi: Indian Queen mother, politician

Franz Anton Mesmer: German physician, developed theory of animal magnetism that led to hypnosis

There is the karmic hint of difficultly find-ing your place in a social time and structure of another period. Perhaps you spoke out sharply in opposition to those who denied people the opportunity to stand up and give their opinions. Maybe you suffered death or punishment for your directness and complaints. You may still feel the unconscious sting of public retribution and try sincerely to be tactful when touching on sensitive social issues of the day. However, it is nearly impossible to keep you away from an opportunity to speak out for the oppressed and the victims of injustice. You are an archetypal personification of one who stands for freedom of expression.

You will find yourself among some of the subcultures and avant-garde segments of society. In your uniqueness, you find commonality among the masses and seek to settle into a path of self-exploration. Your quest for living introduces you to many extreme forms of personal indulgence, and after a while, you find a middle ground of expression that still allows for the pursuit of your unique taste of life.

2nd Degree of Gemini

If this is your sun sign, you are compassionate, kind, and at times controlling. You strive to be fair and equitable, although you may not find it easy to please everyone all of the time. This number-sign combination raises issues of conflict with social mores and customs, and it is very likely that your early years were riddled with conflicts regarding proper behavior and social protocols. There is a kind of natural Gemini tendency toward playfulness and a touch of mischief. Perhaps your childhood

environment did not encourage the full expression of those healthy childhood traits. You can be careful and guarded in your public interaction, and people may think of you as a trifle remote and inaccessible. Some of you may compensate for this through acting or some form of public performance.

You constantly find yourself struggling internally with conflicting codes of behavior. There is the karmic suggestion that in another time and place, you may have been tyrannically controlling of people's behavior and social conduct. You could find yourself experiencing such suppression in your early family situations and throughout this life. Whereas your desire is to be more universally humanitarian, it may not be easy to be able to do so during this life experience. If you are to do so, you will be called on to stand up and use your position of authority to lobby for greater freedom of human expression and social flexibility.

This can be a combination of great humor, healthy childlike playfulness, and unique personality. Your perception of life can be both entertaining and wise. It may take many years for you to find the confidence and circumstance that let you be yourself comfortably. Once the hurdles have been crossed, you are a delightful character of whim, mood, and independent self-expression. You are most comfortable around people of broad experience and expansiveness of thought.

3rd Degree of Gemini

If this is your sun sign, you are witty, wild, and often wonderfully unpredictable as you tiptoe your way through the tests and trials of life. You move like a butterfly and most likely do not sting like a bee. Most of you were blessed with a live-and-let-live attitude that is not quick to judge someone at first sight. This allows people to be at ease in your presence. When they are at ease, you will find that they will trust you and be willing to share very personal information about themselves. This trust is not to be taken lightly or misused. It would be easy to use it against someone and for your own interests.

There is the karmic hint that in other times and settings you have been insensitive and most likely exceedingly cavalier toward other people and their sensitivities. Perhaps you prided your mental prowess and thus considered emotional people as weak and vulnerable. Possibly you were afraid that people who were spontaneous and open about feelings might get out of control and disrupt the statutes of behavior that were set in stone by your position and power within the community. You are learning to appreciate the structure within chaos and the paradoxical orderliness in serendipity. This sounds philosophical and profound, but it pretty much comes down to lightening up.

Your imagination and almost innocent manner of coming to profound yet simple solutions makes you a crowd pleaser and a person who is sought after for solutions and suggestions. This is a great number-sign combination for the entertainer and those who flourish being in front of the public. You attract many friends and go many places as your life unfolds before you. Your diversity of understanding and range of knowledge allow you to get along with people from all levels of status and standing within their communities.

4th Degree of Gemini

If this is your sun sign, you are more likely to be organized and predictable than many of your Gemini family. This number-sign combination can indicate a more stable nature when compared to otherwise often scattered Gemini tendencies. At its best, this combination indicates more staying power when it comes to completing projects or commitments. You are more able to stay focused when other Gemini's become easily distracted by other opportunities and proposals. You likely will find Taurus influences very influential in your chart. There is more caution to your approach and planning before you make important moves.

NOTABLES WITH THIS DEGREE:

Henry Kissinger: U.S. Secretary of State, political adviser

Pio of Pietrelcina: Italian sainted Catholic priest noted for his piety and supernatural events

Miles Davis: American jazz musician, trumpeter, bandleader, composer

John Wayne: American actor, director, producer, political activist

There is the karmic suggestion that in another time and setting, you were involved with some kind of project or endeavor that got out of control and resulted in upheaval and probably the destruction of the lives of many people. Perhaps it was a belief system gone amuck. It might have been a physical project of some magnitude that had been underestimated. There is a fear of losing control that sometimes motivates you toward too much caution and fear. You seek balance between knowing when to take risks and when to pause for further evaluation in order to achieve the most successful results. At best, you reach a midpoint where you move quickly and courageously on queue and pause to ponder when appropriate.

You are worldly, wise, and well traveled. Your Gemini zest for experience has led you to the far corners of Earth in search of life's myriad mysteries. You have many tales to tell and trophies to show from your collection of culture and experiences. In the end, you attract a circle of trusted souls into your life who stay with you through the many trials and tribulations of accomplishment. You have much and are capable of being very generous with those who helped you acquire it.

5th Degree of Gemini

If this is your sun sign, you live on the edge throughout much of your life. This is a number-sign combination that encourages explora-tion, excitation, and at times, the exploitation of life. You become frustrated with standards and norms and take a stand for individuality whenever possible. Never wanting to be tied down by restrictions, you will probably find yourself frequently on the move or starting new endeavors. You embrace sensuality and perhaps human sexuality with great verve and enthusiasm. This may take you into delight-ful experimentation of the body and soul.

NOTABLES WITH THIS DEGREE:

Helena Bonham Carter: English actress

Isadora Duncan: American dancer associated with formulating modern dance

Christopher Lee: English actor

Jack Kevorkian: American pathologist, euthanasia activist, painter, author, composer

There is the karmic hint at having crossed social and political standards in another time and place. This likely resulted in much reaction and perhaps condemnation of your actions before many people. You rally against social restraint but look for the magic social system that you hope will give people the power to experi-ment and decide for themselves. You may find yourself flaunting excess in an attempt to jar loose the tightness of public opinion and repression. You can be funny, fascinating, and flirtatious with others and with life itself. You like to tease and at times taunt those who let inhibitions stop them from experiencing life to its fullest.

This is a number-sign combination that encourages an honest and intense immersion into the plentifulness of life that is offered to us while on this planet. Your quest for living is infectious, and you attract many people who are inspired by your zealous pursuit of expression and freedom of living. While this can result in criticism and dissent by your detractors, it also can serve as a rallying point for those souls who long to reach out and touch real life. Be careful that your aspirations don't turn your behavior into escapist indulgence rather than a breakthrough of self-awareness.

NUMEROLOGY OF ASTROLOGY

6ᵗʰ Degree of Gemini

If this is your sun sign, you may have some difficulty connecting directly to your personal feelings and inner motives. You are keen to see what makes other people tick and might choose to act these insights out on the stage or through some form of writing, singing, or performing. This is a good number-sign combination for those who delve into the human psyche. It is easier for you to find your own inner events than many of your Gemini contemporaries. You are clever at finding alternative ways to motivate those stubborn and weary souls who have given up or just like to be contrary.

NOTABLES WITH THIS DEGREE:

Ian Fleming: English author and journalist, created James Bond character

Jesse Bradford: American actor

Louis Gossett Jr.: American actor

There is the karmic hint of having been insensitive and probably manipulative of other people's emotions in other times. Maybe you were a bit perverse in twisting someone's emotional weak spot in order to get something you wanted that was theirs. You can do this very easily and strive to use that insight for assisting others rather than taking unfair emotional advantage of them. Some of you might be developing instruments and technologies that allow for a more complete connection of the mind, body, and spirit.

You are nimble and quick to adjust to the changes and unexpected events of the times. This flexibility makes you a good consultant and advisor in times of panic and chaos. You are able to articulate very personal and emotional experiences and give definition to what others struggle to comprehend and report. Your facile mind can take intuitive leaps of comprehension and come up with an entirely new set of logical stratagems to deal with the crisis at hand. You will enjoy traveling among many cultures and societies, working to sew the thread of commonality among people into a unified force that can cope more efficiently with the travails of our times.

7th Degree of Gemini

If this is your sun sign, you are a little more subdued than some of your Gemini brethren. You are more internally focused than outgoing. This does not necessarily completely negate the traditional gregarious Gemini, but it may make you more cautious and careful. You weigh, analyze, and measure before plunging into something, and you are cautious in the process of getting to know someone new. In the end, you build solid friendships and alliances once you commit. You take from the general and narrow down to specifics. This can be helpful for matters of research and investigation when you must get to the specific point or issue.

There is the karmic hint of having once been very attached to a source of teaching in which you believed very deeply. Maybe your belief became outdated and dogmatic rather than sustaining and uplifting. Perhaps you defended it vigorously to the extent of causing harm and injustice to others. You are careful about subterfuge and can get rankled when someone gets up on the pedestal and speaks compulsively about theories or concepts that are long outdated. You can become particularly upset with pompous academics who arrogantly hold on to outworn, conventional teachings.

You can spin delightful tales with the best of them and love to debate into the night about time, space, philosophy, spirituality, or scientific matters that are hot topics of the day. You will likely find yourself becoming increasingly curious about extraterrestrial life and its relationship to the evolution of this planet. Since your awareness is boundless, there is no topic that does not get some of your attention and interest. When not reading or speculating, you may well be writing the text or treatise that will inspire yet another generation of scholars and explorers.

NOTABLES WITH THIS DEGREE:

Gopi Krishna: Indian yogi, mystic, teacher, social reformer, writer

John Fogerty: American singer, songwriter, musician

Patch Adams: American social activist, citizen diplomat, professional clown, author

Rudy Giuliani: American lawyer, business executive, politician, mayor of New York City

Bob Hope: English-born American comedian, dancer, actor

8th Degree of Gemini

If this is your sun sign, you are restless, reserved, and ready to mix it up with the circumstances that life brings you. There are always numerous options and choices for you to make, and it may not be easy to manage all of those possibilities easily. You do it better, however, than many of your Gemini brothers and sisters. When they break down under the stress and strain of deliberation, you relish the role of getting on top of the situation and handling each demand with studied discipline. Your quick mental grasp of things, along with a wealth of experience, gives you excellent personal resources to achieve what you want.

NOTABLES WITH THIS DEGREE:

John F. Kennedy: American president

Darrelyn Gunzburg: Australian playwright, astrologer

George Zweig: Russian-born American particle physicist, neurobiologist, financial officer

Annette Bening: American actress

There is a karmic suggestion that you were unwilling to face decisions and responsibilities in another time and place. Perhaps you shirked your role as a leader or avoided the responsibility expected of your title or position. You are now able to overcome past fears and use your assets to a greater degree of effectiveness. Versatility is the name, and action is the game. You are curious about many things and rapidly acquire insight about a subject. This results in a vast reservoir of information from which you can draw when putting the pieces of a project together.

People with this number-sign combination are often interested in matters of law, regulation, and management of events and organizations. This can include an interest in the natural laws of physics, nature, and other sciences. You try to make order out of chaos, and you are intent on understanding the principles and dynamics underlying the evolution of humankind and this planet upon which you live. You mix and mingle among many diverse cultures and people with assorted ideas about life. This makes you an interesting conversationalist and an entertaining person.

9th Degree of Gemini

If this is your sun sign, you can be quite an enigma to those who aspire to figure out your personality traits. The dual nature of Gemini in itself makes it difficult to pinpoint certain traits that might be more evident in the other signs. With the 9 and Gemini combination, the discernment can become an even greater task. Your richness, depth of life experience, and perception of human nature allows you to pick out any role you would like to perform. Thus, it can be difficult for you to identify your own true self. There is a fascination with the perfect and noble in human nature. But at the same time, there are those of you who find delight in exploring the darker side of our human condition.

NOTABLES WITH THIS DEGREE:

Clint Eastwood: American actor, director, producer, composer, pianist, politician

Peter the Great: Russian Czar, known for westernizing Russia

Walt Whitman: American poet, essayist, journalist, humanist, transcendentalist

Wynonna Judd: American country music singer, entertainer

There is a karmic hint that there was a time and place when you engaged in behavior that bordered on the cruel and perhaps sadistic. There is a part of you that wants to be pure, good, and noble. However, there is also that part of you that is guilt ridden, troubled, and at times tormented by the ugliness of past deeds. This is a life of learning, forgiveness, and self-acceptance. You have come to the realization that having done such things before, you can accept the experience and no longer have to be transfixed on it.

Because of your grasp and acceptance of the more murky waters of the human subconscious, you can be effective in assisting others with their own troubled pasts. Many of you will be attracted to counseling or some form of support system for those who suffer more deeply from past transgressions. You may find yourself enjoying the finer forms of music, art, and transcendental philosophies. At some time in your life, you will find enjoyment in humanitarian efforts and reform.

10th Degree of Gemini

If this is your sun sign, you are noted for your versatility of talents and flexibility of manner. You drift and glide through the boardwalk of human endeavor with an air of mischievousness. You toy with the travails that beset you and then tackle the challenges that come to your door head-on. You live with knowledge of the paradox that everything is terribly important, but it really doesn't matter! In that delightful space of serendipitous enchantment, you frolic where others falter and dance when others become depressed. It is not that you are above life. You just can't quite get to the point of taking it so bloody seriously.

NOTABLES WITH THIS DEGREE:

Marilyn Monroe: American movie star

Brigham Young: American religious leader

Andy Griffith: American actor

Morgan Freeman: American actor, producer, narrator

Don Ameche: American television entertainer, Broadway actor

You have an inquisitive attitude and absorb information at a high rate. You will turn over many intellectual stones in your thirst for knowledge and attempt to get a grasp on life. You have a knack for juggling many interests, and you are envied by many for your diversity of talents and abilities. Despite this inclination for multiplicity, your heart seeks to find a kind of grand, unifying theory that will pull the meaning of things together. There is a karmic hint of having used your understanding of duality to divide and separate others in another time and place. Your knack for being able to accept the interplay of dualities allows you to recognize avenues for the reconciliation of conflicts when others are trapped in the ongoing agitation of apparent conflict between dualities.

Your youthful exuberance and meandering way of traveling through life may appear immature to the serious and cavalier to the self-righteous. However, for the most part, people are curious about how you do it, and they secretly want to emulate some of that verve and dash. Quick, cheeky, and — when appropriate — preposterous, you do not allow those around you to become complacent. Because of your ability to react quickly and see solutions while others balk, many of you will find yourselves in managerial positions that require swift decision making.

11th Degree of Gemini

If this is your sun sign, you are not likely to pass through life unnoticed. You manifest a flair for drama, exaggeration, and showmanship at just the right place and time to get the desired results from those around you. This can be an unconscious holdover from the past or a purposeful posture that you are able to implement on demand. Sooner or later, you will find a way to stand out in the crowd, but it's not as if that is your only motivation in life. Your diversity of interest and potential is vast. You want to make an impact, and the primary way of doing so is to be able to reach a large number of people.

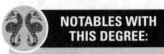

NOTABLES WITH THIS DEGREE:

Karen Mok: Chinese actress, singer, songwriter, animal rights' advocate

Heidi Klum: German model, actress, business executive, fashion designer

Martha Washington: the first First Lady of the United States

Alejandro Agresti: Argentine film director, screenwriter, producer

There is a karmic hint that in another life setting, you took part in disseminating truth that would set people free. Perhaps the effort was sabotaged by a traitor within. Maybe your message was not clearly understood, and it stirred up old superstitions or fears within the group of people you wished to awaken. You witnessed your efforts crumble and blamed yourself for what you believed to be a failure of effort. There is part of you that still fears public reaction. At the same time, there is a part of you that seeks to get public attention. As you find your truth once more, you will attract the right media and method of presentation.

You can scatter your resources and miss the point or utilize your diverse talents to get a lot done. Usually those who are born with this number-sign combination get along easily with people from a wide range of culture, education, and awareness. You seek to mend misunderstandings and heal wounds that have been woven into the fabric of culture over eons of time. Your intuition can be a formidable tool to clearly grasp the needs of the masses and address the specific issues that are important to those you wish to assist.

12th Degree of Gemini

If this is your sun sign, you may feel like you are on a quest to understand the fickle finger of fate. You frequently feel like you are swimming upstream against the current of the cosmic tides. It appears that others seem to sashay though life with relative ease while you more often struggle to earn or attain almost any desired reward. You have the assets and personality traits to get ahead and experience the good things that life offers. It is not clear to you why these things do not seem to happen.

There is the karmic hint that you could have previously impaired the learning of a group of people. Possibly your arrogance did not want them to know as much as you. Maybe you were afraid that things would get out of control if they knew too much. Perhaps you were the pawn being used by those who had control over the population at that time. You felt helpless to prevent the injustice that was taking place. You punish yourself for having prevented others from receiving their just dues. Now you subconsciously sabotage the opportunity to have more for yourself. Now is a good time to work through this karma and move into your rightful place of cosmic inheritance.

At your best, you are buoyant, bright, and blushing with excitement at the bountiful opportunities the universe presents. You are engaging and full of information, ranging from the trivial to the profound. People come to expect something tantalizing and rare from you, and you seldom disappoint. There is much within you that can be of assistance to helping humankind. You can languish in a sense of false humility, but once you shed that age-old behavior, you will blossom into a delight of knowing and giving.

13th Degree of Gemini

If this is your sun sign, you will frequently find yourself dancing on the edge of the dichotomies of life. The mystery of death stirs your quest to get as much as you can from being alive. The brightness of the light serves to stimulate your desire to fathom the depths of the dark side. You relish the dance and tides of flow between the yin and the yang. You move in and out of the crevices of human consciousness with curiosity and, at times, cunning consideration. You know the elation of love and life and have also plunged into the depths of despair. What are you to do with all of this breadth of experience and scope of human condition?

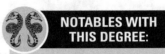

NOTABLES WITH THIS DEGREE:

Antoinette Story: Mayan oracle, intuitive, futurist

George H. W. Bush: American president, intelligence official

George Noory: American talk show host

Angelina Jolie: American actress

There is the hint of karmic residue carried over from another time and experience when you were in a position to do much and assist humanity in its evolutionary spiral. Perhaps you chose instead to take a personal course of self-indulgence, building exaggerated personal esteem. Perhaps fear got in the way, and you were not willing to take the risk involved to improve the condition of the world around you. You will have many choices and opportunities in this lifetime to get going and get something done. The longer you wait to do so, the greater the existential guilt of doing nothing.

You are blessed with many potential tools that can assist you on your path through the web of human accomplishment. You are clever and equipped well to accomplish what you believe is your course of life. It might be difficult at times to select a particular focus and stay with that choice. Your sense of humor and quick wit will help you under many adverse circumstances. Be careful that the wit does not turn to rueful cynicism and painfully acrid assessments of others and their lot in life.

14th Degree of Gemini

If this is your sun sign, you are capable of standing out as a beacon of light in a world that grows dark and foreboding. You are interested in transformation of the body, mind, and soul. Your ability to adapt to the immediate demands of your environment serves you well in times of crisis and chaos. This is a hands-on number-sign combination. You want to see results, not just theorization and speculation. You are capable and willing to take risks that many would scoff at. This

tendency can be taken too far, as some of you are prone to gambling and compulsive risk taking.

There is the karmic hint that in another life sequence, you may well have been a participant in some form of experiment that went wrong. Possibly you blame yourself for mistakes that might have been made. Maybe someone who felt threatened by progress and change sabotaged the effort. You want to believe in technologies or philosophies that transform society and humanity. You can become fearful of advancements or innovations that appear to go too far too fast. It is most important for you to focus on learning discernment and trust of the inner wisdom of higher consciousness.

You are dynamic, delightful, and daring. This zest for living makes you fun to be with, and people seek you out knowing that you will come up with something that excites and entertains. Your curiosity and sense of adventure leads you into all sorts of challenging and demanding activities that would make many mortals pause and doubt. This number-sign combination is common for people who like physical exercise. You may be a dancer or participate in some vigorous form of competitive sporting event.

15th Degree of Gemini

If this is your sun sign, you have a baffling quality of behavior that both mystifies and captivates. This adds mystery to a sun sign already known for unpredictability and paradoxical temperament. You can switch from saintly to sinful, benign to unmerciful, and charming to scheming in the twinkle of an eye. There is a touch of cynicism that you couch in humor and rivulets of mental parrying that confuse just what it is you really are trying to say. Perhaps your internal conflicts get in the way of knowing for yourself just what you do mean.

NOTABLES WITH THIS DEGREE:

Thomas Mann: German novelist, social critic, philanthropist

Geronimo: Indian leader of the Chiricahua Apache

James Connolly: Irish and Scottish socialist leader

Yukihiro Takahashi: Japanese musician and drummer

You are both alluring and standoffish in the same moment. Many will find you engaging and are drawn to further understand your unique and mysterious personality. Perhaps it is because you are bequeathed with so many contradictory character traits that many people are curious to know more about you. In the process, they may secretly wish to find out more information about themselves that has eluded their personal quest for self-understanding. There is a karmic hint of being both a con and a cherub in another time and place. You return now with a desire to integrate and acknowledge seemingly irreconcilable facets of your personality.

This process might be as baffling to you as it can be to those who know you. You remain devilishly delightful in the way you present the story of repentance and release, making you a popular communicator and entertaining host. You have a valuable story to tell about the chronicles of personal growth, and many of you will be drawn to positions that allow you to teach and assist others who struggle on their own paths of personal integration.

16th Degree of Gemini

If this is your sun sign, you are an enigma wrapped in a mystery with a touch of the unpredictable thrown in to make things interesting. Well, maybe that's a little dramatic, but you are born for drama. There is a touch of sadness that goes with this number-sign combination, and many of you will feel like you are always chasing something that is just around the corner but never quite arrives. But the quest is worth it for those who persevere. There is a kind of mystical charm at the far end of the chain of consciousness. For those who are willing to stay the path, the richest form of reward awaits, with a glimpse into the very making of the cosmos and life itself.

NOTABLES WITH THIS DEGREE:

Grant Lewi: American astrologer, author

Anna Kournikova: Russian-American professional tennis player, model

Dean Martin: American actor, singer, entertainer

Muammar al-Gaddafi: Libyan military leader, ruler

Prince: American musician, singer, songwriter

There is the karmic hint that you could have taken the enlightened path in another time and place. Perhaps you got close to the golden grail only to get your hopes dashed after taking a wrong turn and getting burned by a rush of uncontrolled kundalini fire. You seek the highest truth but are leery of what you will find. You pray to the gods for light, but you are afraid that punishment might await you. You dread fate but push it to the limits. Perhaps you are closer than you realize to that truth and the light. Perhaps you just need to *be* there rather than trying so hard to *get* there.

You drift among a rather uncommon mixture of souls who share a similar sense of wanting to go beyond the predictable social norms. You live near the edge, and many of you choose danger as one form of daring. Your characteristics of unconventionality and ambiguity attract many curious souls to your door and can lead to some most unusual life experiences.

17ᵗʰ Degree of Gemini

If this is your sun sign, you are a bundle of energy looking for a place to go. Your boundless enthusiasm and positive outlook toward life is infectious to those who know you. You are dexterous of mind and awareness, which means there are so many things that you could do if you just put your mind to it. You can get yourself overextended and put limitations on your accomplishments. It is a challenge to find balance and perspective in your life. Diversity can sometimes be your downfall, and you will constantly be faced with choices and decisions about where to place your attention.

NOTABLES WITH THIS DEGREE:

Frank Lloyd Wright: American international architect, interior designer, author, educator

Nancy Sinatra: American actress and singer

Barbara Bush: First Lady of the United States, mother of an American president

Happy Rockefeller: Second Lady of the United States

James Darren: American actor, director, singer

There is a karmic hint of having had extraordinary ability and leadership opportunity in another time and setting. Perhaps you got sidetracked by lesser interests and did not attain your desired destiny. You could be hesitant taking on responsibility, but once taken, you can be very successful in leading and achieving. As you learn to focus and stay centered, you will find yourself once again able to both set an example for others and attain your most cherished ambitions. You can find solutions where others would never think to go.

This can be a friendly number-sign combination but not usually a warm one. Some may see you as detached and perhaps even unfeeling. You are achievement oriented and see people as a means to get things done rather than for their intrinsic value. Your enthusiasm is stimulating to others, and you get along best with those who share your aspirations and ideas. You mix and mingle with many but most likely get close to only a few. You are always around those who have power and control. Sensitive to waste and misuse of resources, you do not have much patience for those who are careless and insensitive to their environment.

NUMEROLOGY OF ASTROLOGY

18th Degree of Gemini

If this is your sun sign, you are in search of a steadfast truth that will sustain you and give you strength to carry on in this world of crass superficiality and endless proclamations of empty philosophies. You listen to the constant stream of lies and public misdirection wondering just where this world is going and what it all means. Having been pulled into the seduction of the process many times, you long for connection to the universal principles underlying the eternal wisdom available to all. Your openness and ability to listen to any and all allows you to be privy to information that helps you to better grasp the condition of humanity and its great needs.

There is the karmic hint of having been a participant in treachery and deceit in another life experience. Maybe you were seduced by offers of personal gain that were terribly important to the ego in that moment. Possibly you knowingly perpetrated untruths in order to feed your own vain needs. At times, you can be fooled by the very tactics you have used on others. You seek to find inner integrity and alignment with your source of eternal truth. You are tired of carrying the burden of guilt and shame from your misdeeds of long ago. There is conviction within your heart that now is the time and moment to find yourself and serve others.

You know the inner workings of politics and power. You are cognizant of the tricks of the trade when it comes to manipulating the masses. Your communication skills will serve you well and allow you to work with a diverse socioeconomic spectrum of the population. You hear their message and speak to the concerns that the honest and true population senses in this time of darkness upon Earth. You are blessed with the social and communications skills to be an active spokesperson for awakening.

NOTABLES WITH THIS DEGREE:

Johnny Depp: American actor, producer, screenwriter

Sorrell Trope: American divorce lawyer

Natalie Portman: American-Israeli actress

Michael J. Fox: Canadian-American actor, Parkinson's disease spokesperson

Judy Garland: American actress, singer, entertainer

19th Degree of Gemini

If this is your sun sign, you are inclined to travel and talk about your many and varied life experiences. It is hard to restrain you from speaking out about what you have seen and done, because you become so immersed in the reflection and observation of life around you. You witness the miracle in nature and the evolution of humanity, remaining ever curious about just how it all came about and where it is going. You like to hypothesize and ponder over the rules of evolution and the intelligence behind the laws of nature.

There is the karmic hint that in another time and circumstance, you arrived at rather dogmatic opinions about scientific or philosophical theories about human and planetary evolution. These ideas were perhaps forced on others with intolerance toward dissent. The effect was meant to slow learning and trap your society into a restricted and controlled learning environment. You find yourself wanting to forge new avenues of academic or scientific thinking, but you can become stubborn in your own beliefs. You will be challenged and criticized often, so you must be accurate and forthright in your findings and discoveries.

Your range of ideas and wide perspective of life make you an interesting friend and associate. There is humor that comes from having been around the block a few times and seeing the foibles and follies of life. You are a visionary of sorts, so it is hard for you to come to terms with the deception and corruption that permeates the Earth adventure. You sometimes do not want to recognize the sordid and corrupt, even when it is right in your face. Many of your dreams and realizations come true with a realistic and honest approach toward the multiple facets of human behavior.

20th Degree of Gemini

If this is your sun sign, you are likely to be recognized for your exceptional flexibility of skills and thought. This number-sign combination enhances Gemini's dualistic nature and multiple abilities. You are intuitive, bright, and mercurial of mind. You mix and mingle among all levels of society, as ethnic or religious differences mean little to you. You grasp the common denominator among all people and work to bring unity of thought and spirit back to the human race. The combination of wit, wisdom, and willingness not to judge people's weaknesses brings you much popularity and acceptance among the masses.

NOTABLES WITH THIS DEGREE:

Joe Montana: American professional football player and business executive

David Thomson: British billionaire media mogul

Gene Wilder: American actor

Richard Strauss: German composer of the late Romantic era

There is the karmic hint of having been a public trickster and twister of words in other times and settings. You knew how to keep others off balance in their beliefs and collective actions. By doing so, you could gain a certain amount of control to be used for selfish purposes. This leaves you with distrust for public figures and the manner in which they disseminate information to the masses. You become disturbed over mendacious and misleading acts of public information. Be careful that you are not up to the same tricks.

You jump from one interest to another and find it difficult to stay focused on any one topic. Dexterity is your name and diversity is your game. You can learn and adapt to just about any situation. This is a good combination for travel and interaction with many cultures and races of humanity. You may be attracted to some form of sociological study, perhaps political science, and the dynamics of group consciousness. You are natural entertainers and many of you will find yourselves on some kind of stage in life giving your all to a grand performance.

21ˢᵗ Degree of Gemini

If this is your sun sign, you are quite capable of cute and clever communication. With this number-sign combination, there is plenty of room for constructive bursts of creative consciousness. It will be hard to keep you down on the farm since your appetite for life and experience will not tolerate routine and drudgery for long. That can be the catch. It is easy to step beyond boundaries and go too far in the pursuit of pleasure. There is an elevated probability of sexual excess or abuse in the family pattern. You may choose lyrics or verse to more formally express yourself.

NOTABLES WITH THIS DEGREE:

Luis Walter Alvarez: American experimental physicist, health researcher, Nobel Prize winner

Ally Sheedy: American actress, author

Richard Thomas: American actor

Ban Ki-moon: Korean diplomat, Secretary of the United Nations

There is the karmic hint that during another soul sojourn, you may have severely stepped beyond the bounds of acceptable behavior. Perhaps you were addicted to stimulants or some hard-core source of pleasure. You likely wasted both body and mind growth by staying attached too long to behavior that was taking you nowhere. Even now, you search to find that balance between learning from experience and moving on at the right time to something new in your evolutionary journey. You do not like to think that you might have missed anything.

You most likely enjoy some form of teaching, training, or informing others. Most of you are attracted to some form of communication-related outlet as a career, vocation, or perhaps just a hobby. You are the life of the party and keep entertaining into the wee hours. You collect information about a lot of things that make you appear knowledgeable and informed. However, you may not delve as deeply into issues as others. For the most part, people enjoy your antics, and your gregarious nature allows you to meet and mingle with many maddening, mischievous, and magical people.

22ⁿᵈ Degree of Gemini

If this is your sun sign, you have a manner and way of going about things that easily catches the attention of those around you. Your ability to absorb various information makes it easy for you to mingle among a wide range of social settings. You are curious and mercurial in your thinking and actions. You are not easily pinned down to any one position, since you operate from such a wide variety of perspectives on matters.

You are easily immersed in the weight of acting out some broad plan or destiny you feel must be fulfilled. Your work and purpose can take precedence over personal matters. At times, you can seem distant and not easily accessible when it comes to personal intimacy. Your exterior persona is often aloof and put-offish. In some cases, this can be seen as arrogance. There is a karmic hint that you previously were unable to channel and discipline special knowledge and abilities. As a result, there was much chaos and disruption affecting many people. Your personal drive and sense of purpose make it likely that you will achieve some level of prominence in the endeavors you choose. You possess a keen sense of judging the public pulse, and this acute skill can be of value in matters of commerce and entrepreneurial efforts. Your desire is to see the benefit of such efforts reach the masses.

In public, you are dynamic and get attention easily. However, you really can be very private and reclusive. There is a deeper insecurity about being publicly scrutinized. You want acceptance, but you are fearful of public ridicule and reparation. You will likely be a part of large organizations or someway affiliated with large groups whose purpose is directed at better organization and production from global resources. There is a curiosity about the greater purpose of humanity. When you are not busy working, you are likely studying or searching through the deeper mysteries of our origin and true metaphysical nature.

NOTABLES WITH THIS DEGREE:

Steffi Graf: German professional tennis player

Che Guevara: Argentine political leader, activist

John Forbes Nash Jr.: American mathematician, game theorist

Donald Trump: American real-estate magnate, television personality

William Butler Yeats: Irish poet, dramatist, politician

23rd Degree of Gemini

If this is your sun sign, you can be weird, wild, and wonderfully willing to try out almost anything in life — *once*. It's not as if you are totally out of control, but you do seek thrills in places the meek would melt into hesitation or retreat. Your go-for-broke nature can get you places fast and gain you much success. And it can take you on compulsive trysts that can be tantamount to travesty. You are sensual, sensitive, and sentimental in many ways. Your *bon vivant* approach to life attracts other people who dare to be bold. This can lead to the most creative and imaginative forms of accomplishment.

NOTABLES WITH THIS DEGREE:

Helen Hunt: American actress, director, screenwriter, activist

Anna Torv: Australian actress

Lakshmi Mittal: Indian billionaire industrialist

Pierre Salinger: American news correspondent, White House press secretary

You may attract some jealousy and at times criticism for what may be seen by the more conservative as an outlandish manner of living. There is the karmic hint of having crossed over the line of constructive behavior into madness and mayhem. Perhaps you were driven by ego. Perhaps you let your vision lead you beyond reason and into irresistible regions of the irrational. You are learning to walk the fine line of balance between genuine genius and gaudy display of the garish and gosh.

You are effective at using a quality of entertainment to communicate your ideas and intent. Many of you with this number-sign combination may find yourselves on some kind of stage of display or performance. You are a fashion setter and rarely cling to the style of the day. Your wide spectrum of experience among so many dissimilar components of society allows you to draw from numerous styles of life and manners. You are a master at storytelling and keeping your audience spellbound with tall tales of travel and telltale trivia of other people and places.

24ᵗʰ Degree of Gemini

If this is your sun sign, you can be a jittery gem of a jester, jumping through the hoops of human relationships. You dart in and out of relationships and associations with the daring of a pirate from Dread. It is not easy to pin you down to either commitment or responsibility. Once you are in the right setting and with the right person or people, you bring an enlightening amount of dexterity and different options to the attention of all. You see possibility where others see a dead end. You make something out of virtually nothing or put together seemingly impossible combinations of options in a marvelous mix of success.

NOTABLES WITH THIS DEGREE:

Courtney Cox: American actress

Adam Smith: Scottish social philosopher, pioneer of political economy

James Belushi: American actor, comedian, musician

François Michelin: French entrepreneur

Zadkiel: English astrologer

There is the karmic clue that in an earlier go-around on this planet, you found yourself trapped in an environment of hopeless rigidity, dogma, and death by doctrine. Perhaps you were influenced by a partner or spouse who held sway over your decision making. Maybe you were afraid of change and linked yourself to an organization that shared the same concern. There is a constant tug of war going on inside you between wanting to get involved and wanting to stay away. You are learning who and when to trust and where you're best combinations of commitment occur.

As you settle into trusting yourself and your choices of partners and associates, you can make your way through the maze of dichotomies with the skill of a magician. Wherever you find yourself or whatever the situation you are in, you are ready to take another course of action at the drop of a hat. This can be an asset in times of chaos when quick decisions are needed and an intuitive sense of the right option comes readily to the forefront of your awareness.

25th Degree of Gemini

If this is your sun sign, you love to step into situations that are out of control, bringing order where there was once chaos. This may be the number-sign combination of a military general or a crisis center supervisor, to mention just a couple of vocations in which you might be found. At the same time, you may have a dislike for undue regulations and compulsive forms of discipline. This paradox can cause you internal strife at times when you are trying to get things organized. You find yourself fearful of being out of control, yet you are at your best when things get into such a state of affairs.

NOTABLES WITH THIS DEGREE:

Starhawk: American author, anarchist, activist, self-described witch

Alice Bailey: English writer and lecturer, occult teacher

Barry Manilow: American singer, songwriter, producer

Joe Piscopo: American actor, comedian

There is the karmic hint of having played a role in anarchy and disruption of culture in another place and time. Perhaps you gallantly led a coup of an oppressive regime only to see those you supported end up establishing a society with the same troubling results. Perhaps you mistakenly conquered a social order that was working well simply because you had been misled by someone who had a personal grudge and agenda toward that establishment. You have an almost compulsive need to see things done right and can be very harsh in your criticism of those who waste or abuse their positions of influence.

This combination often leads to those who are urbane, educated, articulate, and likely opinionated. You pride yourself in your preparation and foreknowledge of what you undertake. There is a tendency with those of you who have this number-sign combination to have your fingers in many pots, and it is easy to spread yourselves too thin. You are curious, cautious, and clever in your approach to matters and are always looking for some deeper motive or explanation as to why we do the things that we do. Your dramatic manner of doing things gets attention, and you are not above play-acting to motivate those around you.

26th Degree of Gemini

If this is your sun sign, you can become mired in the mud and malfeasance of justice, commerce, and contemporary social mores. The breakdown of morals and high standards of ethics troubles you and may lead to personal trouble as you encounter misrepresentation and possible malignment. It's not as if you are a perfect specimen, but you strive to be an honest citizen in a world where honesty has little value. You are particularly interested in the role of the individual in society as well as how the masses are administrated and maneuvered. Many of you will be attracted to roles of service and assisting those who experience social injustice and wrongdoing.

NOTABLES WITH THIS DEGREE:

Paul McCartney: English singer, composer, musician

Art Bell: American radio talk show host

Newt Gingrich: American history professor, conservative political leader, author

There is the karmic hint that in another life episode, you may have been severely rigid about matters of justice and ethical behavior. Perhaps you witnessed the deterioration of society around you and tried in vain to stem the tide by overreacting to disregard for the law and the citizenry. Perhaps you put on the face of taking the high road while selling your soul to the pressure of illicit and even illegal operators. You have been confused about where and how to take a stand against impropriety in social discourse. You may well be placed into a position once again that requires the utmost of discernment and integrity in the administrative matters of society.

For the most part, you are well respected in your social circles and have the knack for being tolerant of the myriad cultures and belief systems that abound across this globe. You can be firm, but you retain an element of caring and compassion when confronting tension and issues of debate among your contemporaries. You can be splendid in the role of adjudicator because of your sense of fairness and recognition of essential emotional issues that play a part in human behavior. This is a busy combination, rich for learning about the evolution of community, nation, and race.

27ᵗʰ Degree of Gemini

If this is your sun sign, you can easily drift through a world of dreams, swashbuckling your way through collisions with imaginary foes and feats as if in a movie-like fantasy. More likely, you have some deep conviction within your being that prompts you to seek outlets for your imagination that turn into productive, mundane activities. You have a somewhat exaggerated, idealistic expectation for humanity and for yourself. It is not easy to live up to the expectation, and you can become disenchanted with the race and at your worst even cynical or loathing.

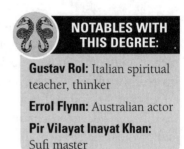

NOTABLES WITH THIS DEGREE:

Gustav Rol: Italian spiritual teacher, thinker

Errol Flynn: Australian actor

Pir Vilayat Inayat Khan: Sufi master

There is the karmic hint of having been previously trapped in a setting where the belief structure of the collective was harsh, dogmatic, and very controlled. It was thought that such careful management of society would make a safe society. Perhaps you rebelled against such control. Perhaps you were a part of creating the propaganda to convince others how happy they should be and how good the system was for them. Perhaps the majority turned against you because of their misery and futility of living in such a restrictive bubble. When under stress, you can cling to thoughts of control and safety. However, when your highest self comes through, you realize the importance of giving each citizen the opportunity to learn and develop his or her own potential. In return, society prospers and grows because each citizen can then give back to the collective the very best contribution possible.

Practicality does not come easy to such dreamers, so you may have to exert more effort than some people to keep your feet grounded and your rhapsodies of imagination channeled into usefulness. It can be tempting to escape into drugs or alcohol or some other addictive way of life. As you come into contact with similar aspiring souls, you can form associations that foster genuine feats of human progress and realignment with the destiny of the planet and of humankind.

28th Degree of Gemini

If this is your sun sign, you find yourself frequently around opportunities to improve your image, income, and inventory. You enjoy the challenge and opportunity found within the marketplace of life. Many of you will be attracted to rules, regulations, and the improvement of efficiency in trade. You are always looking at ways to improve the process of getting through the many hoops of bureaucratic living with less fuss and more ease. Matters of ethics and regulation are never far away, even if you are not directly involved in them.

NOTABLES WITH THIS DEGREE:

Paula Abdul: American singer, choreographer, television personality

Fred M. Baron: American trial lawyer, political fundraiser

Olympia Dukakis: American actress

Vikram Seth: Indian poet, novelist, travel writer, biographer, memoirist

You are often at odds with the behavior codes and social taboos of your day. You could be known for your roustabout behavior and dalliances into the sensual. There is a karmic hint to times before when you have flaunted disregard for convention and acted in complete hostility toward the community and its codes of behavior to the point of probable violent and criminal activities. This part of your dark side may flare up under times of stress and ego drive. Your inner self is now working at releasing ancient anger and hostility in order to contribute to making society more aware and evolved.

This number-sign combination can help to mitigate some of the vacillation that comes from the dual nature of Gemini. You are more focused than many of your Gemini contemporaries and, in most cases, better organized and capable of taking a leadership role when called on to do so. Your love for the consumption of input is undeterred, and you are well equipped to put information into practical application. You are very capable of handling the politics of an organization and weaving your way through the pettiness and power plays. You can come through this with your integrity intact and personal principles left uncontaminated.

29th Degree of Gemini

If this is your sun sign, you are puzzled, piqued, and frequently found pondering the dichotomies of nature, particularly the dizzying dance of human nature. You struggle to be perfect and find yourself perplexed with your many flaws. You seek a spiritual path, but you are also enamored with the trinkets of material wealth. You seek meditative quiet, but you are thrilled when given public attention. You are outspoken about the breakdown of public morals while secretly hiding some rather extreme indulgences. Where does one go to find the ultimate peace of mind? That question may have plagued you for many rounds of life on this third rock from the Sun.

NOTABLES WITH THIS DEGREE:

Edward Snowden: American CIA employee, concerned whistleblower

Jean-Paul Sartre: French novelist, screenwriter, existential philosopher

Nicole Kidman: Australian actress, singer, producer, activist

Maggie Siff: American actress

Richard I. Neal: U.S. Marine general

There is a karmic hint that in another time and sequence of your searching soul, you aspired to live a utopian life with other souls of pure intent. Somehow dysfunction and inappropriate behavior crept into the population and the entire group structure became corrupted and crumpled. Perhaps you were one who was first tempted and fell to unacceptable behaviors. Perhaps you were disillusioned by the hidden, perverse behavior of one who claimed to be a leader. Perhaps you tried to cover up someone's inappropriate behavior to protect the reputation and public image of the group. You find yourself seeking to build a better society but feeling that it may be futile as you bear witness to the massive breakdown of good all around you.

You seek to live by a high standard of integrity and are constantly in search of those you feel meet your high standard of conduct. There is an air of refinement and sensitivity to your environment, and you expect the people around you to have the same. You are intuitive, have an eye for creative accomplishment, and are attracted to actions that elevate community consciousness. Many of you will be called on to lead and administrate changes in the community.

CANCER

0 Degree of Cancer

If this is your sun sign, there is a part of you that is like the all-embracing Mother Earth figure. Even in the male chart, there is a special feminine capacity for embracing and nurturing all of humankind. You are observant about the culture, class, and socially conditioned behaviors of human beings. This makes for excellent researchers, investigators, and students of human nature. Many of you are astute at mimicking the many nuances of expressions. You are curious and considerate in many ways of the foibles and weaknesses of the human race. Your ability to accept people just as they are makes you universally popular and respected.

NOTABLES WITH THIS DEGREE:

Prince William: Duke of Cambridge, military airman

Dianne Feinstein: U.S. Senator, Democratic Party spokesperson

Meryl Streep: American actress

Nicola Sirkis: French guitarist, singer, lyricist

Erica Durance: Canadian actress, producer

There is the karmic hint that in another time and setting, you were perhaps extremely prejudiced and biased toward certain ethnic, religious, or social groups. Your intolerance may have led to much conflict and injury resulting from the defense of what you thought to be righteously correct. There is much guilt and a strong desire to be fair and balanced in the way you look at all people. For the most part, you are learning to do a good job of such. You could find yourself in the position to become a healer between races, ethnic groups, or religious believers.

There are so many things you could do and want to do that it is essentially impossible to get them all done in one lifetime. It is easy for you to believe there may be more lifetimes to come. You have an unquenchable thirst to know more about humanity and are aware of the unlimited possibilities of human growth. You have become interested in promoting the conscious development of human growth and potential and will likely become aligned with people or organizations whose goal is tapping into the resources of unused human potential.

1ˢᵗ Degree of Cancer

If this is your sun sign, you are dashing, emotionally daring, and willing to push through tight situations when others are restrained by sentiment or codependent insecurities. Many of you will be attracted to positions that deal with dysfunctional families and the socially disturbed. If you are attracted to the arts, you will set new standards and open new avenues of theatrical performance and modes of expression. You are a little more assertive than many of your Cancer contemporaries, and you know how to work the undercurrents of social consciousness for better or for worse.

NOTABLES WITH THIS DEGREE:

Cyndi Lauper: American singer, songwriter, actress

June Carter Cash: American singer, songwriter, actress, comedienne

Erich Maria Remarque: German novelist, editor, librarian

Maryse Gildas: French television and radio hostess

There is the karmic hint of having been afraid or negligent of being open and confident in the expression of your feelings in previous life settings. You may have feared reprisal, or perhaps you were a victim of abuse and did not want to get in touch with repressed anger and hostility. Maybe you go a little overboard and become excessively lavish in praise and adulation when you are caught off balance and want to impress others. You will be placed in situations that require you to make quick and decisive decisions that require trust of feelings and connection to your true inner motives.

You will find yourself among those in the avant-garde of communication and awakening the mass consciousness. This can be terribly frustrating when you realize how much most of the public are afraid of their own repressed emotions and seem to be hypnotized by the media into believing they should continue to be silent and unresponsive to oppression. You enjoy the company of companions who are open and candid in self-expression, particularly those who have the ability to see the seriousness of the human condition through the eyes of humor. You sense the multidimensional shifts taking place and help make it easier for the masses to absorb the intensity of new energy arriving on the planet.

2nd Degree of Cancer

If this is your sun sign, you are attuned to the emotional mood of the masses and seek to better comprehend the manner in which the collective consciousness works. That curiosity at times takes you deep into the strata of the collective unconscious as well, and that means deep into your own hidden recesses of being. Such visitations can yield sublime clues about your divine potential as well as terrifying secrets of your dark past. You seem to be intimate with fear and are puzzled about the magnetic hold it has on so many people.

There is a karmic hint of having preyed on the fear and collective angst in other times and settings. Perhaps you used fear to control the masses or to sway a population toward a selfish endeavor. You could easily do the same once more and may experience the temptation to do so. Because you intuitively grasp how to find the path to higher awareness, you may also be led to inspire and uplift the masses toward a more enlightened awareness of their true destinies. Some are drawn to drugs or artificial stimulants in an attempt to crash heaven's gate. More likely, you will find the natural progress of meditation and contemplation the more desired avenue that leads to the fullest manifestation of divine wonder.

This is a natural combination for those who serve in educational roles or in medical and healing professions. Your concern for the welfare of others, along with natural, intuitive instincts matches well with such positions. You are soft spoken but deft at getting people motivated, and even though you speak softly, you often carry a big stick. Interpreters, mediators, and negotiators will often be found with this combination because of the associated ability to work patiently with both sides in a conflict.

NOTABLES WITH THIS DEGREE:

George Orwell: English novelist, journalist, critic, political and cultural commentator

Edward VIII: English king who abdicated the throne for a woman

Rich Bach: American metaphysical-oriented author, transformation theorist

Emmanuella Vaugier: Canadian actress, model

3rd Degree of Cancer

If this is your sun sign, you are frequently one of the more entertaining and colorful characters of the Cancer spectrum. Even if you never get behind the camera or on stage, much of your lifestyle can be effusive and full of star-quality moments. You may choose drama as one of your ways to have an impact and get the desired reaction from those with whom you interact. You enjoy having people over to socialize and share the latest of life experiences. Your environment is tasteful, trendy, and decorated in such a manner as to create comfort, having a touch of softness that puts people at ease when visiting.

There are less-glamorous moments in your life that stir up repressed memories and hidden issues on the dark side — which eventually happens to all of us. Hidden sexual issues are likely within your family and perhaps your own childhood. These hidden experiences can interfere with your creative expression. Karmic clues suggest other life cycles during which you were caught in the misuse and abuse of emotional development. Perhaps you prevented another or others from the opportunity to have freedom of emotional expression and independence. Perhaps your own fears prevented you from taking opportunities to have an abundance of love and human warmth. You seek to find a true center within your soul from which your eternal sense of self-worth and self-expression naturally flow.

At best, you have a flair for fun and are the consummate host or hostess. People thrive and flourish in the nurturing atmosphere you present. Your sense of emotional acceptance and inner strength allow others to be comfortable and open with their own core beliefs and values. You attract accomplished and talented people to your circle of trusted friends and associates.

NOTABLES WITH THIS DEGREE:

Karisma Kapoor: Indian actress

Alani "La La" Vasquez: American disc jockey, television personality

Ricky Gervais: English comedian, author, actor, director, producer

Isabelle Adjani: French multilingual actress and singer

Carly Simon: American singer, songwriter, musician, children's author

4th Degree of Cancer

If this is your sun sign, you display tendencies to be more grounded than some of your other Cancer contemporaries. This can allow you to channel your feelings and emotions more directly into feats of accomplishment. There is a fruitful mix of intuition and practical know-how that enables you to get to the heart of matters. Your interest in science may not just be intellectual. You could very well apply a scientific method in what you are doing, even if it is not science per se. Just be careful that you don't let your fierce need for accuracy and deliberateness cause you to forsake input from your intuitive nature.

NOTABLES WITH THIS DEGREE:

Willy Messerschmitt: German aircraft designer, manufacturer

Carl Levin: U.S. senator, lawyer

Derek Jeter: American professional baseball player

Salvadore Allende: Chilean president, physician

There is the karmic hint that in another life setting, you may have been overly sentimental and foolishly misled or misinformed about the reality of events around you. Perhaps you were too idealistic or sentimental about what was happening and overlooked inherent danger or possible abuse. You are learning to trust valid intuitive input and then put it to use in a structure that is consistent and reliable. You will be appreciated by many for your contribution to your community and to the world.

At best, you work hard and play hard. You don't want to become so serious as to miss out on the lighthearted side of sharing. You may not get there as fast as others, but when you do arrive, it is in a grand fashion. That is because you have put in the right preparation and perseverance to reach the highest levels of achievement. You are capable of deep and devoted love, and once you are connected to the right compatible partner, you both will share the most profound and committed relationship imaginable. You are certainly not adverse to the finer things of life that success can earn.

5th Degree of Cancer

If this is your sun sign, you are likely to experience a wide range of intense human experience while traveling this round of life. Your sensitivity and attunement to other people's moods and manners serves you well when involved with programs that assist in the social and psychological enhancement of human consciousness. This combination intensifies the emotional swings that Cancers normally experience. You will travel on a roller coaster of highs and lows during the course of life events.

NOTABLES WITH THIS DEGREE:

Betty Hill: American social worker and UFO abductee

J. J. Abrams: American television producer, writer, actor, composer, director

Ross Perot: American electronic business magnate, aspired presidential candidate

Tony Leung Chiu Wai: Chinese actor

It can be a test of character as you struggle through some of the depths of emotions and feelings of the dark side. This may also include, however, the joy and ecstasy of soaring into the mystical realms of joy and peace beyond the daily range of emotional experience.

There is a karmic hint at having been indulgent and abusive to the body and senses in previous lives. You are learning to live in harmony with the body and senses — not overdoing and abusing, but also not ignoring and rejecting the experiences that come from sensual input. Your connection to body and sensory awareness combined with a wide range of experiences enables you to deftly assist others who are unable to connect with their feelings and inner conflict.

You enjoy life fully and may be fortunate to travel enough to see more of the world than most people. For some of you, this may include the capacity to travel to other worlds as well. You are psychically attuned to many higher vibrations. Some of you will develop this as a tool for providing guidance, counseling, and teaching others. You find yourself meeting unconventional and interesting personalities from all over the world. This gives you breadth of understanding the diverse nature of culture and human experience.

6th Degree of Cancer

If this is your sun sign, you will be placed in situations that test your emotional fortitude and integrity. One of your major tests will be to consciously process feelings and expressions rather than repress and deny them. There is the karmic suggestion of having been in situations where you were calloused and indifferent to the suffering of people around you. There is an opportunity now for you to accomplish much healing and to be a part of giving other people the tools to more effectively deal with suffering. There will be many opportunities for learning compassion and empathy. Many of you will be attracted to pursuits in the arts and communications.

NOTABLES WITH THIS DEGREE:

Helen Keller: American deaf and blind author, activist, lecturer

Kathy Bates: American actress, director

Mel Brooks: American director, writer, comedian, actor, producer, composer

Gilda Radner: American television actress, comedienne

Your wide range of sensitivity and attunement to subtleties makes your work of interest and intrigue to those who discover it.

You struggle within yourself over myriad conflicting emotions. There is a likelihood of coming from a home environment of conflict between parents. There may have been ethnic, religious, or social status issues that compounded the daily tension. You had to internalize much of your frustration, and that can result in a lot of repressed anger showing up in your adult life. You see suffering in others and will take a stand when you see abuse taking place. Unfortunately, you may not be aware of your abusive patterns. Many people in the counseling, medical, educational, and service-oriented professions have this combination.

You will have an opportunity to mix and mingle among myriad social groups and cultures. During life, you are introduced to a rich mixture of ways that people express themselves and to the variety in cultural development. You are learning to expand your humanitarian perspective and overcome innate prejudices that are inherent from your past. Out of conflict comes healing, and you will be placed in many situations that give you a chance to be a more sensitive and aware leader.

7th Degree of Cancer

If this is your sun sign, you are a little more reserved and remote than many of your Cancer contemporaries. You weave your way between the emotional sea within and the tantalizing call of the intellect to run your life and rule your day. At best, you train the rational mind to confirm the deep inner truths that emerge from the depths of your heart and soul. More often, you are caught in the confusion of hearing a truth from within and your mind rationalizing an excuse to deny the obvious . Your consciousness works overtime trying to ferret out the real truth amid the clamor of lies and misdirection that dominate communication in these modern times.

NOTABLES WITH THIS DEGREE:

Lauren Green: American television newscaster

Dr. William J. Mayo: American physician, medical innovator

Gary Busey: American actor

Alain Finkielkraut: French essayist, author

Henri Proglio: French business magnate

There is a karmic hint that in another time and place, you once possessed God-given cosmic wisdom that set you apart from many mortal minds. Perhaps arrogance took over, or you may have succumbed to the lure of power and control that come with having privileged knowledge. With time and the misuse of wisdom, you fell into a period of confusion and endless intellectual search to regain lost awareness. You are once again seeking to get back on the path that leads to infinite consciousness and connection to eternal truth.

Your depth of soul searching and your passionate quest to get to the bottom of life's secrets attract you to other powerful and stimulating thinkers and searchers. You love to sit around the fire in long conversations about the mysteries of life and existential paradoxes that mystify humankind in its onward journey. You can go to the deepest depths of human emotion when circumstances stir your quest. There is deep compassion within your soul, and many of you can be found supporting causes that encourage reform and social programs that educate and encourage others to know themselves.

8th Degree of Cancer

If this is your sun sign, you have a little more drive and flair for taking the lead role than many of your Cancer contemporaries. There is a sense of power and dynamism that catches the attention of other people and may very well put you at the forefront of the endeavors you choose. You are emotionally attuned to the collective consciousness and are often one step ahead in anticipating the trends and thoughts of society. This knack for knowing can result in finding yourself at the forefront of trends and changes. You may well end up in a career that directly benefits from this personality trait.

NOTABLES WITH THIS DEGREE:

Mike Tyson: American professional boxer, actor

Michael Phelps: American Olympic swimmer

Pamela Anderson: American actress, model, producer, author, activist

Chan Ho Park: Korean professional baseball player, first South Korean in MLB

You are not immune to stepping on someone else's toes as you tiptoe your way to the top. There is a karmic hint of having been a user and manipulator in other times and places. You have a keen grasp of people's emotional weaknesses and are frequently tempted to use this to exploit rather than benefit. You feel as if you sometimes owe others some kind of debt and may become compulsive about helping. Music, art, and mood are central to your lifestyle, and you often find yourself emotionally venting through an artistic venue.

For the most part, you are liked, welcomed, and in many cases, adored by those close to you. There is a gentle charm associated with this combination that puts others at ease and allows them to communicate openly and honestly. You may worry a bit too much about what others are thinking, but for the most part, your contentment comes from being aligned from within rather than trying to guesstimate what is wanted from you by others in your outer world. Luck and financial gain can come your way rather easily when you are confidently in touch with your true self.

9th Degree of Cancer

If this is your sun sign, there is an air of the sacrificial lamb about your number-sign combination that suggests the path of martyrs and myths. Your heart weighs heavily with the hardships and suffering of humanity. You are driven to do something to lessen the burden so many endure. In the early part of your life, this will not be so easy, since you could likely be overwhelmed by emotional pain and hardships of dysfunction that affect your behavior. There is the karmic suggestion of previous self-indulgence. So you may have much given to you that will later be taken away. You are learning the true value of reality in contrast to attempting to live an ideal. As you know your true self, you will understand who you truly want to be.

NOTABLES WITH THIS DEGREE:

Diana Spencer: Princess of Wales

Raymond Moody: American parapsychologist, near-death researcher

Amantine Lucile Aurore Dupin (George Sand): French feminist author, novelist

Kalpana Chawla: Indian-American astronaut, mission specialist

Your high ideals and buoyant attitude toward humankind are an inspiration to those whose lives you touch. You can be unrealistic at times in your expectations of others. You are susceptible to being used and manipulated for others' agendas. Strong emotional fluctuations are a natural part of your life, and you will likely choose a path of therapy or professional assistance during your life. Many of you are gifted with rarefied talents or creative abilities that tap into powerful archetypes within the human psyche.

You have an eye for art and the finer things of life. You might pursue an artistic talent of some sort. This may be a vocation or perhaps full-time profession. The drama and excitement pertaining to your life make you a magnet for friends and associates who like to bathe in the aura of your wide-ranging experiences. You seek the comfort of a loving relationship and will devote yourself to the one you love. Your high expectations and unwillingness to look at dysfunctional issues in advance set you up for disappointment in the intimacy department.

10th Degree of Cancer

If this is your sun sign, you will find yourself out in front of many of your other Cancer cohorts. This combination likes to be at the edge of emotional experience, some of you taking more than your share of risks to get an emotional high. For others, you may find pleasure in exploring different and new ways to lessen the emotional discomfort and pain of humanity. Many with this number-sign combination are healers, counselors, educators, and ministers. The things to do with home are also important to you, and you look for the latest and best of different and refined furnishings and flourishes of décor.

NOTABLES WITH THIS DEGREE:

Franz Kafka: German author

Hermann Hesse: German-born Swiss poet, novelist, painter

Ahmed Ouyahia: Algerian prime minister, diplomat, politician

Valentinian III: Western Roman emperor

There is a strong gambling aspect with this combination, and with poor aspects, this could indicate becoming addicted to the rush. The upside is the ability to take risks at the right time with positive results. While the Cancer personality is well known for cycles of moodiness and potential sulking, you are less likely to stay in such emotional doldrums. There is the karmic hint that in a previous life scenario, you may have taken careless and selfish risks that resulted in the loss of many lives. At best, you see underlying causes and decide to work on the deeper issues. At worst, you continually find something new to distract you from underlying resentments and anger.

You are a keen observer of social behavior, and you pay considerable attention to recurring events throughout the evolving history of nations. You may very well be involved in political reform or social movements associated with human rights and alleviating the afflictions of humanity. You may defy the inclination to back away from conflict like the crab retreating into its corner. In fact, you are likely to be the one to stand up and become the leader or organizer of such activity. You can be a breath of fresh air in a world gone emotionally amuck.

11ᵗʰ Degree of Cancer

If this is your sun sign, you will soar to heights of emotional and intuitive consciousness rarely experienced by the masses. This number-sign combination adds a range of awareness far beyond the already sensitive Cancer consciousness. You are lifted by the aid of angels and higher beings into glimpses of divine possibility. This inspires you to lift others up to new heights of human expansion and leaps of faith. This combination is found in the charts of many of those people who are involved some way with the healing arts. You could be one of those people who choose to develop your expanded gift of giving.

NOTABLES WITH THIS DEGREE:

Tom Cruise: American actor and producer

Gina Lollobrigida: Italian actress, photojournalist, sculptor

Geraldo Rivera: American television host, journalist, lawyer

There is a karmic hint of having been blessed with some form of paranormal or spiritual gifts in another soul journey. Perhaps you were punished for defying the conventions or religious rules of the day. Maybe you were humiliated for being different from other people in your village or community. Whatever path you choose to take in your life, there will always be a certain curiosity about the afterlife and other worlds that seem so close to your awareness. Your interest in social issues may take you into public service or a communications profession in which you are part of educating and informing the masses.

You enjoy mixing and mingling among the many diverse cultures and clans of planet Earth. You possess a natural sense of empathy that allows others to trust you and respond in an open and revealing manner. At best, you have a lightness of being that illuminates and uplifts those who are touched by your presence. Once you make a fully aware commitment to developing your higher self, there are immense possibilities for expansion of awareness and reception of powers that bring you eternal insight and lasting joy.

12th Degree of Cancer

If this is your sun sign, you may feel at times that you have no control over your life, yet somehow you end up being where you believe you should be. Kismet can play funny games with those who have this number-sign combination. You may end up being known for what you have done rather than for who you are. History will put many of you in prominent places, whether it is in your small group or on the world stage. You may very well be called away from what you plan to do in order to do something for someone else.

There is the karmic hint of having placed yourself in front of others in other times and places. Perhaps you had no concern for others as long as you attained or acquired what you wanted. Perhaps other people experienced personal loss or misfortune because of your selfish decisions. There is a part of you that feels like you owe a debt to others and may not have much of a chance to live for yourself. Some of you may be driven by feelings of guilt for not having been more aware of other people and their needs. Perhaps you feel like you deserve very little and sacrifice your life in the act of supplying the need of other people around you.

Your emotional sensitivity to people around you can make you a major candidate for enmeshed relationships and codependency. You will struggle to learn how to separate your own consciousness from others. Once you find yourself, you may very well realize that you do enjoy being of assistance to others and serving where you can. Many good martyrs have come from people with this combination. You will be known for the legacy you left and the deeds that you have done.

13th Degree of Cancer

If this is your sun sign, you will be involved in the evolution and rebirth of human consciousness. You are keenly aware of the disintegration of social stability and the moral fiber of humanity. You are like a Phoenix figure who transforms the dysfunction and darkness of humankind, bringing out a rebirth and resurgence of light. Where others see deterioration and disaster, you see determination and transformation in motion. While sensitive to the plight and insecurity of the masses, you grasp that a greater plan is unfolding, thus giving hope and encouragement amid the chaos. You are, at your best, patient and consoling to those who panic at the upheaval in their temporal world.

NOTABLES WITH THIS DEGREE:

Cecil John Rhodes: English mining magnate, diamond-market wielder

Merv Griffin: American television host, musician, actor, and media mogul

Janet Leigh: American actress, author

Inayat Khan: Sufi master, spiritual leader

There is a karmic hint of having been a participant in the purposeful destruction of a society or large mass of people in another time and situation. You are keenly aware of the perilous times of transformation in which we live, and you seek to bring out the best in humankind rather than stimulate the dark side of human nature. This is a number-sign combination of destiny, and you likely feel that you are a part of some greater plan to restore dignity and the rightful place of healthy human life on Earth.

On the personal side, this combination often gives one a concerned and pleasant personality pattern. You are a good listener and trusted confidant. Life may find you among the counselors and caregivers of society. You are a trusted companion and careful lover. Once settled into a trusted relationship, you are loyal and attentive to the needs of your partner and family members. There is an animated side of your personality that can light up a whole room and bring a smile to the face of the most forlorn and disenchanted souls.

14th Degree of Cancer

If this is your sun sign, your quotient for compassion runs high and your concern for others makes you a great counselor and healer. Many of you will find yourselves in this kind of role, but not necessarily in a professional capacity: parent, friend, or confidant. You are dexterous, diligent, and discerning when it comes to dealing with the issues around you. Your intuitive brilliance can be developed to such an extent as to be almost miraculous in its powers of perception. A downside of this combination is how easy it can be for you to slip into a pattern of compulsive codependency.

NOTABLES WITH THIS DEGREE:

Paul Solomon: American transcendental channel, spiritual teacher

Gian Carlo Menotti: Italian musician, opera composer

Ringo Starr: English musician, actor

Nancy Reagan: actress, First Lady of the United States

There is a karmic hint of having been emotionally irresponsible and indifferent to others in another life setting. Perhaps you selfishly manipulated and used other people with cold disdain, resulting in destructive repercussions for those who did not respond to your spell. At times, you feel compelled to make right some deep-down sense of injustice. Guilt associated with this pattern is a trigger mechanism that can lead you back into becoming used and abused once again. You seek higher awareness and to open your door of inner light so that your pure radiance can be felt by all you contact.

You are fun-loving and enjoy getting outside to engage in hiking, sporting, fishing, or almost any sort of activity that connects with nature and helps to keep the body fit. People enjoy being around you because of your lighthearted nature and great sense of humor. Because of the many life experiences that you have enjoyed, you can be most gifted when it comes to telling stories and recounting your numerous adventures. Your get-it-done approach to responsibility earns you kudos from supervisors and coworkers alike. There is a lot of ardor and passion mixed into almost everything you do.

15th Degree of Cancer

If this is your sun sign, you are active, vital, and distinctly determined to experience life. You absorb experiences like a sponge and use the memory of these to add flourish and spice later when giving presentations and performances. This is the combination of an active soul who may dance, perform athletically, or find other physically challenging activities for personal joy and cathartic benefits. It is not so easy for you to be disciplined in what you do. That very issue can come back and bite you in the bottom right at the moment when you are able to reach an elevated level of achievement.

NOTABLES WITH THIS DEGREE:

Michelle Kwan: American Olympic skater and spokesperson

Elizabeth Kübler-Ross: Swiss-American psychiatrist, author, spokesperson for death and dying

Annalee Skarin: American metaphysical author, proponent of physical immortality

There is a karmic suggestion of having been a master manipulator and user of others in another time and place. Perhaps you saw weakness in others and worked it in every way for your own self-gratification and personal indulgence. Possibly you have hurt many and trusted none. Many of you are attracted to psychology or some form of counselor and mentor. You fancy yourselves as helping others. You probably do. But what you may not see is that you really seek to resolve your own dysfunction and rediscover your true inner self.

People with this combination are complex and puzzling characters to discern. You cannot overlook the misery and apprehension that so many allow to control their lives. While you have some sympathy for their condition, you also get annoyed to see people seeped in the victimhood of martyrdom and abuse. There is a brighter side to your nature, and all is not as negative as may appear. Once on a path toward harmony and balance within your inner and outer self, you blossom onto a regenerative path of service and restoration of a healthy human society and healthy individual consciousness. Your candor and directness is refreshing and inspiring to those who hide and sulk behind the face of denial and dysfunction.

16th Degree of Cancer

If this is your sun sign, you will transverse a multitude of emotional highs and lows before this especially challenging life sequence has run its course. Before your cycle is through, you may feel like you want to be a psychiatrist because of all the sorting out of complicated consciousness you feel you have to do (and may have done). You are expansive, exploring, and seek to encourage those who suffer through the many afflictions of being human. You especially become revolted by abuse of others and by those who would consciously perpetrate a pattern of abusive behavior for their own gain and even amusement.

NOTABLES WITH THIS DEGREE:

O. J. Simpson: American professional football player, actor

Judalon Rose Smyth: American model, author, astrologer

Hassan II: king of Morocco

John D. Rockefeller: American industrialist, oil magnate

There is the karmic hint of having purposely messed up other minds through manipulation, possibly terror, and perhaps even to the extreme of torture. Maybe you vented a sadistic streak developed from having been seriously abused yourself. You may have gotten caught in a web of some else's dark ministrations because of delusion or misplaced loyalty. You have likely trampled through the pits of darkness and despair and now live at the threshold of a potentially brilliant breakthrough into the light. You are imminently aware of the vast range of human consciousness and seek to render education and service to the cast of struggling humanity.

Your complicated personality and somewhat unpredictable nature can be an attractive feature to many with whom you come in contact. You are frequently found among the strata of subcultures that live on the fringe and espouse philosophies that do not resonate with the conventional, programmed social thinking of your day. You enjoy intellectual speculation and have the type of original mind that takes a flight of fancy into sublime realms and comes back down with a brilliant breakthrough of a mind-changing nature. Serendipity can be your best friend, and an open mind will benefit you immensely in opening to your true purpose.

17th Degree of Cancer

If this is your sun sign, you find yourself full of optimism about human evolution and, at the same time, perplexed by the many things that people do to seemingly deny the opportunity for personal growth. It is not as easy for you to display the range of human emotion as some of your Cancer brothers and sisters. You may be a fine mimic or actor in your attempt to explore your personal feelings and reactions to living. The study of psychology or sociology might be an outlet for some of you, providing understanding of human emotions (primarily your own).

NOTABLES WITH THIS DEGREE:

Tom Hanks: American actor, director, producer, writer, activist

Nikola Tesla: Serbian-born American inventor, genius engineer, physicist, futurist

Barbara Cartland: English author

Alexia: Princess of Greece and Denmark

There is a karmic hint of having used deception and emotional tyranny over others in another time and place. Perhaps you coveted power and used fear and threats to prey on the emotional vulnerability of others. This may cause you to feel vulnerable to public opinion and social attitudes toward your own personal behavior. You want to see the best in people and portray human experience in a positive light. However, you want to be careful that you don't overlook or ignore deception and the work of those who tamper with the dark side.

You will find yourself a little more proactive about life than many of your Cancer contemporaries. Whereas they may be more subjective and contemplative about feelings, you put your emotions on your shoulder and go out and do something about how you feel. Your sensitivity to others makes you a natural when it comes to counseling, coaching, consulting, or performing in some field of public service. While money is not a priority to most of you, if that becomes your area of interest, you will make an excellent portfolio manager or financial consultant. As a sideline, you keep an eye on the weather and have a knack of knowing what it is going to do.

18th Degree of Cancer

If this is your sun sign, your heightened Cancer sensitivities will be tested to their extreme limits. That includes both sides of the emotional spectrum. The intuitive reach of the Cancerian consciousness is already widely known. The emotional mobility of the Cancer personality is also a given. You will find yourself experiencing a wide fluctuation of emotions that might even eclipse those of your other Cancer brothers and sisters. You seek to heal and help, yet there is a distrust of how other people really feel about you and what you do. The underlying issue is: Just how much do you trust your own emotions?

NOTABLES WITH THIS DEGREE:

John Quincy Adams: American president, diplomat

Elie Lison: Belgian actor, comedian, director, producer, astrologer

Elijah Blue Allman: American musician, artist

Georgio Armani: Italian fashion designer, business mogul

There is a karmic clue that in another lifetime, you might have been a malcontent capable of stirring up both mayhem and misdirection. A simple way of saying the same thing might be: It was easy for you to lie. After a while, you may have even started to believe your own tall tales and perhaps purposeful untruths. Maybe it was for a political ploy. Perhaps it was to stir up controversy against opponents. Possibly you were richly rewarded to misrepresent someone else who held a position of power. You are searching to find the path back to a trusted equilibrium with your highest of divine sensitivities.

Once you feel empowered from your true source, you have an energy reserve to get things done that would make many mortals envious. You may very well find yourselves in roles of leadership where you aptly direct and inspire confidence and emotional security in those who rely on your guidance. You are able to read the mood of the crowd and can adapt to almost any social environment when called on to blend and mingle. You are likely to mix with many prominent and powerful people within the circle of your contacts.

19th Degree of Cancer

If this is your sun sign, you will be blessed in many ways during your lifetime and be placed in situations that allow you to have impact on the society or community in which you live. You have deep convictions of faith and a generally optimistic outlook toward human experience. You seek to bring out the best qualities of humanity and strive to find a spirit of cooperation between races and religions of a diverse nature. The overall benevolent quality of this combination softens some of the blows of fate and smoothes out some of the bumps along the road of life. Be careful not to take that feeling of grace for granted, because you might get a crisp cosmic wake-up call in the form of a most unanticipated occurrence.

NOTABLES WITH THIS DEGREE:

Bill Cosby: actor, comedian, writer, producer, educator, author, activist

Louis XI: monarch of the House of Bourbon, king of France

Caroline Wozniacki: Danish professional tennis player

Pablo Neruda: Chilean author, Communist politician

There is the karmic hint of having doubted a deity and denounced humankind in other times and places. You are striving to restore a working relationship in your belief about God and humans. You seek to understand and share with others the seeming complexities of administering and interpreting divine fiats. Whether you adhere to a religious denomination or not, your life plan includes an attempt to live in alignment with what you believe to be higher law.

Your diversity of interests and inquisitiveness about virtually everything allows you to blend in with people of radically differing viewpoints about life. You may be fortunate to get around to many points on the globe. Your travels will be rich with stories and anecdotes about the most amazing and amusing people. There is a childlike innocence that many of you will manifest. That quality enables others to be freer in expressing themselves around you. This allows you to have intimacy in sharing the truth and more personal information with one another.

20th Degree of Cancer

If this is your sun sign, you are concerned about health, harmony, and happiness within yourself and for the disconcerted masses all around you. Your keen intuitive sensitivity enables you to attune to both the individual and collective unconscious within the human animal. For some of you, it may be hard to turn this sensitivity off, and you can become overwhelmed with the negativity and angst you detect. Your innate diplomatic skills may serve you well in the troubled times that plague the planet. You could very well find yourself traversing between the cultures or dimensions of human and other-worldly kingdoms.

There is a karmic clue suggesting that you have been privy to transcendent and transformational information that could change the planet and human evolution in a positive direction. There is a hint that at some point, you used such information in a manner that misdirected or misled the population. You are now in conflict with your feelings when trying to tune into the highest and noblest of data while lingering in the negative aura of the dark side of self and humanity. Do you sell yourself out or rise to the occasion and once more bring forth the noble truth? Once you find inner harmony, you may well reconnect to the higher plane energies that will allow you to receive new archetypal plans for developing earthly transformation.

Your gracious nature and soft-sell approach to confrontation and Earth dramas may find you acting as a mediator among classes or ethnic groups struggling in the illusion of their differences rather than recognition of their similarities. We will all be dealing with harsh social and natural breakdowns and catastrophes, so those who can restore calm and give intuitive directives will be cherished and heard in times of cataclysm. You are a natural at social interaction and moving delicately within group dynamics. Your presence and manner is calming and has a settling impact on the restless.

21st Degree of Cancer

If this is your sun sign, you are moody, mercurial, and motivated by your heart. In many instances, the heart plunges when the head is doubtful. The strange thing is that more often than not, the heart is right. Be careful not to take that too far. When your logic and intuition are in sync, you flow with imagination and amazing success through the rigors of life. Life is your stage, and you relish your role, particularly when you know deep inside what it is and where it leads. In this time of rapidly expanding consciousness, you could very well be the first kid on the block to make that connection. At your best, nothing would give you more satisfaction than to assist others in the process of finding their true destinies.

NOTABLES WITH THIS DEGREE:

Ricardo Lindemann: Brazilian astrologer, theosophist

Gerald Ford: American president, statesman

Xavier Darcos: French scholar, politician, Minister of Labor, General Inspector for national education

Robert F. Overmyer: U.S. Marine test pilot, astronaut

It hasn't always been this way. The karmic clues suggest that in other times and circumstances, you selfishly retained information that was intended to be shared with others. By doing so, you may have impeded the collective growth of group (including your own). Perhaps you enjoyed believing you had some kind of ownership over the information. Perhaps you felt superior and did not believe that others were ready for the profound message you could render. You look forward to teaching, and as your cosmic connection becomes stronger, the moment will arrive for you to do just that.

You love the stage of life, and some of you will find yourselves in the entertainment industry. There is a special effect you have when communicating that catches attention and comes across as most convincing. You are colorful and can be charismatic. Your environment emanates a particular aesthetic flair that has the distinct mark of your creativity. You could be envied by some and copied by others. More often than not, you will be appreciated for the lovely contribution you make to the world in which you live.

NUMEROLOGY OF ASTROLOGY

22nd Degree of Cancer

If this is your sun sign, you are determined to get to the bottom of what it is that impels you to think about getting something special done with your life. You are fascinated by the stories of people who seem to sense they have some special destiny, and that kismet will bring a welcomed opportunity just around the next corner. You find yourself looking for that corner. You are learning to trust your inner instincts and recognize how the eternal part of your soul communicates through the many avenues of your earthbound personality. You find yourself among people who want to get something special done that will change the negative direction of the planet's population.

NOTABLES WITH THIS DEGREE:

Shelley von Strunckel: American astrologer, columnist

Jane Lynch: American actress, comedienne, singer

Jesse Ventura: American professional wrestler, politician, actor, author

Alexander the Great: Greek military commander, king of Macedon

There is the karmic hint that in a previous life sojourn, you may have scattered your resources or somehow squandered the opportunity to accomplish something significant that you were given the ability to do. Perhaps you placed too many kettles in the fire and just could not concentrate enough attention in one place to get things done. Perhaps you were so distracted by the superficial temptations of status and ego that you were dissuaded from the course of your soul. You are willing to give up temporal longings if you know your eternal aspirations will come into focus and you can fulfill the eternal aspirations written eons ago on the script of your soul.

You are an emotional stalwart to the confused and insecure people who make up the majority of the population around you. You project a kind of lofty compassion that allows people to accept their past transgressions and overcome patterns of guilt and shame that, until now, have negated their personal paths of progress. You enjoy physical sport and rigorous exercise of the body. You are a champion of physical disciplines that honor the body and espouse the need for integration of body, mind, and soul.

23rd Degree of Cancer

If this is your sun sign, you can be carefree, cunning, contagious, and captivating in your pursuit of life. There are few barriers that limit you and many outlets of self-expression that come along to knock on your door. Your already recognized emotional Cancer temperament will be tested by the whirlwind tour of emotions that you traverse on your roller coaster ride through life. You are usually unwilling to settle for the conventional. Your sentimental and sensitive approach to things makes you a favorite in many circles and endears you to a following of close friends and associates.

There is the karmic hint of having passed through other lives of penitence, abstinence, hermitage, and perhaps self-flagellation. You may have gone to extremes to avoid life indulgence, overdoing, or extravagance. The pattern suggests earlier times when your behavior became so extreme that it caused you needless self-destruction — and likely harm to others as well. You were wild and out of control. There were many other life experiences spent going to extremes out of guilt and fear of losing control. You have come to find a balance between living life to the fullest and keeping focus on the central issue of your soul growth.

You will find yourself wanting to share your gifts with others who have less. There is so much you seek to experience and to try out that it will not always be easy to know when to slow down and focus your efforts and growth on the most important issue at hand. This is a number-sign combination of travel and exposure to myriad cultures and social variations for living. You travel among this world and at times peek into others as your consciousness is blessed and elevated by your good works.

24th Degree of Cancer

If this is your sun sign, you are particularly attuned to the collective unconscious, especially the unrest within your social environment. You feel the unrest around you and are sympathetically drawn into some form of response to this condition. The Cancer personality is a natural caretaker and healer at heart, and with this number-sign combination, that quality takes on a more urgent nature. Many of you will find service in the healing and medically related arts. Many of you will fill roles of social service and counseling to the many who suffer and seek relief from the pressures of modern unrest.

NOTABLES WITH THIS DEGREE:

Alexandre of Belgium: Prince of Belgium

John Jacob Astor: German-American business magnate, investor, merchant

David Hasselhoff: American actor, musician, producer

Priyanka Chopra: Indian actress, singer, Miss World

At times, you will find yourselves in total crosscurrent with public opinion and behavior. There is the karmic hint of having been a part of social tyranny and upheaval in other time frames. You experience horror at the atrocities and cruelty that humans are capable of performing. There is a deep sense of guilt when flashes of memory pop up to reveal your own part in such previous behavior. You are determined to assist in the awakening of humanity and preparation for the upheaval that is growing around you. This might be in your local community or on a large global scale according to how your fate has been charted.

You cling to memories both bad and good and can hold on to guilt with an efficiency that would cause many to marvel. This guilt can lead to external behaviors of impulsive counseling and codependency. You may do your best to do what you think society wants you to do. It is important to take care of your own emotional needs before trying to take care of the needs of others. Your ability to care and love is boundless, and this makes you a wonderful mate and partner both in the intimate and commercial senses.

25th Degree of Cancer

If this is your sun sign, you may find yourself busy, bothered, and bewildered by all of the choices, challenges, and chances that come from living in this material world. Whew! Take a deep breath, and then take a long and hard look at the circumstances you have chosen. You will find that as busy as things seem to be, your greatest opportunities for growth come when you take time to be reflective, contemplative, and in touch with your inner wisdom. You have a pretty good grasp of the motives of humanity and the whims of society around you. The negativity you see troubles you. You have little control over many global issues. You can take control of your own personal issues and be the captain of your voyage.

NOTABLES WITH THIS DEGREE:

Nelson Mandela: South African president, political activist

Richard Branson: British business magnate, airline executive

Giacomo Balla: Italian artist, musician, futurist painter

Madame Soleil: French astrologer, radio broadcaster

There is the karmic hint of having lost track of your true purpose in a previous life sojourn on this planet. Perhaps you became smitten with the pleasures of the senses and addicted to satiation of the physical body. Maybe you found it easier to avoid responsibility to self by gambling with the distractions and amusements of a purposeless social order. Possibly you were unable to reconcile the duality of the physical plane and forgot the union with the One. You have been lost and forgotten, but now you can be found. You now realize it is time to reconnect to that which you have never lost.

You can be most charming and attuned to the culture in which you find yourself. Your lessons and observations gained from travel, trekking, and tarrying among the subcultures of humanity temper your soul and enable you to embrace diversity. The wealth of experience makes you a valuable asset when it comes to assessment and evaluation in matters of commerce, politics, and interaction among different populations.

26th Degree of Cancer

If this is your sun sign, you are attuned to the social atmosphere and political climate of the workplace. You walk a fine political line between the power brokers and plebeians of the marketplace. You would like to be a powerbroker, but you are wary of the abuse of power. You identify with the plebs but do not want to be caught up in victimhood. You can sometimes get caught up in caring for people even when they do not seem to care about themselves. What is one to do? Once you have cleared out your own stuff, you can be very effective in some form of counseling or human consulting capacity.

NOTABLES WITH THIS DEGREE:

Carlos Santana: Mexican-American musician

Edmund Hillary: New Zealand mountain climber, first to climb Mount Everest

William Scranton: Pennsylvania governor, U.N. Ambassador

Samuel Colt: American inventor, industrialist, gun manufacturer

There is a karmic hint of having previously placed yourself in an environment that was murky with mixed emotions and misplaced intentions. Perhaps you manipulated and toyed with other people's most-cherished and personal hopes, plans, and participation in the pools of personal interaction. Maybe you felt you were above the trivial pursuit of such childish entanglements. Possibly you were the pawn of people in power who held little or no regard for human aspirations. You seek to find balance in the external life that matches the balance you desire within your inner being.

More often than not, those of you with this combination carry yourselves with a quiet dignity and a consuming sense of caring for others. There is a likelihood of literary interest with this combination. You may find yourselves somehow connected to publishing or some aspect of communication through words. At best, you find yourself comfortable mixing with any race, gender, culture, or caste. This universal acceptance of the human plight on this planet enables you to work in positions of translation and intercommunication between seemingly irreconcilable groups of discontented souls.

27th Degree of Cancer

If this is your sun sign, you are one of the more baffling members of the Cancer family. The elusive relationship between your mind, emotions, and the intrigues of the material world are a constant swirl of dichotomies and possible continuous inner tension. Your sensitivity to the emotional experiences of others around you can be a blessing or a source of considerable unease. Your natural inclination is to step in and help wherever you find suffering or hurt. However, as time goes on, you realize that there is so much of it going on in the world that it is impossible to relieve it all.

NOTABLES WITH THIS DEGREE:

Veronica Lario Berlusconi: Italian actress, wife of Italian Prime Minister

Natalie Wood: American actress

John Calvin: French protestant theologian, clergyman

A strong inclination toward idealism and reach toward perfection infuses your soul. It can be painful to witness just how short humanity falls in the quest toward being the best. Some of you turn depressed and cynical as you witness the waste of human energy in the corruption and out-of-control manipulation of the masses. You seek to improve society, but it is not easy to know where to start since there is such dysfunction throughout. There is a karmic hint that somewhere in your soul progression through the planet you got blinded by false idealism and deceived into supporting dark and nefarious forces. You seek to find your true path to enlightenment and service to pure light.

Much of your life can feel unsettled as you search to find the right place and right group of people with whom you experience trust and comfort. Things can seem a bit unstable in your world, and this can be reflected in the people and experiences you manifest. Once centered within your own place of peace, you are effective at reform and reconciliation of those who are discordant and at odds with society and each other. Many of you will become keen peacemakers and healers of the existential crises that so many suffer from in these times.

28ᵗʰ Degree of Cancer

If this is your sun sign, you are driven by strong internal emotions that shape and mold your path through life. There is a bit of ego associated with this combination and a karmic implication of having been ruthless and overbearing in another time and place. You are learning to direct your aggressive nature into caring for and assisting others who struggle with victimhood in an already oppressive world. You seek public attention and acceptance. At the same time, you believe you can disregard commonly accepted mores and guidelines. It is not uncommon to have a closet of hidden emotional traumas that continue to stir the unconscious emotional stew throughout your life.

NOTABLES WITH THIS DEGREE:

Baldur Ebertin: German astrologer, esoteric healer

Ernest Hemingway: American novelist, short story writer, and journalist

Robin Williams: American actor, comedian

Sarah Biasini: Italian actress

This combination stirs up a bit of turbulence in an already emotional Cancer chart. There is a conflict with the integration of the animus energy. In a man's chart, there is an indication of excessive influence from a strong-willed (probably domineering) mother. You will likely go through several relationships and disappointments with women. In a woman's chart, there is the presence of much willfulness and male assertiveness. You wrestle with your inner emotions and have trouble relating in an open and direct manner.

There is much zest for life and searching for emotional harmony. You can fluctuate from bombast to shyness in a flash, and you are prone to turn on the drama when eyes are focused on you. Like most of your Cancer brethren, you seek peace and contentment through your relationships. You are intuitively aware of the mood and pulse of the collective unconscious, feeding off of the public pulse of the day. This combination gives diversity of potential and offers you many possible paths of accomplishment and fulfillment in the world.

29th Degree of Cancer

If this is your sun sign, you may find yourself frequently in search of dreams and ideal remedies that just do not fit into the real world. This should not keep you from pursuing your fondest wishes. You just may have to make some adjustments over time regarding practical expectations. You are sensitive to the emotional suffering and abuse that you see around you. You have experienced it firsthand. You often wonder if there is a better way for people to emotionally interact and communicate.

NOTABLES WITH THIS DEGREE:

Bruce King (Zolar): American astrologer, columnist

Margaretha-Marie Alacoque: French saint, mystic

Danny Glover: American actor, director, political activist

There is the karmic suggestion that in another time and setting, you presented a very optimistic and practical method for people to elevate their emotional consciousness and communicate it to others in a healthy and considerate manner. Perhaps that teaching was distorted by others who resented your efficiency. Perhaps it threatened those who had control over the masses for self-interest and personal gain. There is the hint that your work got turned against you and resulted in your suffering and pain. You long to get back to a world of openness and honesty of emotional expression that is not cluttered with so many unconscious blocks and disorders.

People with this number-sign combination frequently display a kind, ethereal quality and refined manner or taste. You can radiate an air of elegance that makes you alluring and desirable to those seeking a quality associate or mate. Your manner is often poetic and you move in and out of social interaction in a mysterious manner that piques the curiosity and captures other's attention. Your idealistic views lead you to groups and organizations that can be utopian in nature or motivated to improve the culture. You may very well utilize some form of artwork or other creative outlet in order to get the word out to the world.

LEO

0 Degree of Leo

If this is your sun sign, you are curious, cautious, and willing to scrutinize anything that offers new ideas that might improve and add to the world. There is an exuberance and refreshing openness with this number-sign combination that allows people to be direct and sincere. You can obtain much valuable information and build a great networking system by putting your best foot forward. This allows you to be right at the start of something new and different. Another side of this would be the informant, or spy, who reports on the progress of others in order to interfere or undermine their efforts.

NOTABLES WITH THIS DEGREE:

Max Heindel: Danish mystic, author, astrologer

Haile Selassie I: Emperor of Ethiopia

Daniel Radcliffe: English actor

Rose Fitzgerald Kennedy: American philanthropist, Kennedy matriarch

Alexandre Dumas: French novelist, playwright

There is a karmic hint of having been involved before in loss and destruction. Perhaps you were responsible for taking the lives of many others. You may fear your own life or become deeply involved in some form of crime prevention or hostility negation. There is guilt from having needlessly torn down something, and now your desire is to be a part of building something good for all concerned. You attract people offering a wide range of abilities and expertise who are ready to help you with your dream of starting over and doing things right. You bring hope when others have lost it, and you strive to overcome despair when it raises its ugly scepter.

You are, at your best, a whirlwind of enthusiasm and sweep up numerous followers who become caught up in your zest for accomplishment. Often there is a kind of charisma associated with this combination. It feeds the Leo ego in a healthy way when you are on the right path doing what you know in your heart and soul to be the best you can do. Even when things get you down, you don't stay there long and can always find the path toward renewal and reconstruction of the project or circumstance at hand.

1ˢᵗ Degree of Leo

If this is your sun sign, you are daring, dynamic, and downright fascinated by a challenge. When others pause, you move. When others doubt themselves, you plunge ahead with confidence (or maybe guile). Most of you not only get it done but you also do it with flair! You are often the go-to person when something needs to be done. That's fine, because you do enjoy the attention and glory that goes with being in the limelight. You have a flair for excitement with the way you go about doing things. This can attract appreciation, envy, and at times resentment or jealousy.

NOTABLES WITH THIS DEGREE:

Jennifer Lopez: American singer, actress, philanthropist

Matt Leblanc: American actor

Elisabeth Moss: American actress

Karl Malone: American professional basketball player, conditioning coach

Azim Premji: Indian billionaire software mogul

There is a high energy level associated with this number-sign combination, and many of you will demonstrate a high metabolism and a muscular body bent on action. There is a karmic suggestion of previous hubris. Some of it lingers and can be a hindrance to your progress at a critical moment of possible advancement. You will want the cooperation of others in the quest that befalls you. It will require that you set aside willfulness in order to create the spirit of joint effort necessary to accomplish the inspired goal within. Your daring and excitement will be a magnet to attract capable and inspired associates who share a similar sense of accomplishment.

There is a sense of adventure associated with this combination. You will find yourself at the forefront of trends and new directions of social thinking and behavior. Always entertaining, you are bestowed with the an inclination toward the dramatic and fanciful. Your ambitious nature serves you well once you know what it is you are after. You will be determined in your desire to get to the bottom of the truth that drives and motivates you. Your curiosity takes you to the brink of knowledge that would overwhelm and perhaps frighten more fragile souls.

NUMEROLOGY OF ASTROLOGY

2nd Degree of Leo

If this is your sun sign, your Leo temperament may be more subdued and perhaps less overpowering than the dramatic Leo personality can often be. You use your charm in a more beguiling and subtle manner than some of the other Leo combinations. This may actually work to your advantage in many situations. While traditionally the Leo mostly uses personal will to motivate people and get things done, you connect with the other people involved. This allows you to consider their points of view and input with more compassion and concern.

NOTABLES WITH THIS DEGREE:

Gracie Allen: American actress, comedienne

Helen Mirren: English actress, social critic

Kevin Spacey: American actor, director, screenwriter, producer

Amelia Earhart: American aviation pioneer, author, women's rights activist

There is the karmic hint of having been frightfully frank, rude, and overbearing in another sequence in the sojourn of the soul. You can dominate and overpower others in the quest for personal supremacy. On the other hand, you can empower and awaken potential within others, thus bringing out the very best in them and yourself. You are admired for your strong personality and timely assertiveness. You are able to emanate this confidence and sense of strength to other people, thus allowing the others to also accomplish much and do well.

Leos with this number-sign combination often exhibit a style and grace that makes their already regal demeanor even more conspicuous. Whatever you choose to do will be done with a special touch of taste and refinement. You find yourself among community leaders and public figures. You want to be known and enjoy being around those who already are. Those who bear the number 2 seek to understand both sides of an issue and be respectful of differing viewpoints. They often see the ironies and foibles of situations and may comment on things with comedic flair. You like to be around things that are happening, and if nothing is happening, you are more often than not the one who gets things going. At best, you are persuasive and inspiring to those who would otherwise be hesitant to take further steps in life.

3rd Degree of Leo

If this is your sun sign, you are an artist of the mind, body, and society. At some time in your life, you will relay your message to the masses. That does not necessarily mean you will be the figure at the front, as with some of you it could involve a behind-the-scenes role within a large creative troupe or institution. Most likely, you will find your way to a position related to media, communications, sales, entertainment, or a similar art form. You want to have your message heard and seek to get the attention of others. You may take some emotional risks, and some of you will take this to the edge of human endurance just for the challenge and thrill. Sexual issues can arise dramatically for you.

NOTABLES WITH THIS DEGREE:

Sandra Bullock: American actress, producer

Mystic Meg: British astrologer, psychic, columnist

Stanley Kubrick: American screenwriter, director, producer, cinematographer

Aldous Huxley: English novelist, essayist, travel writer

You might find yourself torn by a conflict between your ego and your inner feelings. There is the karmic hint of a previous setting in which you were called on to compromise your inner self for the aggrandizement of someone in a position of enormous influence. There is much conflict within you regarding when to sacrifice artistic integrity for the betterment of the masses. You question just who should be making such decisions. The question becomes even more poignant when you realize that the representatives of the masses are grossly corrupt and untruthful.

You are colorful and carry out matters with drama and a touch of panache. It is a good combination for the stage and entertainment roles. People like to be around you and what you are doing, because in most cases, it is unique, theatrical, and good for a full-fledged rush. There will be some highs and lows as you take a ride on the emotional roller coaster of life.

4th Degree of Leo

If this is your sun sign, you are determined and headstrong in your way of getting things accomplished in life. You can muster a little more tenacity than many of your Leo contemporaries. This gives you staying power and a greater capacity to get the job done, whatever that might be. However, this tendency can work against you if your stubbornness gets in the way of recognizing newer and better options for you to take into account. There is the karmic suggestion of having gotten to a high-level position of accomplishment in another time and place. Rather than taking the next step to further growth and responsibility, you sat on your laurels and became enamored with the ego gratification of power and recognition.

NOTABLES WITH THIS DEGREE:

Hugo Chávez: President of Venezuela, politician

Dorothy Hamill: American Olympic champion figure skater

Maya Rudolph: American actress, comedienne

It is easy for you to assume that you deserve things without having to earn them the old-fashioned way. It is true that some things will come to you easily. However, those that really mean the most will have to be acquired through preparation and demonstration of your qualifications to fulfill the opportunity that is presented to you. You love the challenge, and the probability is high that you will attain your heart's desire this time around. You are driven, dynamic, and daring once you feel you have found the right course toward your life's desires.

Once on course toward your destiny, your fixed sense of purpose and dynamic personality attract those to you who are similarly qualified and have the appropriate complimentary skills to help you reach the highest pinnacle of success. To many, you will appear single-minded as you pour so much energy into your dream. There is often little distinction between divine obsession and obsessive-compulsive disorders. You will want to have healthy and aware people around you who can distinguish between the two.

5th Degree of Leo

If this is your sun sign, you will entertain and surprise many as you progress along your passage through this planet. You travel, talk, and train as you take off on a wonderful trip through life. That is not to say there won't be moments of doubt, disappointment, and lessons for you. This is a number-sign combination of the 5's zest for living and the Leo's drama that results in an opportunity for rich and rewarding living. You meet and mingle with people from diverse and remarkable backgrounds. You will have to learn to focus and discipline yourself in order to keep up with all of the things you want to do.

NOTABLES WITH THIS DEGREE:

Peter Jennings: Canadian-American television journalist, newscaster

Jacqueline Kennedy Onassis: First Lady of the United States, Doubleday book editor

Benito Mussolini: Prime Minister and dictator of Italy

Sanjay Dutt: Indian actor, producer, politician

Despite the appearance that so much of your life is going well, you can be plagued with self-doubt and recurring insecurity. There is the karmic hint that you may have been in a very visible public position in another time and sequence of your soul. Perhaps you overstepped your position or created a very embarrassing situation for yourself and many of the people who supported you. There is a deep-seated fear of public rejection and concern that you will be misunderstood by the masses. You are learning to be true to yourself and recognize that other people have their own expectations and values about life that are to be respected in the proper perspective.

Like many of your Leo family, you radiate a regal quality that gets respect and adoration for some of you. You realize that it is important to give something back to life and to those who do not have the opportunities that you have. You support charities and philanthropic institutions when you believe in their causes and trust that they do what they say in assisting others. Faith is important to you, and many of you observe a meaningful spiritual reverence and devoted practice.

6th Degree of Leo

If this is your sun sign, you may very well live with a little less of the lion ferocity than many of your Leo family members. It is very easy for your Leo ego to become firmly centered in yourself. The number 6 clearly encourages more consideration of the many. As your ego returns to an alignment with your inner core, you will see the need of the many. Then you can dynamically and assertively apply your Leo daring and dash to get results in a manner that can amaze. You are far ahead in the caring and compassion department.

Your lion ego will be challenged, and humbling experiences will manage to find a way into your life on a regular basis — that is, until the issue at hand is recognized and brought into cosmic balance. This most likely raises the question: Just what is this issue? The key may be trust. There is the karmic hint that in another life sequence, you put your faith in a person who also represented a collective of believers. Something went terribly wrong, and you felt that a word of commitment was broken. You retain anger and judgment from having been part of the terrible consequences of others. You seek to regain trust related to other people, your creator, and your inner guidance.

You are a devoted friend and companion. You pride yourself in your loyalty, and for the most part, this brings you the reward of good associates. Sometimes loyalty can make you blind to flaws in those you trust. You are learning that the most important relationship is the one with yourself. When the masculine and feminine, divine and human, and higher self and lower self are all in balance, you are clear in your assessment of others. At that point, it becomes easier to read the cosmic signals of your destiny and to move forward with the most important eternal matters of your soul journey.

NOTABLES WITH THIS DEGREE:

Henry Ford: American industrialist, founder of Ford Motor Company, social activist

Arnold Schwarzenegger: Austrian-American movie actor, politician, Mr. Universe

Clara Bow: American silent-movie actress, early sex symbol

Peter Bogdanovich: American writer, director, critic, actor

7th Degree of Leo

If this is your sun sign, you can be pensive, proud, and prone to pondering while your Leo contemporaries are out getting it done. There can be an advantage to your propensity to wait. Once you are certain, you most likely get it done right. Meanwhile, the more impulsive Leos have to concede or redo what they have accomplished. You can be most profound and spin a magical yet intelligent yarn about both the common and most arcane of subjects. You do not lack the bombastic Leo mannerisms. It's just that you are a little more sneaky in your approach, thus catching people by surprise with your strength.

NOTABLES WITH THIS DEGREE:

Paul Anka: Canadian singer, songwriter, actor

Vivica A. Fox: American actress, producer

Patrick Modiano: French novelist

Delta Burke: American actress, comedienne, producer, author

You can become downright arrogant and at times cynical. There is a hidden side of you that fears being ignored or overlooked by the crowd. You feign humility but rarely mean it. There is a karmic hint that in another soul journey, you staunchly defended an idea or position of principle that turned out to go wrong. Perhaps you were too vain to see the error of your ways. Perhaps you were flattered and deceived by others who used your position or influence to persuade others. You can be too cautious when the moment demands action. You can overcome any lingering doubt as you learn to trust the combination of intellect and intuition when arriving at moments of decision.

On the lighter side, your keen insight into human nature lends itself to a great sense of humor and often-profound analysis of the given situation at hand. You enjoy research that leads to immediate application and confirmation of the data at hand. You are sure to be noticed when you turn on that dynamo Leo spirit and take it upon yourself to carry the evening or occasion on the weight of your words and deeds.

8th Degree of Leo

If this is your sun sign, you have a gift for grandeur and empowerment as well as a flair for drama that allows you to make your point with convincing accentuation. This gives you a drive for power and heightens the chance of success. For many of you, money will come into your lives with abundance and ease, but without some discretion and discipline, it can also slip right through your fingers. Your ability to embellish can lead you into fields of communication or media. This is the number-sign combination of the fervent and passionate stage performer. The stage gives you the opportunity to flush out personal feelings long suppressed from earlier childhood trauma. There is the likelihood of issues with a parent who showed a compulsive need to control.

NOTABLES WITH THIS DEGREE:

Sebastian Kresge: American founder of S. S. Kresge Company, Kmart business magnate

J. K. Rowling: English author

Herman Melville: American author

You will likely have been exposed to many forms of abuse by those who have power or who are in positions of authority, perhaps in your childhood. You are keen to have those who abuse power brought to justice and publicly reprimanded for their assault on society. There is a karmic hint of past abuse of power in another time and place. You admire strong personalities, especially those who take on a cause to protect and improve the lives of people who are not able to protect themselves against predators and abusers. Your proclivity to be enamored with the noble and pure may lead you into groups or organizations that preach personal empowerment.

You have a kind of indomitable spirit that takes you through life and often attracts those who are dazzled by your strength and brilliance. You have a magnetic personality that inspires others to have courage and fortitude in the midst of the most distressing events. Your flair for general issues may cause you to overlook details and minor concerns that can grow to become major obstacles. You seek a strong partner but will end up competing with him or her. You can find one who is both strong and gentle. That person is there, even if not so obvious.

9ᵗʰ Degree of Leo

If this is your sun sign, you are somewhat softer with your approach to matters than many of your Leo contemporaries. This combination takes a little of the edge off of the strong Leo ego and directs some of the energy from the individual to concern for the whole. You are a humanitarian at heart and may serve with philanthropic organizations or give to them generously when you are able. That can apply to personal relationships as well. You can be a most generous friend and lover, and your bright and fiery personality lights up the show wherever you go. You are doggedly determined to somehow contribute to a better world, and you will take a leadership role to do that when you believe in the organization or people you support.

NOTABLES WITH THIS DEGREE:

Yves Saint Laurent: French fashion designer, business executive

Peter O'Toole: Irish actor

Isabel Allende: Chilean novelist, dramatist

Wes Craven: American director, writer, producer

Placing too much trust in others, however, can sometimes lead to grave disappointment. You must guard against becoming so idealistic that you do not see red flags in the behavior of those you trust. There is the karmic hint of having been so blinded in another time and place that you did not see those you believed in causing actual harm or abuse to others. Once discovered, you were shocked and thrown into remorse, distrust, and despair. You are clearly learning discretion at this time. Be careful how you choose and who you choose.

You may well find yourself in some dramatic role either on stage or in life itself. Along with the usual Leo magnetism, there is a certain ethereal quality about many of you that intrigues people to know who you are and how you got to where you are. You are most happy helping to awaken and enlighten others to the joy of self-discovery.

10th Degree of Leo

If this is your sun sign, you have a way of getting noticed, and you love it. Most likely, when you do get attention, you will be able to hold that position because you have something worthwhile to present. Your penchant for being the center of attention is a very strong drive, and it puts you near other high-powered people who are also going far. You are at your best around strong, innovative people who feed on change and perpetual rearrangement. There is the suggestion of developing some cautionary tactics to prevent stepping on others' toes so that you don't seriously offend someone rather than inform them.

NOTABLES WITH THIS DEGREE:

Martha Stewart: American business magnate, author, television personality

Lambert Wilson: French actor, singer

Evangeline Lilly: Canadian actress, writer

Youssouf Fofana: French leader of the Gang of Barbarians, convicted murderer

You do not like to stay with things very long, although your ego can attach itself firmly to what you have just done. In that case, you may defend against change more from personal attachment than against the threat of change itself. There is a karmic hint that you were overbearing and used will to control people and events. Those with this number-sign combination are usually entertaining and have the drive to fend off people who might threaten their position. You are often found at the forefront of reformation or challenging the status quo. With adverse aspects, this can lead to rebellious and hostile actions. In these instances, you may step outside of the law or social dictates because your ego believes you are above such petty restrictions.

In most cases, the person with this combination is highly energetic, talented, and full of adventure. You will do things on the slightest provocation. Your willingness to take risks is often an asset that puts you ahead of competitors and gains you respect for your decisiveness. Your personal life is rich in diversity and constant flirtation with plunging into the unknown. You leave a lasting impression with whoever you have chosen to share your life.

11th Degree of Leo

If this is your sun sign, you are fastidious, fair-minded, and dislike façades. You desire to be idealistic and optimistic about humankind and human endeavors. Life, however, may place you where you are forced to look at the depressing and sometimes despicable acts that people commit. Your dramatic Leo nature combined with the effervescence of the 11th degree can make for an interesting personality, positioning you in the thick of some pretty important human affairs. You have a nose for truth and oftentimes people will open up with some of their most personal feelings and confidential knowledge.

NOTABLES WITH THIS DEGREE:

Tom Brady: American professional football player

Lance Alworth: American professional football player

Martin Sheen: American actor

Mary Decker: American Olympic runner, World Championship gold medalist

There is the karmic suggestion of having been in a previous position that made you privy to the thoughts and actions of a powerful potentate. Your inside knowledge gave you responsibility, putting you on a tightrope of delicate balancing acts between factions of power and intrigue. Perhaps you were misled by a colleague and compromised by deception. Maybe you had a disagreement with the leader and were disposed or disclaimed. You will once again find yourself in the position to choose to speak the truth or compromise yourself to nefarious forces that operate around you. You could be disposed of for pointing out the truth about those who desire that the public remains ignorant of what goes on in the back rooms of power.

With this combination, your fiery Leo personality may be somewhat more subdued. This does not, however, diminish your flair for the dramatic and entertaining. You are informative and fair when sharing information with others and dislike the pettiness of rumors and demagoguery of deception. This makes you a trusted friend, associate, and colleague. You may very well meet many people who are powerful and influential in their community or circle of influence.

12th Degree of Leo

If this is your sun sign, you are creative, cautious, and capable of accomplishing much if you stay focused. Things may not come easy for you, and many of you may be recognized for what you have done after the fact. However, this does not deter you from pushing ahead as if you are driven by some kind of destiny. You are sensitive to the rhythms of life and move like a sonata as if in tune with the music of the spheres. You may not be as much in tune with your deeper, personal feelings and sensitivities. It is as if you are a step behind acting on what you know to be the truth deep inside.

You seem to spend a lot of time catching up and getting into the moment. You might place yourself into situations as a martyr and target of mistreatment. There is a karmic hint of having previously failed to step in when a major injustice was taking place. Perhaps you pulled back when you should have pushed or submitted when you should have taken a stand. Indecisiveness can be your worst enemy. You know there is something that needs to be done, but you have trouble finding the right direction. With focus and fearlessness, you can get back in touch with the direction and purpose of your soul.

Your bent toward being multitalented can cause you some consternation when seeking to decide how to best focus energy. You are admired by those less gifted and can sometimes attract envy or jealousy when demonstrating how talented you can be. Your Leo independence can make it difficult for you to admit how important it is to have support and trust. You can soar high when connected with the right collection of friends and associates.

NOTABLES WITH THIS DEGREE:

Sydney Omarr: American astrologer, author, lecturer

Neil Armstrong: American astronaut, pilot, professor, first person to walk on the Moon

Guy de Maupassant: French author, short-story originator

Louis Armstrong: American jazz trumpeter, band leader, actor

John Huston: American screenwriter, director, producer

13th Degree of Leo

If this is your sun sign, you are creative, cautious and ever on the alert for cues regarding the nature of changes to come. You learn very quickly in life that nothing is constant. Therefore, you are far more prepared for the vagrancies of life than many around you. Be careful, as this preparedness can become a neurotic obsession that leaves you completely out of touch with others and the real nature of change taking place. At best, you recognize when something has come to a close of its cycle and get out before being caught in the pitfalls of closure. When the large Leo ego gets too involved, your pride makes it difficult to admit you must give up or retreat.

NOTABLES WITH THIS DEGREE:

Lucille Ball: American actress, comedienne, model, studio executive

Marine Le Pen: French politician, lawyer

Andy Warhol: American commercial illustrator, pop artist, film maker

There is the karmic hint that in another soul setting, you may have failed to warn others about impending doom or a possible calamity to the group in which you belonged. Perhaps you were blamed for losses or punished for a lapse of judgment. You are hesitant to speak out about faults or threats that you see. You have become weary when making decisions and can become erratic in your actions and behavior. Once you reconcile your fears and find peace within, you chart a stable course through the muck and mire of the social chaos around you.

Though often impulsive and self-serving, there is a dash and flourish about the way you do things that makes it hard for some to resist your verve and daring. Many with this combination have a natural vent for seductive maneuvering and can be persuasive in the pursuit of something or someone they desire. You are there when things go wrong and are helpful demonstrating to others how to survive when things have gone terribly wrong.

14th Degree of Leo

If this is your sun sign, you may be in store for some marvelous twists of fate in the journey of consciousness. The proud and regal quality of the Leo personality is somewhat subdued with this combination. However, it does not diminish the drive to reach a plateau of accomplishment and recognition. People with this combination often possess a special flair that captures the imagination and interest of the masses. In the positive sense, this can work to your advantage when you have something to offer that is of interest and benefit to many. On the other hand, if you dabble in the nefarious, the same qualities can make you stand out and get caught.

NOTABLES WITH THIS DEGREE:

Caetano Veloso: Brazilian musician, composer, political activist

Roland Kirk: American multi-instrumentalist musician330, comic, satirist

Charlize Theron: South African–American actress, model

Sheldon Adelson: American gaming and entertainment billionaire

Zander Schloss: American musician, composer, actor

There is the karmic hint of having been especially blessed in another time and setting. Perhaps you were not appreciative of the gift or chose not to develop some unique potential bestowed on you by the creator. You have the chance to develop a very special talent or ability that could potentially render great things for many people. There may be social resistance to your quest, and you may upset some people of the status quo with your alternative renderings. There will be a challenge to find the right people who support you and understand the significance of your contribution.

You will need to pay attention to discipline and the willingness to stay with challenging and sometimes delayed developments. You are a hands-on kind of person, and this can cause you trouble turning things over and trusting someone else to manage your concepts. You have a sense for understanding the nature of matter and the mechanics of reconstructing form. You may well work at the forefront of quantum science and at the very edge of exploring human and cosmic consciousness.

15th Degree of Leo

If this is your sun sign, you are loaded with enough ammunition to get just about anything you want. One question that may often recur with you is: "Just what do I want?" You understand the motives and whims of the human animal and grasp the seamy and saintly sides of human behavior with equal clearness. You often vacillate between a burning desire to help others and scathing criticism of their ignorant and easily manipulated nature. There is the rush to enlighten that can also stir up the old subconscious pattern of wanting to enslave others.

There is the karmic hint that in another sequence of the soul, you may have been in a position to abuse your power and advanced psychological insight into human nature. Perhaps you were an arrogant overlord who ruled with fear and terror in order to keep the masses under your whip. Perhaps you were in an academic or religious position to influence social change from your seat of power within the setting of another time. You alternate between craving public attention and then wanting to hide like a hermit and not be seen. It is time to resolve old guilt patterns and move into your highest level of self-expression.

Whatever you do, it is likely done with a flair for the dramatic. You do like the limelight, and there will be many of you with this combination who have a lifestyle that places you in the public eye. There is a natural athletic quality about this combination. At a minimum, you like to do exercise that is demanding and has a reward besides self-accomplishment, such as yoga. You can be very caring about others, but you may not be directly affectionate or comfortable with outward displays of devotion. However, you will proudly display your partner to others as a sign of your good taste and skill in selection.

NOTABLES WITH THIS DEGREE:

Mata Hari: Dutch exotic dancer, courtesan, convicted spy

James Randi: Canadian-American stage magician, scientific skeptic, author

David Duchovny: American actor, writer, director

Altaír Jarabo: Mexican actress, model

Sky Dylan Dayton: American entrepreneur, computer software magnate, founder of EarthLink

16th Degree of Leo

If this is your sun sign, you do not expect your life experiences to follow the same path as those of the ordinary scripts given to most mortals. You will be tossed and turned about by tides of fame and fortune that would have the meek scurrying to find shelter and safety. It is a great ride if you choose to work with it willingly and with an open awareness of its deeper purpose. You have a personality pattern that is not easy to predict or decipher, and this makes you an intriguing and mysterious friend and associate.

You may find yourself repeatedly placed in situations where you almost always come up with a surprise. Many of you adopt an almost fatalistic philosophy in order to cope with the unusual and unexpected twists of kismet that come your way. There is a karmic hint of having experimented with explosive ideas and strategies that may have resulted in upheaval and loss of many lives. You are keenly aware of the weaknesses of humanity and how readily ideas and plans can turn corrupt and tainted. You may wonder about activities of the dark side or be found searching in all avenues of human consciousness while looking for a path of redemption and restoration for the noble human being.

If you do not seek excitement, you seem to find it. You are attracted like a moth to a flame when it comes to being around exploratory ventures and far-out experimentation. Many of you will be called into disaster relief work and renewal projects in which you are at home giving directions and working with those who are panic stricken. If attracted to the performing arts, you will express a wide range of talents and convey a complex range of human behaviors. You may get a mischievous delight at times creating shocking and frightening scenes with your behavior.

17ᵗʰ Degree of Leo

If this is your sun sign, you are likely to see opportunity everywhere you go. Your openness and belief that things will turn out well make you a popular figure among your crowd. Your natural Leo leadership can be lifted to an even higher level when this number-sign combination is present. Other people find your positive outlook convincing and are willing to go in with you on investments or new adventures. This can be a favorable combination for attaining the influence and fortune that you desire, whether it is of a materialistic or more transcendental nature.

NOTABLES WITH THIS DEGREE:

Gillian Anderson: American actress

José Silva: American psychic educator, author, parapsychologist

Devon Edwenna Aoki: American actress, model

Rosanna Arquette: American actress, director, producer

Amedeo Avogadro: Italian physicist, educator, savant

Perhaps you can become guilty of overselling. There is the karmic hint of having been reprimanded or punished in another time sequence for overestimating a situation. Things may have gone terribly wrong. Possibly you were misled by someone else. Maybe you were a con artist who preyed on other's weaknesses. You are learning once again to trust others and to trust your highest inspirations. When you do, things go well for you, and your actions will lead to significant benefit for other people who listen to you.

Your natural flair for the dramatic will lead many of you to the stage of some sorts. That might be acting or getting on the public podium to rally people to a beloved cause. Despite your innate optimism, you may find yourself caught in situations in which you must act out your pessimism and contempt for the deceit and fabrication that is so prevalent in the world around you. This combination gives an air of refinement to the Leo nature, and you consciously expend the necessary effort to project the kind of public persona that will get you the things you seek. Your studious and direct approach to matters allows you to organize and motivate those you oversee.

18th Degree of Leo

If this is your sun sign, you will find your life full of dramatic encounters and a merry-go-round of unpredictable events. You thrive on uncertainty and are at your best taking the lead when others falter out of fear and inability to adjust to unexpected setbacks. Your energetic personality attracts people who like to get things done. You will have to be wary of behind-the-scenes power struggles among your followers and associates. This is a combination of action, and you will be found participating with those who are active in making change in the world.

You are focused on the need to have your convictions known to the world. This combination accentuates the Leo drive and interest in power. There is a karmic suggestion of past inclination toward hypocrisy and misleading others about your life and intent. You are learning to be true to what you say and forthright in your proclamations to others. The pitfall can be that you believe what you say to be true but may not be true to what you say. You are learning to be respectful of others' viewpoints and wary of falling into the trap of dogma.

While you are as capable as any of affection and personal relationships, this is more a number-sign combination of destiny. You feel some sort of calling in life and will not be content unless you feel you are somehow fulfilling that calling. Those who are close to you must understand just how important this is to you. In that case, you can experience the satisfaction that comes from home, family, and attention to the domestic issues. You may be found in commerce or in a leadership role within an institution. It is natural for you to take the lead, and many will follow your commands.

19th Degree of Leo

If this is your sun sign, you are fiery, idealistic, and full of drama. Ever trying to discover the golden rainbow of idyllic social life, you may find yourself attracted to political reform or sweeping social changes. Your inquisitive and engaging manner will find you in the company of many influential and sometimes powerful personalities. You relish the limelight, and when given the stage, you are capable of generating quite a performance. Although curious about humanity, you keep a more detached approach to matters rather than a hands-on one.

There is the karmic suggestion of having been involved in power struggles and mass control of large populations. You strike out at injustice, but can be guilty of doing the very thing that you criticize in others. If ego takes over, you may find yourself gluttonous and ruthless in pursuit of power. There is the opportunity to release many souls from the bondage of fear and social domination. You have the opportunity to contribute to the enlightenment and release of the masses, but arrogance and self-importance may get in the way and distort this aspiration.

You are an inspiration to many and can have followers of your faith and fate. If attracted to technology, you can be quite an influence in the innovation and development of advanced communication and scientific technologies. This is more a pattern of greater destiny rather than a personal number-sign combination. It is easier to see yourself in the context of the times and events going on around you rather than being directly connected to your inner core and living from the essence of your being. Twisted idealism can lead you to believe your actions are pure and beneficent when they can in fact be myopic and tyrannical. After reaching self-enlightenment, you strive to truly enlighten the many.

NOTABLES WITH THIS DEGREE:

Fidel Castro: Prime Minister of Cuba, communist leader

Miss Cleo: American psychic, psychic telephone reading spokesperson

George Soros: Hungarian-American business magnate, philanthropist

William Wallace: Scottish military leader, freedom fighter

Sridevi Kapoor: Indian actress

20th Degree of Leo

If this is your sun sign, you may appear some-what softer and more subdued than many of your Leo brethren. This number-sign combination brings out the desire to better understand others and work together harmoniously rather than overwhelm and conquer as the ego-driven Leo personality is so often known to be capable of doing. When you are at your best, your wonderful exuberant Leo personality flashes out in all of its typical brilliance. This combination makes it possible for the brilliance to be seen and appreciated by more people because you present yourself in a manner that is in touch with what the collective consciousness seeks, not just giving them what your ego wants to give.

NOTABLES WITH THIS DEGREE:

Alfred Hitchcock: English director, producer, suspense specialist, TV host

Koffi Olomide: Congolese soukous singer, producer, composer

Wim Wenders: German director, playwright, author, photographer, producer

There is the karmic hint of having been in previous positions of control and lordship over a segment of the population. Perhaps you trampled the hopes and aspirations of the people by imposing your own rigid policy of living. Perhaps you defended an outworn dogma to the point of desperation and degrading acts to keep your underlings subjugated.

You have access to higher codes of living and long to recognize and apply them in your life once again. You seek to unite and grow rather than split and divide. Your grasp of the social complexities can be of substantial meaning to you as you go forward with your life purpose.

Your attention to detail and your Leo pride come together to help you create tasteful and touching surroundings wherever you dwell. You enjoy hosting important people as well as discussing the politics of commerce and community. The Leo personality is strongly inclined toward drama and the arts. If you choose such a pursuit, you will touch the hearts of those who view your work because of your nuance of interpretation and presentation of the material at hand.

21st Degree of Leo

If this is your sun sign, you can be stunning, creative, and quite accomplished. Most likely, you will find yourself involved with some form of communication, media, or artistic endeavor. The natural inclination for expression can easily combine with the dynamic Leo personality to put you into the public limelight sometime during your life. You communicate in a swift, direct, and effective manner that quickly achieves what you want. There is a kind of spark in your personality that makes you easily recognized, causing you to stand out in a crowd. This can work to your advantage given the circumstances, but it can also be somewhat frustrating when you desire anonymity.

NOTABLES WITH THIS DEGREE:

Steve Martin: American actor, comedian, musician, author, playwright, producer

Tim Tebow: American professional football player

Deborah Meyer: American three-time Olympic champion swimmer, coach

Dalia Hernandez: Mexican actress, dancer

There is a karmic suggestion of having used your glib tongue deceptively in another time and place. Perhaps you were a con artist or agent of deceit for purposes of intelligence or spying. You have a hidden side that is protected vociferously for concern that others may find out about your sordid past. The result is that you may be seen by many as elusive and remote. It can also result in confusing messages that you give to others when you are under stress. There will be times of struggle as you endeavor to reconcile the differences with your past and establish harmony once more.

The lighter side of your nature loves to mix and mingle with other life achievers. You enjoy the trappings of success in the company you keep, your home, and your travels. Your flair for the dramatic may find you attracted to some form of entertainment as a hobby or second career. You are acutely aware of the power of communications and may study or spend time regarding marketing and the art of public persuasion.

22nd Degree of Leo

If this is your sun sign, you may at times feel almost driven by an obsession that there is some particular project that you need to get done in this life. Once you determine just what this is, your Leo drive kicks into gear. The upside of this Leo boldness is the presence of abundant energy and a sustaining personality profile that enables you to pull off your desired accomplishment with much gusto. This combination favors the organizational skills and savvy to benefit from your knowledge of both physical and social sciences.

NOTABLES WITH THIS DEGREE:

Napoleon Bonaparte: French leader, military general, TV host

Sri Aurobindo: Indian philosopher, guru, political activist, poet

Fu Mingxua: Chinese Olympic diver, multiple gold medalist

Forrest Mars Jr.: billionaire confectioner, founder of Mars Inc.

There is the karmic hint of emotional mistrust from another life sequence. Perhaps you were betrayed by someone who promised emotional support. Maybe you invested considerable emotional energy into a cherished cause only to see things fall apart, ending in total disappointment. You have all of the necessary tools with which to obtain your highest aspirations. It is now a matter of trusting your own inner feelings and being willing to make the proper discernment when it comes to their expression of feelings and sentiments. Once in harmony with your own feelings, there is passion and unequaled drive toward that which you desire the most.

You may be seen by many as impersonal and self-motivated. That may be true of those within this group who have not reached the turning point of consciousness when the need to release ego control has been recognized and addressed. Even with higher awakening, your motives may be seen as self-generated since it is not easy for you to directly express your most intimate of feelings. You are inclined to let actions do the speaking as you put your energy into the cause of helping to open the heart center of a closed and troubled human race.

23rd Degree of Leo

If this is your sun sign, you can stretch your imagination to the limits and take experience to the extremes of social acceptance. When the Leo ego gets out of control, this may lead to shocking public displays and hostile reactions. Under less negative aspects, people with this number-sign combination like to push the envelope of convention by experimentation with behavior that breaches standard community taboos. Within limits, such an adventurous effort may loosen up restraints that repress the natural progression of self-awareness. When taken to extremes, such behavior can break down time-honored norms that have proven to be the backbone of a stable society.

NOTABLES WITH THIS DEGREE:

Madonna: American singer, songwriter, actress, author, director, philanthropist

Matthew Manning: English author, psychic, healer

Taissa Farmiga: American actress

T. E. Lawrence: British army officer known for affinity with the Arab culture

There is the karmic hint of previous practices of extreme behavior that attracted the wrath of the authority of the day, such as the church or government office that set the laws and codes of behavior. You may have been severely punished and you may now hold deep resentment toward such institutions, or perhaps you were the one who arrogantly and self-righteously imposed unjust and overly excessive restraint on those who did so. You will find yourself in an internal struggle to determine for yourself just what constitutes proper behavior and when it is appropriate. This may turn you toward more inward guidelines and spiritual standards of behavior that come from the inner self.

Your tendency toward the lavish and luxurious attracts you to people of means and power. You want to be careful about living beyond your means, as you may be prone to displaying a lifestyle that you might not be able to financially support. You can be generous and trusting to a fault, especially if you are out to win friends and influence people. People may hope to bleed off some of your excess.

24ᵗʰ Degree of Leo

If this is your sun sign, you have chosen a somewhat arduous path through the sticky wicket of power, passion, and the predicaments of a pernicious society gone wild. What? Your heart strives for compassion in a cold world. You strive to speak softly in a strident and harshly critical social environment. You strive to be strong under the pressure of leadership that encourages passive followers. You work hard to bring about humane and considerate results for those you represent as you watch the incompetent and lazy get credit for less. You recognize that forces are in motion to bring about the transformation and restoration of this world to a place of honor and high ideals. You know within your heart the time grows nigh.

NOTABLES WITH THIS DEGREE:

Larry Ellison: American billionaire business magnate, cofounder of the Oracle Corporation

Sean Penn: American actor, screenwriter, director, politician

Tarja Turunen: Finnish singer, songwriter

Donny Wahlberg: American singer, actor, producer

There is the karmic clue of having participated in previous life processes in which you were involved in the emotional disturbance of large numbers of fellow earthlings. Perhaps you lost your faith and hysterically promoted programs of fear and hopelessness. Perhaps you purposefully participated in someone else's secret agenda to keep the masses unstable in order to maintain a hold on their fate. You seek to find emotional equilibrium within and to restore emotional empowerment to the many. You are blessed with a flair for the daring and dashing. There comes a time when these traits will be of considerable value in rallying the weak and fearful to stand up and regain dominion over their due heritage of the heart.

You have the pride, patience, and pugnacity to stand up against those who would oppress and restrain others from the right to joy, harmony, and contentment of heart. Your compassion and sense of self-forgiveness are growing stronger, and the fear that you once had to confront negativity is waning. When you are inspired from within, your prominent Leo personality roars to life with a dynamic presentation of inspiration, truth, and timely solutions to the challenges at hand.

25th Degree of Leo

If this is your sun sign, you are constantly in a state of forlorn uncertainty in your efforts to fully grasp the importance of individuality within the context of social norms and taboos. As you better understand just how psychologically and morally dysfunctional the institutions of our modern day have become, you turn disillusioned and perhaps cynical. The usual direct Leo approach to matters may be a little tempered by the more mental approach indicated by this combination. You may ponder while other Leos take the plunge. Sometimes this may suit you better than flying in impulsively.

NOTABLES WITH THIS DEGREE:

Roman Polanski: Polish-French director, producer, writer, actor

Isabel Hickey: American author, astrologer

Edward Norton: American actor, screenwriter, director, producer, social activist

Willem Koppejan: Dutch author, astrologer

There is a karmic hint that in another life setting, your lifestyle may not have met the approval of the community in which you lived. You may have been defiant and even rebellious toward the system. You may still remain rebellious toward those who are in authority. Perhaps the repressed anger gets in the way of letting you achieve your aspirations and truly getting the attention of those who can make a change. You may find yourself exploring the kinky and unconventional side of human behavior. Some of you will choose to focus on life in one of the subcultures of your environment.

You love a debate and getting into the spirit of controversy. You would have been a good cowboy in the American West since you so enjoy a good fair fight. Because of your innate grasp of many social subtleties, you mix and mingle among the diverse cultures of the working classes with playful and sometimes mischievous abandon. You are liked wherever you go and can have an impact wherever you have been. You are not easily forgotten, because you leave a big imprint on the territory that you have visited.

26th Degree of Leo

If this is your sun sign, you may not be as bold and bombastic in your display of force as some of the Leo family. Nevertheless, you are often found in the center of power struggles and debates. You are ardent, alert, and ready to become involved in matters that pertain to oppression and wrongful application of administrative management. You could find yourself placed in the position of standing up against those who abuse power, particularly when happiness is being denied. You may be somewhat more diminutive in stature and standing than your adversaries, but you can be a tough cookie to discourage when you have taken on a cause in which you believe.

There is a karmic clue that in an earlier go around, you may have become overly involved and emotionally dependent on someone else. Perhaps you took on someone else's grudge only to find out you had been deceived. Maybe you imposed a doctrine of controlled emotions, scarcity, and extreme self-denial as a way of gaining favor of the gods. Possibly you still retain guilt and choose to passively punish yourself by preventing happiness, joy, and love. You seek once more to find a balance between an open heart and clear mind. You are in search of the rhythm of the spheres and the dance of the cosmos.

It is easy for you to confuse the difference between discipline and denial. You chafe at restraints while at the same time worrying about becoming overly emotional and out of control. You are fortunate to find friends who recognize the dilemma and provide you with excellent psychological insight and sincere support. Your literary interests take you far and wide into texts and treatises of boundless human experience. You may well pen a missive that gives thought to the empowerment of human freedom to live well and prosper.

NOTABLES WITH THIS DEGREE:

Bill Clinton: American president, lawyer, business executive

Robert Redford: American actor, director, producer, environmentalist, philanthropist

Benjamin Harrison: American president, military leader

Coco Chanel: French fashion designer, singer, entrepreneur, social trendsetter

27th Degree of Leo

If this is your sun sign, you may actually be a little less bold and daring than many of your Leo family members. The idealism of the Leo is channeled into more detailed matters, micromanaging more than the sweeping grandeur of the proud warrior lion. This is not to say you won't take larger issues under your belt. This number-sign combination strengthens the Leo intellectual inquisitiveness and can make for excellent communicators. If you take the path of drama and entertainment, you flourish in roles of minute scrutiny and subtlety that explore the eccentric and bizarre corners of human nature that other performers might reject.

NOTABLES WITH THIS DEGREE:

James Marsters: American actor, musician

H. P. Lovecraft: American fantasy, horror, and science-fiction author

Kenny Rogers: American country music singer, producer, songwriter, actor, author, producer, entrepreneur

There is the karmic hint that in an earlier life setting, you may have become overwhelmed by the tides of human emotion, going out of control. Perhaps you caused great embarrassment to your family or some socially prominent leader. Perhaps you scoffed at the rules and regulations of the time. There is a likelihood of having been punished severely for flagrant transgressions of the social codes. Your expansive soul still wants to make the grand appearance and rousing performance. However, you have chosen to build some restraint into your personality this time around in order to have some time to ponder the consequences before plunging.

You will find yourself enjoying wickedly wise and wondrous people who push the limits of conventional human behavior. You enjoy exploring transcendental experiments that offer the tantalizing enticements of opening the door of the universe to let your inquiring soul take a look. You will do well with a partner who places some restraints on your expansive personality. But you are more likely to find someone who is able to stay with you on your roller coaster rides through life. Too much restraint will drive you away.

28th Degree of Leo

If this is your sun sign, you will be active among your social environment and often at the forefront of things developing on the fringe of advancement and change. Your innate Leo tendency to want recognition and attention is augmented by this numerical combination. You possess certain diplomatic skills that let you interact with a wide range of cultural races and religions. This number-sign combination is one that can attract money and social status, so you could be found among the upper classes of society. This can be a tedious and sometimes treacherous course as you touch the toes of the dark side of society along the way.

There is a karmic hint of having been part of nefarious activities in other times and settings. You understand human weakness and emotional vulnerability well, and there is a lingering temptation to use that knowledge for personal gratification and gain. You can relieve some of the human suffering or participate in its continuation. If you detach and look down on humanity with superiority and arrogance, you may continue the karmic loop. If you choose to awaken and enlighten, you can create a new strand of evolutionary growth.

You possess many excellent social attributes that gain you favor and appreciation. You understand the complexities of commerce and the organizational competency to lead or manage large organizations if that is your destiny. There is a regal Leo quality that likes the things of luxury and fine living. For many of you, there will be the opportunity to have fine surroundings and the things that reflect a level of high success. There is an element of technical understanding that lets you stay current with breakthroughs and allows you to be at the forefront of advancements in technology.

NOTABLES WITH THIS DEGREE:

Norman Schwarzkopf: American Army military general

Claude Debussy: French impressionist musician

Jennifer Finnigan: Canadian actress

Tori Amos: American pianist, singer, songwriter

Sergey Brin: American billionaire computer scientist, Internet entrepreneur who cofounded Google

29th Degree of Leo

If this is your sun sign, the raging lion side of your personality is tempered somewhat, and you are more likely to use tact rather than your raging roar to motivate others to get things done. The Leo ego is given a chance for refinement and resolution by the influence of the ideals and sensitivity to others that come with this number-sign combination.

You are learning that you don't have to take criticism as a personal affront and that very often there is good advice laced within the words of the speaker. This number-sign combination allows for some impersonal distancing for you to think things over before impulsively replying out of injured Leo pride.

NOTABLES WITH THIS DEGREE:

Ray Bradbury: American fantasy, horror, and science-fiction author

Roland Orzabal: English musician, songwriter, record producer

Henri Cartier-Bresson: French innovative photographer, founder of modern photojournalism

There is the karmic suggestion that you have previously been within a life structure in which your pride and perhaps arrogance may have gotten in the way of your personal development. There is the suggestion that you were very talented or a virtuoso in some creative endeavor. You may have believed that you were bigger than all the people who appreciated you and forgot that each one is equally big in his or her own world. You likely flaunted tradition and ignored social protocol and consideration in your hasty and harsh rebuke of any criticism. You are now learning humility and to be respectful of certain rules of social order.

The Leo drive and competitive spirit are very much present, and you want to stand out from others and be recognized. Through your accomplishments, you are placed in situations that allow you to have a large positive effect on the public consciousness. You can inspire many to make things better or irritate many and bring the house of rancor down on your back. You associate with the accomplished and elite, and together you can form a powerful organization for encouraging the attainment of dreams and the most elevated aspirations.

VIRGO

0 Degree of Virgo

If this is your sun sign, you are driven to perform at high levels and believe that you deserve to get the best of rewards for having given the best performance. You are a bit of an actor and enjoy the limelight coming your way. With this number-sign combination, it is difficult to appease that Virgo tendency toward wanting everything done right and proper. Your early years can be restless and confusing. While your contemporaries seem to find their purpose in life, you struggle through dead ends and seeming misadventures. Once you find an inner purpose, you are dynamic and flushed with the possibility of fulfilling a deep soul need.

NOTABLES WITH THIS DEGREE:

Kobe Bryant: American professional basketball player

Jorge Paulo Lemann: Swiss-Brazilian billionaire banker

Lisa Najeeb Halaby: Queen Noor of Jordan, social activist

Jorge Luis Borges: Argentine author, poet, essayist

You tend toward being witty, wonderful, and perhaps a bit more wild than some of your more conservative Virgo mates. You have a sense of organization combined with the ability to recognize multiple options. This unique gift allows you to explain complicated matters easily to others, thus making it possible for them to move through otherwise complicated learning experiences. There is a karmic suggestion that in another life sequence, you were in a situation that presented enormous opportunity for personal and social growth. Perhaps out of fear you chose not to seize that moment. Now you know there is something special you are here to do. However, it might elude you until you make a conscious effort to get back on the soul track.

You observe life from a broad expanse of mind and spirit. Your intuitive grasp of situations amazes people when you hit squarely on a topic that is in right front of their eyes, yet to them has remained unseen. This combination is beneficial to the process of innovation and inventiveness. You will leave the world a different place at each step along your path. You touch others with inspiration and abundant practical insights.

1st Degree of Virgo

If this is your sun sign, you can be more assertive than many of your Virgo contemporaries. You move when others pause and confront when others defer. There is a little less of the Virgo caution with this number-sign combination. That can be either a blessing or a curse. Too much impulsiveness can get you into sticky situations faster than desired. On the other hand, if you move quickly, having absorbed the material and information your Virgo computer has arranged and assembled, you will impress and amaze others with your combination of astute timing and analysis.

There is the karmic suggestion that in another soul sequence, you may have become excessively attached to a belief system or intellectual concept. Perhaps out of arrogance

NOTABLES WITH THIS DEGREE:

Sean Connery: Scottish actor, producer

Cecil Andrus: governor of Idaho, U.S. Secretary of the Interior

Leonard Bernstein: American conductor, pianist, author, composer

Marlee Matlin: American actress

George Wallace: governor of Alabama, conservative political leader

or power, you could not budge from a position even when all of the evidence proved otherwise. You are learning to integrate new concepts when appropriate so that you are more efficient in your accomplishments. You can stretch your mind in order to allow more immediate and applicable concepts to come in and be recognized for their appropriateness. Your potential strength is to introduce ideas that are functional as well as brilliant and original.

You can be chipper, dapper, and in frivolous moments, dowdy. You may break the rules of tidiness with less conscience than many of your Virgo contemporaries. Your humor is crisp, cagey, and can keep your friends and associates off-guard with its spot-on insight. You will find yourself doing work or routines that involve short trips and frequently getting out and about, as you are not inclined to sit still very long in one place. You could be drawn to journalism or a position in which you present commentaries on the human way of life. A touch of quirkiness and a twist of wit make you a recognized part of your community.

2nd Degree of Virgo

If this is your sun sign, it is not an easy num-ber-sign combination to assess. There is the possibility of expanding the Virgo trait of pickiness to hypercritical heights. Paradoxi-cally, there is also the possibility that your Virgo critical inclination is less obvious and perhaps even refined. Favorable planetary aspects would lean you toward the latter. More likely, you possess keen insight into sensing other's moods and intents. People are inclined to reveal details to you about themselves that are often reserved only for trusted friends or associates. Your flair for detail enables you to remember personal information and specifics that other people appreciate.

Some of you like to flaunt yourselves in public and disregard convention. There is the karmic hint that you have been strongly antisocial in other times and settings. Perhaps you liked to mock the morality of others or were inclined to interpret eth-ics in any manner that best suited your own gains and ends. You will walk a tightrope between wanting the support of the public and respecting the status quo while at the same time desperately seeking your own self-expression and interests. You understand the fickleness of public opinion and may become some form of advisor to those whose positions depend on the ever-changing climate of social trends.

Although you may be active in the public arena, you tend to be shy and more introspective than you may appear. You seek approval and to be accepted, but there is a deeper issue with trust that makes it difficult for you to be completely open with others. You use your skill with words to weave your way through myriad personal whims and moods of those around you. There is a quality of class associated with this combination, and for the most part, it helps you gain respect from your peers.

NOTABLES WITH THIS DEGREE:

Mother Teresa: Albanian born, Indian Roman Catholic Religious Sister, activist

Jo Dee Messina: American country music singer, Special Olympics ambassador

Alexander Skarsgård: Swedish actor

Thalía: Mexican actress, singer, author, business executive

Regis Philbin: American media personality, actor, singer

3rd Degree of Virgo

If this is your sun sign, you struggle with conflicting emotions between the desire for spontaneity and the Virgo inclination toward being careful and methodical in self-conduct. You are cautious in the expression of feelings and can be controlled when it comes to making any striking and bold creative gesture. Once you find your comfort zone, you are capable of striking bursts of imaginative and innovative brilliance. You may surprise other Virgos with your sporadic outbursts of emotion and celebration. This number-sign combination is common among many authors and people who love to spread the word.

NOTABLES WITH THIS DEGREE:

Lyndon B. Johnson: American president

Zipporah Dobyns: American psychologist, astrologer

Guillaume Apollinaire: French poet, playwright, critic

Yasser Arafat: Palestinian leader, statesman

Cheng Yu-tung: Hong Kong billionaire, real-estate magnate

There is a karmic hint that in another life sequence, you may have been the perpetrator of gossip resulting in harm to and suffering for the target. Perhaps this was by intent or perhaps you were unaware of the misleading nature of the information. You experience guilt for having seen someone suffer badly from your actions. It is also likely you have been the victim of misleading information. You are overly sensitive to what people say and to the process of propaganda and prevarication. You strive to be accurate, honest, and fair in your assessments and statements about others. You would make a great journalist or perhaps a judge, but you are certainly not limited to these vocations.

This combination often is associated with people who have a little extra spark of openness and an almost magical quality that shines amid the majority of average personalities so prevalent among societies. You are at your best when this combination just shines on the basic Virgo personally traits, getting you recognized for your refreshing presence amid the collective. You have the knack for taking something quite ordinary and routine and turning it into a moment that stands out, or perhaps a product that just happens to be right for the moment in which you present it.

NUMEROLOGY OF ASTROLOGY

4th Degree of Virgo

If this is your sun sign, you are cool, calm and work hard to appear collected. Sometimes you reach that degree of control, but most of the time you strive to get there. This number-sign combination can make the Virgo personality even more tedious than it is regarded to be. On the other hand, the elements are there to reach your aspired goals and to excel in the work that you choose to do. The combination of Virgo attention to detail along with the 4's steadiness and perseverance allow you to be thorough and accomplished in whatever you do. You are willing to put in the extra overtime and effort necessary to get the job done right.

There is the karmic suggestion that in another time and setting, you were placed in a situation of opportunity to improve yourself and contribute to the advancement of humanity's potential. Perhaps you were too proud, possibly lazy. This suggests an opportunity missed and the restless need of a soul to get caught up. Once you move through the compulsiveness of catching up and find the natural stride of your soul, you will settle happily into a situation of great contentment and realization. Your capacity to rebound from setbacks is second to none. You are willing to overcome any hurdle that fate or circumstance place in your path.

Because of your stable nature and dependability, you are often sought after for advice regarding myriad aspects of life. You are appreciated for your trustworthiness and reliability under pressure. Although not ostentatious, many of you will find comfort, and your experience will include the better things of life. Your fertile mind and search for knowledge may take you on a path of exploration into an obscure event in history.

NOTABLES WITH THIS DEGREE:

Sarah Chalke: Canadian actress

Elizabeth Ann Seton: American Catholic saint, educational pioneer

LeAnn Rimes: American country music singer

Donald O'Connor: American actor, dancer, singer, comedian

Amanda Tapping: English-born Canadian actress, producer, director

5th Degree of Virgo

If this is your sun sign, you long to assert your individuality, hoping at the same time for public acceptance. There is a kind of tension in your life about being who you are while trying to gain attention and acceptance from others. You see yourself as conforming to the tenets and norms of society. However, public perception of your life and actions may not see you as conforming to standard operating procedures. You will likely be found in circles that seek to stretch taboos and open doors that are usually considered unmentionable. You experience guilt when overindulging but resentment when not allowed to pursue your indulgences.

There is a karmic suggestion of previous lifetimes in which you have tried to hide personal excess from public scrutiny. You are now trying to learn to live within the norms of society while being able to explore and express your personal uniqueness. Your behavior at times can border on the bizarre and extreme, which can attract an opposite reaction from the public you most want to please. You are an excellent student of human behavior. Your perceptive analysis earns you recognition and awards. Your sociological observations are astute and influential in your area of expertise.

Your sense of humor borders on the satirical, and even so, you are often the center of gatherings with your wit and marvelously entertaining insight into human and social behavior. Many public spokespeople, lecturers, and entertainers share this number-sign combination. You are less attentive to detail than many of your Virgo kin. On the contrary, some of you share almost an aversion to painstaking detail and time spent on preparation. This can be a shortcoming when circumstances demand thoroughness in every facet of the project at hand.

NOTABLES WITH THIS DEGREE:

Michael Jackson: American singer-songwriter, dancer, actor, philanthropist

Vernon E. Clark: American astrologer, author, psychologist

Johann von Goethe: German novelist, painter, theorist

Rebecca De Mornay: American actress

Charlie Parker: American jazz musician

6th Degree of Virgo

If this is your sun sign, you will struggle to be genuinely connected and aware of your true inner feelings that emanate from the depths of your soul. Your desire is to be of service to humanity, and you will find yourself attracted to the types of careers that relate to service and assistance to others. For many of you, this may take an indirect path toward giving to others. For instance, you may find yourself called on to perform in the business arena. Since it is extremely difficult for you to directly experience and relate deep personal feelings, you become enamored with providing huge amounts of material goods to the masses. This can lead to huge success in retailing or in expanding the distribution of goods and services. There are some of you who will gravitate toward a political path of liberal causes.

NOTABLES WITH THIS DEGREE:

Fred MacMurray: American actor, political activist

Warren Buffett: American billionaire mogul, philanthropist

Lauren Collins: American actress

There is a karmic hint that in another time and place, you were terribly selfish and inconsiderate regarding the needs of the less fortunate. You withheld the very necessities of life, causing the tragic suffering of many souls. You may currently find yourself driven by an almost compulsive need to give back what you realize you took away. This can drive you to produce on a mass scale. Yet another outlet for some of this repressed guilt may be the need to give generously to charitable causes and organizations.

You are cautious, calculating, and at times conniving as you go about managing various matters of commerce. At times, you are indifferent to the human equation when calculating your possible gains and successes. You are attentive to image and appearance, and you take care of your possessions with noted fervor. You can be very generous to those you admire and to those you perceive to have been loyal to your dreams and aspirations.

7ᵗʰ Degree of Virgo

If this is your sun sign, you are cerebral, careful, and at times cantankerous. This number-sign combination adds a mental quality to the already analytical Virgo personality. You like to be logically correct and have your informational package in neat order for presentation. Virgos with this combination need to be careful that they do not hide from their emotions and feelings behind a lot of mental pontification and pretense. You may be ignoring a tendency toward your own abusiveness and rage. Even if you have your emotions in line, it is not easy for you to display warmth or affection in a direct manner. Some of you will do it on the stage or perhaps in some role of advice or consulting.

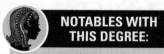

NOTABLES WITH THIS DEGREE:

Cameron Diaz: American actress, model

Raymond Buckland: English-American author of Wicca and the occult, Wiccan High Priest

Rania Al Abdullah: Queen of Jordan, global humanitarian

Maria Montessori: Italian physician, education system pioneer

There is a karmic hint of previous life experiences in which you were intellectually arrogant and emotionally detached from the real needs of others. You are almost compulsive in your effort to be caring and can use a professional cloak to mask your own repressed anger. As you face your own issues and become more natural, your message will receive greater attention. You will be found around research and investigative types of occupations. Many of you will excel in areas of philosophy, religion, and social sciences.

As you become comfortable with yourself, you exude wit and wisdom that many find intriguing. Once you work though the tendency toward abuse and repression, you can be a loyal and committed partner. What you cannot emotionally display openly, you express through working to create a stable home environment. You enjoy classification and the arrangement of information, and you may find yourself attracted to communications. You may find yourself attracted to ancient cultures that have unusual centers of wisdom and advanced information. You pride yourself in your historical perspective toward the evolution of culture.

8th Degree of Virgo

If this is your sun sign, you long to assert your ideas and intellect in an effort to spread information to the many. You feel at home when you can manage the affairs of commerce or whatever endeavor you enter. Your attention to detail and orderliness catches the attention of your superiors, giving you the opportunity to move up quickly through the ranks of your organization. There is a proclivity toward wanting to control issues and matters, and this desire for control will follow you through your life.

NOTABLES WITH THIS DEGREE:

Rocky Marciano: American professional boxer, undefeated heavyweight champion

Richard Gere: American actor

Nicolas Sarkozy: French president, political activist

James Coburn: American actor

Dr. Phil McGraw: American television personality, psychologist

When taken too far, you can be seduced by the temporary high of having control over the many. It is easy to be persuaded by manipulative personalities into compromising your own identity and that of the many in order to feed the appetite of the few. There is a karmic hint that you have made similar pacts in other times and places. Do you wish to sell out once more, or do you wish to use your access to information in a manner that enlightens the mass consciousness? Time will tell. Whatever your destiny, you will at some time find yourself fascinated by education, communication, and sharing knowledge. Perhaps you will be a part of establishing new technologies and mediums of sending information.

You are likely admired by many for your accomplishments and are capable of attracting quite a cast of characters around you in your pursuit of the pleasures of life. You enjoy collecting the trophies that indicate success and reaching a point of prominence beyond that of your peers. You enjoy the games of power, and you will likely be amid the fray and fracas of politics and posturing of the powerful. You enjoy studying cultures and history in order to better grasp just how society functions and how you can get the most out of maneuvering through the web of social intrigues.

9th Degree of Virgo

If this is your sun sign, you may be a little more idealistic and hopeful than many of your Virgo contemporaries. Your ideas and expectations can seem pretty far-out for someone who is expected to be grounded and rooted in old Missouri skepticism. At its best, this number-sign combination stimulates your dreams and gives you the necessary equipment to fulfill your schemes. You inspire others with your vision and possess the tenacity to stick to it until you see it come into fruition. Your charm and persuasive manner lend a hand to helping with the public relations portion of your quest.

NOTABLES WITH THIS DEGREE:

Keanu Reeves: Canadian actor, director, producer, musician, author

Gloria Estefan: Cuban-American singer, songwriter, entrepreneur

Salma Hayek: Mexican-American actress, director, producer

Aimee Osbourne: English singer, actress, columnist

There is the karmic clue that perhaps you were in a position to inspire and uplift others in another time and place. Perhaps you sold out to personal power or greed. Perhaps you feel as if you failed to accomplish the soul's desired intent. There is lingering guilt and doubt regarding your ability to accomplish anything of meaning. You will be placed in a position that allows you to once again make a spiritual move that can substantially enhance your inner growth. People who share the same dream and aspiration to help humanity will enter your life at just the right time.

You mix and mingle with unique and unusual souls as you go about your life on this plane of existence. You travel to exotic places and are introduced to arcane and esoteric teachings that are both ancient and divinely applicable in this time. Your cultured manner and gift of story make it easier for you to attract capable and dedicated accomplices who are both qualified and motivated to see your mission through to the end. You see a vision of an uncorrupted world and strive to prepare yourself and those who believe they are ready to bring that possible world into reality.

10th Degree of Virgo

If this is your sun sign, you live in a world of ups and downs and turns of fate that will keep you and everyone in your life constantly wondering what is going to happen next. This gives additional pizzazz to an already ever-changing Virgo personality. It is particularly hard to pin you down to anything or anyone, because you are always interested in something different and someone new. Yet amid this seemingly nonsensical persona, your vast range of experience and information make you a magnet to others and an exciting addition to anyone's entourage.

NOTABLES WITH THIS DEGREE:

Shaun White: American ski board champion, Olympic athlete, professional skateboarder

Anthony Louis: American astrologer, psychiatrist

Christa McAuliffe: American teacher, crew member of Challenger Space Shuttle

Charlie Sheen: American actor

There is often some kind of drama or perhaps crisis going on in your life. Some of those close to you may not be able to survive all of the stress and uncertainty that comes with being around you. However, when you do find loyal friends, you have more to share than your scattered exterior antics may indicate. There is a karmic suggestion that in another time, you were hesitant to stand up for your beliefs, leaving many people disappointed and at the mercy of other persuaders with less than benign intent. At your best, you are lighthearted, fanciful, and fun to be with. Your candor and sometimes guileless comments catch the repressed and evasive off-guard. The pretentious may find it uncomfortable to be around you, because you see right through the façade.

When you are not having fun, you are busy pursuing activities of intrigue. You wish to live and let live, but you find those around you have plenty to say about how you should live your life. You recoil at the restraints and taboos of society that rob individuality while leaving the masses lined up in a row singing the politically and socially correct slogans impressed on them by authoritarian mindbenders. At some point in your life, your behavior will push right up against the tight barriers and rigid restraints that quell the positive evolution of the human experience.

11th Degree of Virgo

If this is your sun sign, you may feel at times like you were born to shine. You may experience a kind of "I have a destiny" feeling, and many of you will be drawn into the limelight at some time during your life. You share a keen attunement to the human race and are very much aware of what is going on around you. At times, this can become disconcerting, since your sensitivity can easily pick up on the unconscious angst of the population around you. It can also be a blessing for your business or career since you have kind of an intuitive grasp of what people want, and then it is just a matter of providing that.

Sometimes it is easy to get pulled down into the collective victimhood and dysfunction that predominates your world. There is a karmic suggestion that in another time and place, you used a prominent position to unjustly and unmercifully criticize and condemn your opponents. You were not above bending the truth to make things sound worse than they were. There is part of you that is very careful and cautious with your tongue in order not to provoke. On the other hand, you may very well be called on to speak up truthfully about matters that might be taboo and touchy to the public. You have the inner fortitude at this time to do so.

Your attention to detail and cautious approach to matters can be very valuable in decision-making or consulting roles. Many of you will be found around public figures or prominent people within the community that you choose. There is an air of confidence that you exude that makes it easy for people to believe what you say and what you represent. You will meet quite accomplished souls along the path and assist others to meet their own highest standard of accomplishment as well.

12ᵗʰ Degree of Virgo

If this is your sun sign, you are gracious, composed, and quite capable. There is a certain charm about this combination that tends to make people want to be on your side in matters of choice. You may be tempted to take this phenomenon to the extreme. In such cases, you can become manipulative of group dynamics. This number-sign combination usually results in people with admirable communication skills and creative abilities. You could find yourself in public relations or positions that involve public service. Your attunement to the mood of the masses will come in handy at some time in your life.

There is the karmic hint that in another time and setting, you may have stumbled in your responsibilities to an institution or congregation of people to whom you had an obligation. You may feel almost compelled to be true to your word and any obligation that you have made to your organization or those who follow you. This can be a burden, but it also can motivate you to do as well as possible under the conditions of stress that come with commitment. There may be moments in your life when you do not feel you have the choice or freedom to act on your own.

The combination of the number 12 with the Virgo personality often results in someone being articulate, meticulous, and tasteful in dress and in the presentation of social persona. Your attention to detail is rewarded by the results you attain and the appreciation of those you represent. You may appear shy and uneasy in a group, but once you get control, you are quite the entertainer and spinner of yarns. There is a kind of humble aura about this combination, and you naturally put people at ease. This allows others to be comfortable with you, revealing their deeper attributes of personality and friendship.

NOTABLES WITH THIS DEGREE:

Arthur Koestler: Hungarian-British author, journalist, social philosopher

Louis XIV: long-reigning king of France

Frank Yerby: historical novelist, first millionaire African-American author, also first African-American author to have book commissioned for Hollywood film

Jesse James: American outlaw, bank robber, gang leader, murderer

13th Degree of Virgo

If this is your sun sign, you may long to take a somewhat alternative path in life from many of your contemporaries. However, circumstance may place you into a situation that is terribly conventional and routine. There is a sense of dissatisfaction with many things in life. In your mind, things could be much better and work much more efficiently. You see so much waste, loss, and misuse of resources and human effort. There is a thread of reform that runs in your blood, and you feel an almost compulsion to get involved in reformation projects.

Despite this, you may find yourself stuck in a role that limits your individual freedom and makes it virtually impossible to speak your true mind without repercussions. Per-

NOTABLES WITH THIS DEGREE:

Jane Addams: American author, socialist, women's suffrage advocate, Nobel Prize laureate

Raquel Welch: American actress, sex symbol

Pippa Middleton: English socialite, Catherine Middleton's sister

Joseph P. Kennedy: American business mogul, political advocate, patriarch of Kennedy family

haps you were in a highly elevated role of leadership in another life setting. Possibly you had a chance to bring positive changes and social transformation. Maybe you were afraid to go against the authority of the time. Maybe you hesitated in fear that you would lose your position or perhaps even your own life. Possibly you were just a coward. Life will place you in situations in which you will have to choose between living your inner truth and being held to the whims of public perception. You will find yourself attracted to those who have the courage to speak out and advocate for the alteration in convention that is called for in your time.

You are determined and quite capable of taking a project or theory to the point of completion and proof. People appreciate you for your loyalty and ability to keep company secrets removed from public scrutiny. Your style of discipline and ability to keep things in an orderly fashion earn you respect and admiration from many. The paradox of this trait is that you can find yourself locked into having to maintain the status quo that you have espoused, even when your heart knows it is time for revision of that position.

NUMEROLOGY OF ASTROLOGY

14th Degree of Virgo

If this is your sun sign, you are blessed with a kind of effervescence that mystifies others and can even be baffling to your more studious Virgo nature. The analytical Virgo mind and need for quantification and explanation may not even solve the riddle about your own uniqueness of personality. You can be skeptical when others believe but have faith in the most doubtful of situations. There are many paradoxes about this number-sign combination, and your imagination and investigative mind will be busy, constantly searching for answers.

NOTABLES WITH THIS DEGREE:

Michael Emerson: American actor

James Foxworthy: American actor, comedian

Evan Rachel Wood: American actress, singer

Claude Pepper: U.S. Senator, advocate of senior citizenry

Swami Sivananda: Hindu spiritual teacher, physician, yoga leader

There is the karmic hint of having come close to accessing a great truth in another time and place. You may have misinterpreted the information or failed to earn access to the final answer. There is still great anger about not having been given the final elucidation. You may blame God or someone of authority for not granting you what you believed to be your earned reward. Hence, you are envious and skeptical about anyone claiming to have any extraordinary powers or gifts. You do not realize that the biggest gift is within you.

Your intellectual ability, acute memory, and knack for detail make you an excellent researcher and cataloguer of events and information. This combination adds the likelihood of travel and exposure to others cultures and perhaps other realms or dimensions of life. If you do not travel physically, your mind will always be actively on the go in the pursuit of answers to questions that constantly arise in your quest for knowledge. You have a knack for the practical. Part of the paradox of this combination is to find practical ways to apply intuitive information and the gifts of spirit that do not always have immediate instructions for use in everyday dilemmas.

15ᵗʰ Degree of Virgo

If this is your sun sign, you struggle with the dichotomy of conscience and strong instinctual needs. Your sense of refinement is grossed out by some of your rude and thoughtless behavior patterns. At the same time, you can flaunt condescension and brutish criticism at those who strive to maintain a wholesome sense of public demeanor. There is the karmic suggestion of having been totally irresponsible and callous toward the conventions and life choices of others. You desperately want to fit in and be accepted, but you find the irreverent part of yourself unwilling to comply. This can put you into positions of compromise.

There is a curious mix of caution and careless abandonment about life responsibilities. The normally discreet Virgo can get out of hand when this number-sign combination is under stress and going through adverse aspects. You can be irreverent at the wrong time and overly pious when straightforwardness might be more appropriate. You just don't know when to rein it in before things become awkward or even ugly. Your keen sense of the public angst makes you an excellent diagnostician of public opinion. You are at your best when called on to render assistance to others in recognizing unconscious behavior that leads to disruption of social communication and evolution. Your social commentary can be biting and satirical, but it is usually accurate and direct.

You are sensitive to social injustice and may be a spokesperson for abused and exploited victims of society. This combination makes for meticulous investigators and researchers. Your desire to be fair takes you through more than the ordinary number of hoops to get your facts straight and information confirmed. As you become more at ease, you put others at ease, which allows them to appreciate the intensity and uniqueness in your presentation of self.

NOTABLES WITH THIS DEGREE:

Michael Shermer: American science writer, founder of the Skeptics Society and *Skeptic* magazine

Grace Metalious: American author known for bestselling, racy novel *Peyton Place*

Alisher Usmanov: Russian billionaire, investment speculator

Peter Sellers: British actor, comedian, musician, dancer

Patsy Cline: American country music singer

16ᵗʰ Degree of Virgo

If this is your sun sign, you will find your life experience riddled with the unexpected and unexplained. At a very early age, this could lead you into some type of research or investigative pursuit. You are curious, cautious, and careful in your emotional and mental approach to life. You will study many fields and explore numerous philosophies in an attempt to answer your thirst for understanding what and why events happen as they do. You have the knack to go out of the way and yet come up with the most practical solutions. Gadgets and unusual machines are no match for your understanding. You dabble in many realms and come out with good results most of the time.

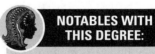

NOTABLES WITH THIS DEGREE:

Hugh Grant: British actor, producer

Arnold Palmer: American professional golf player, business executive

Michael Bublé: Canadian singer, songwriter, actor

Bill O'Reilly: American television commentator, syndicated columnist

Perhaps you find yourself constantly looking around the corner expecting disaster. There is a karmic hint that you have contributed to some destructive event in your past, and at times, you can be haunted by the fear of repeating this pattern. You may find yourself going through a period in your life when you attract mistakes and weird incidences of calamity. As you work through your unconscious patterns, this tendency will decline and pretty much pass away. Many of you will be quite comfortable with matters related to security and safety issues at home or in the marketplace.

At best, you are a problem solver and task master. Your innate sense of wanting to know how things tick makes you a good investigator or researcher. Life is full of mysteries, and you will be found right at the front of the line attempting to get the scoop on the answers. Although you are a bit eccentric and inclined to rather unpredictable behaviors, for the most part, people are intrigued by your penchant for self-expression and individuality.

17ᵗʰ Degree of Virgo

If this is your sun sign, you are scrutinizing, sagacious, and searching. There is an eternal hope that wells in your heart, and unless that is shattered, you are cautiously optimistic about what is around the corner for you and for humankind. You are prone to take every precaution to make sure that you get around the corner to see what is there. Your mind is always in gear, and you run experience through the mental file to sort out what is meaningful and educational. This can sometimes get in the way, and you will want to guard against using it as protection from your feelings and inner reality.

NOTABLES WITH THIS DEGREE:

Ferdinand Marcos: Philippine president, attorney

Leo Tolstoy: Russian novelist, essayist, dramatist

Colin Firth: English actor

Cardinal Richelieu: French Catholic clergyman, diplomat

Ulrika Ericsson: Swedish actress, model

There is a karmic suggestion that you have been sassy, sarcastic, and purposefully undercutting toward opponents in other times and places. Misinformation was the name, and arrogance was the game. By misguiding, you divided forces against you. It is a real ego rush to feel superior, presuming you have outsmarted someone. It is always a temptation to fall back into such an attitude, especially when the compensation and pressure are great. Your wish is to accurately inform others about the circumstances at hand.

This number-sign combination gives a command of language and penetrating insight into the nature of law and the legal process. You appreciate the noble intent of the law. At the same time, you are keenly aware of how it can be distorted and used to undermine good and allow the dark side of humans to prevail. You are heady, intense, and appear to be assured of yourself in most situations — especially in public. Your tedious nature and detailed dedication to protocol make you an excellent researcher or investigator. You have a nose for scandal and must be careful that you do not become the source of such.

18th Degree of Virgo

If this is your sun sign, some negative quali-ties can be very obvious in your personality makeup. Your disposition inclines toward skeptical. You can be overly suspicious and critical of others with a lot of issues revolving around trust and loyalty. Depending on other aspects of your chart, you are defensive and proud about the position you take and do not like to be outperformed by those around you. Without the addition of some more mellow-ing aspects, this can be to your undoing. This is a combination of keen awareness and deep wisdom about human nature. You can draw from this vast storehouse of knowledge to be a fine teacher or trainer of personal growth.

This can be the aspect of a paid provocateur who purposely stirs up trou-ble to divert attention away from more serious matters of concern. The karmic pattern hints at having been a spy or person involved with intentional lies and deception in other times and places. It is not an easy task restoring integrity and trust in yourself. There is a strong existential quest associated with this number-sign combination, and you long to be back in touch with your spiri-tual core and the deeper attributes of your soul.

Many of you will be drawn toward the fine arts or routes of articulation and expression of self. Your very nature is dramatic, and some of you will act this out on stage or in some form of entertainment. Whatever your calling, there is almost an obsession to get things done right, and perfection is always at the forefront of your attention. You expect no less of others and can become very critical of what you see as weakness in others. It is not so easy for you to see that the same weakness lies within you.

19th Degree of Virgo

If this is your sun sign, you may demonstrate somewhat less of the picky and critical nature that is sometimes associated with the Virgo clan. This number-sign combination encourages openness to new thoughts and opinions. It welcomes the expansion of consciousness and the awakening of the spiritually refined side of the human personality. You can be blunt, but your grasp and presentation of the facts makes your observations welcome to those who recognize the wisdom in your grasp. You are not above guarding your vulnerability, however. You can be wary of emotional sentiment that obscures the light of truth. You prefer to prove things with facts and evidence rather than go with blind trust.

There is the karmic hint that in another life sequence, you may have been vulnerable to criticism and attack by acting on faith while having no real factual support at hand. Perhaps you were undermined by skeptics or displaced by the deceitful who demanded proof positive of the principle of faith on which you stood. Your pride, ego, and position in life all suffered. You inherently trust the inner faith that guides your highest esteem but are cognizant of the leverage that comes with being able whenever possible to back your beliefs with factual and experiential evidence.

You enjoy being around those who are willing to take a step toward modernization, building on the lessons that history has revealed. You invite freethinkers and visionaries into your circle of associates because of the stimulation to consciousness they bring. Despite your direct nature of approaching matters, you are quite capable of literary sensitivity, and when called on, you demonstrate a compelling poetic sense of destiny and an elevated look at the steps humankind is taking toward the stars.

NOTABLES WITH THIS DEGREE:

Mylène Farmer: French-Canadian singer, songwriter, actress, author

Han Suyin: China-born Eurasian novelist, author, physician

María de Zayas y Sotomayor: Spanish novelist, early feminist

Alfred A. Knopf: American book publisher

Henry Hudson: English sea explorer, navigator

NUMEROLOGY OF ASTROLOGY

20th Degree of Virgo

If this is your sun sign, you may demonstrate exquisite skills when it comes to diplomacy and getting along well with other people. For some of you, that skill could apply to other kingdoms, such as animal, alien, angelic, or extradimensional. There very well could be otherworldly matters that occur during the lifetimes of those with this number-sign combination. But for the most part, you find your life centered around the issues of daily matters right here on ole terra firma. You find it difficult to cope with the little issues since your grasp of things tends to be more universal in breadth.

NOTABLES WITH THIS DEGREE:

Sam Neill: New Zealand actor

Dmitry Medvedev: Russian Prime Minister

Milton Hershey: American confectioner, philanthropist

J. B. Priestley: English author

There is a karmic hint that in another time sequence of the soul, you may have become aware of information that was not easy to consume by your community, or perhaps you experienced visions of events that exposed the fraud of those in power. Maybe you tapped transcendental forces that frightened the public and potentates alike. Perhaps you simply had an intuitive grasp of the dysfunctions of that time that the private person and collective public consciousness did not wish to address. You may have suffered at the hands of witch hunters or fearful fanatics who were stirred into action by behind-the-scenes manipulators. You are wary of those who disseminate information and keen to recognize misinformation in the media of your times. You are learning who you can trust and what to say as inspiration comes to you from your inner source of light.

Many of you with this combination enjoy a solid education and strive to become cognizant of the processes and precedents of public interaction. You are appreciated for your conversational skills and grasp of events around you. Your sense of taste and a touch of refinement adds a certain charm that allows you to mix with the elite as well as the unfortunate. It is important for you to pay attention to details since you have a tendency to be more infatuated with the grand scale of things, and thus fail to recognize that the miniscule can be as important as the great and grand.

21ˢᵗ Degree of Virgo

If this is your sun sign, you are articulate, outgoing, and earnestly interested in the art of living. There is a verve and flavor for life that many of you exude. This can be most invigorating to those around you who are not as inclined to be so energetic. Many of you are attracted to writing or some form of communications-related endeavor. Your intense curiosity and attention to detail makes you a good researcher and recorder of facts and events. You are keenly aware of the principles of cause and effect. This fascination leads you into the study of motivation and how people make decisions in life.

NOTABLES WITH THIS DEGREE:

Ingo Swann: American artist, author, psychic, developed remote viewing

Ayo: German singer, songwriter

Oliver Stone: American director, screenwriter, producer

Tommy Lee Jones: American actor, director

There is a karmic hint of having been in situations when your insight and superior knowledge could have been misused to abuse others. Perhaps you naively gave information to people who used it with bad intentions and dark ulterior motives. Perhaps you were forced under duress to reveal information that lead to death or destruction. You wish to see people work through dysfunctions and evolve into more productive and self-sufficient beings. There is an inherent distrust of those who are given too much authority in matters of the dissemination of information without double checks and countermeasures built into the system of government or administration.

You wonder with delight in the realm of mind and soul. You are convivial and conversational, and you enjoy the process of soliciting information from people who rarely share with friends, let alone strangers. For the most part, you would never use access to such private revelations in a manner that would cause embarrassment or regret from your source. You are more inclined to keep storing the input from all of your intimate exchanges for the purpose of formulating hypotheses and possible helpful guidelines to greater living.

22nd Degree of Virgo

If this is your sun sign, you are dedicated and determined to diligently discovering and defining your destiny. There is a knowing feeling within your heart and soul that there is some task that is important for you to get done well during this go-around. Your Virgo knack for neatness and detail may serve you well as you prepare yourself carefully with the necessary accouterments for success. You can be witty, wicked, and fun with your grasp of language and innuendo in human experience. Your air of detachment can cause some people to consider your actions impersonal.

NOTABLES WITH THIS DEGREE:

Dan Marino: American professional football player

William Howard Taft: American president, U.S. Chief Justice

Harry of Wales: Prince of Wales

Faith Ford: American actress, model

However, there is a deep humanitarian concern within your heart and soul, and you aspire to contribute to uplift human awareness.

There is a karmic hint of having gotten careless with power in another sequence of your soul journey on this planet. Perhaps you used transcendental power to harm or maim. Perhaps you used such powers out of anger or ego before completing the necessary training to fully comprehend and control such forces. You know you have some extraordinary potential, but you labor in doubt about its possible misuse. You may want to seek a trusted one who has knowledge of such forces and has already learned to better master them.

You are a loyal and reliable companion and friend. Once given an assigned task, you work diligently and determinedly until you have finished as much as possible. Money issues come and go, but you always seem to have enough to get through. If you set your sights on wealth and material success, you are quite capable of maintaining a high standard of living. For the most part, you are likely to place more energy on spiritual prosperity and harmony. Things may come to you later in life, but the wait will most likely be worth it.

23rd Degree of Virgo

If this is your sun sign, you vacillate between rigorous vigilance and unchecked gusto in your desire to stretch the boundaries of knowledge and the perimeters of human inquiry. You are attracted to experimentation in a safe way. There is a leap of faith suggested with this number-sign combination that will push the careful Virgo personality to the limits. An unabashed curiosity combined with a serious scientific caution can lead to an outcome of discovering very important information and triggering commanding original events. With poor aspects and total lack of moderation, this combination is inclined toward serious delusion and neurotic preoccupation with fantasy.

NOTABLES WITH THIS DEGREE:

Mickey Rourke: American actor, screenwriter, boxer

Lauren Bacall: American actress

Edgar Mitchell: American pilot, NASA astronaut

Elgin Baylor: American professional basketball player, NBA general manager

There is the karmic hint of previous excessiveness and out-of-control behavior. Perhaps you strenuously thrashed out against convention to prove someone wrong. Maybe you were out of control and someone tried to warn you of the consequences only for you to react violently. Possibly your intellectual arrogance caused you to take chances with dangerous, unknown forces. You might have stepped over a line and brought about negative consequences to many people. This has left you uncertain and fearful of going to excess once more. You are learning to balance your daring by collecting factual evidence and proceeding into matters by measured stages of precaution.

You can be playful and lighthearted, which makes it easy for people to be with you. Humor comes easily and your mischievous side is capable of some hilarious pranks and pratfalls. Caution: don't take this too far, or you might slip into the realm of the risky and dangerous. Although many people might take you lightly, you have a lot of savvy regarding human nature, and there are many with this number-sign combination found in therapeutic or counseling positions in which they mix their street smarts with academic training. This combination softens some of the potential Virgo prickly personality traits, making you popular and appreciated among family and friends.

24ᵗʰ Degree of Virgo

If this is your sun sign, you are critical, cogent, and calculating. Your early childhood environment was emotionally unsettled, leaving you with many questions and concerns about what is going on in the world. There are issues of trust involved with this number-sign combination. As much as you desperately look for it, you seem to run into people and situations where mendacity rules. This is a combination of much internal emotional conflict that finds you caught between two or more conditions that evoke different emotional needs. You become torn and confused trying to sort out all of the emotional variables, and oftentimes, you choose to simply shut down and go into your head.

NOTABLES WITH THIS DEGREE:

Lord Jamar: American actor, musician, emcee

Andrew D. Basiago: American lawyer, author, proclaimed time traveler, social activist

Robert Blake: American actor

Aisha Tyler: American actress, comedienne, author

This quest to get to the bottom of issues causes you to be ardently committed to getting to the crux of hidden events that are going on in your community or sphere of living. You are outspoken in your disgust with the misuse and abuse of human emotions and the exploitation of people for the purposeful gain of the select few. There is the karmic hint of having fervently believed something in another time and place that may have turned out not to be so. You had been such a vocal spokesperson only to find out there had been distortion and deceit taking place right under your nose. You may have desperately defended yourself, but could not convince the public of your innocence. To this day, you can become overly compulsive in your effort to prove yourself correct.

You seek a committed and loving relationship, but previous emotional trauma and your own picky analytical Virgo mind can make you appear distant and defensive to a potential partner. Many of you find happiness later in life, as you are driven to get other things done during your earlier youthful years.

25th Degree of Virgo

If this is your sun sign, you will find your life becoming more rewarding when you get out of your head and decide to smell the roses. Well, that does not mean giving up that splendid mental acuity. Unfortunately, many of you use the mental processes to avoid getting into your feeling nature. As you learn to explore and trust your feelings, you will find that your intellectual insights become more astute and meaningful. You benefit by traveling and coming into contact with contrasting cultures and sociopolitical foundations. The wider the range of your human experiences, the broader and more far-reaching your conceptualizations of people will become.

NOTABLES WITH THIS DEGREE:

Lance Armstrong: American Olympic bicyclist

Greta Garbo: Swedish actress, early silent film star

Alexandra Vandernoot: Belgian actress

Joan Lunden: American journalist, author, television show hostess

There is the karmic hint that you may have sat in the proverbial intellectual ivory tower and pontificated on the behavior and mores of humanity. Perhaps your observations were thoughtful and well considered but lacking in the compassion and perspective that comes from actual participation in the human ethos. Maybe intellectual bias and arrogance made you partial to some groups and creeds. Possibly you harbored ill will toward certain groups of people because of past negative interactions. As you mix, mingle, and discover the universality of all humanity, you will find a manner of presenting your suppositions that will be noted and recorded by others for their value and contribution to human understanding. A little opening of the heart always helps.

You are well versed in many areas of knowledge and can be a splendid conversationalist and witty entertainer. You lighten up parties and social gatherings with your vast array of information and clever ditties about human nature and experience. For some of you, the temptation to be unconventional is too strong to overcome, and you can be found as an ardent spokesperson for a minority group with a determined agenda.

26th Degree of Virgo

If this is your sun sign, you will experience a varied life fraught with matters of self-image and the role you perform in society. Early on there can be emotional conflicts with authority figures, and you may struggle with institutional delays and oversights during portions of your life. You want to get along and are intimately in touch with the angst of the collective unconscious. This is the number-sign combination of caretakers and natural healers.

NOTABLES WITH THIS DEGREE:

Sophia Loren: Italian actress

Rinat Akhmetov: Ukrainian billionaire business mogul

Cass Elliot: American singer, actress

Kavya Madhavan: Indian actress, artist, dancer

Mia Martini: Italian singer

You will likely be caught up in the many vagaries of social injustice, change, or instability during the course of your life. There is the karmic hint of having been unjustly harsh and critical of public figures. Perhaps you used lies to undermine the leadership of your opponents. You may experience sacrifices to be made and burdens to bear, but you can rise above these struggles to do much good, touching the lives of many. Power issues and social image play into this combination with the suggestion of possible abuse or misuse of authority figures in your early years. This combination often has to do with passive abuse. It is not so much what was done to you; rather, it was what you did not have and did not receive that lurks with troublesome tremors in your memory.

You have a compassionate side that touches many and allows people to relate to you with comfort and ease. You make a devoted mate and loyal associate who wins ventures of partnership. There is much evidence of the Virgo concern for details and proper etiquette. You do want to make a favorable impression on others. Even though you have a tender side, you do like the position of power and to feel in control of the moment at hand. Some may find you a bit uptight in your insistence on following rules and regulation right to the dot, but your lighter side often disarms tensions and gets you through rough moments of personal interaction.

27th Degree of Virgo

If this is your sun sign, you are deft, discerning, and desperately looking for the best in human nature. You search for the altruistic and divine in others but are confronted with the stark reality of the dark side of human nature. It is not easy for you to reconcile the two aspects, and you search for the answers to human origin and the path of evolution. This is the number-sign combination of one who looks and hopes for utopia only to run into a cesspool of human behavior. Many of you are involved in research or academic studies that seek to sort out more understanding about humankind.

There is the karmic hint of having been part of developing a grand society of perfect politics and human commerce. You fell prey to the temptation of corruption and sold out for personal reasons only to see the venture turn into a disaster. There is much guilt left within your subconscious, and when you have trouble seeing that, you project it into your perception of the vile and distorted around you. Even though you encourage and aspire to reach for the best in others, it is easy for you to become disenchanted with the extent of human weakness and willingness to suffer in dysfunction and disastrous behaviors.

You can be charming and delightful when called on since you know how to turn on the entertainment button and give the audience what it wants. More often than not, you are drawn toward the more liberal and global aspects of politics and organizational endeavors. You have an interest in the esoteric and magical, and you may find yourself sifting through old texts of the occult in an effort to find clues to the hidden secrets of our personal nature. You may become disenchanted and escape through drugs or other forms of addiction. Once you overcome this, you can be very productive and successful at shoring up your image of life with others.

28th Degree of Virgo

If this is your sun sign, you are quite sensitive to the legalities, liabilities, and labyrinth of innuendos woven within the lines of human communication. You thrive at sorting out and simplifying communications that have gotten complicated and buried in long-winded bureaucratic legalese. Detail does not have to become burdensome, and many of you have the knack of being able to cut right through the clutter of detail to get directly to the point. You make detail simple. It may not have always been this way.

There are karmic clues that hint at the likelihood you have been trapped in other times and places amid the mess and tedium of detail. Perhaps you were afraid of error, so you had to spell everything out in such infinite detail in order to leave no question about what it was you wanted. Perhaps you were worried that without strict detail and guidance, matters would get out of control so badly that great damage or harm might occur. You could very well have imposed oppressive, detailed, restrictive measures on the masses. Such measures left little room for the freedom to learn and grow from open experiences with life. An archetypal project for this number-sign combination might be creating a simplified manual of personal growth. You are learning to appreciate how each person is unique and deserving of the opportunity to carve out his or her own destiny.

You are a collector of facts and figures of sometimes obscure topics. It is somewhat ironic how frequently possessing such knowledge favors you when you are able to supply a timely tidbit that becomes valuable advice in the moment. Many people find you a bit stiff, perhaps formal, and might believe that you are not easy to get to know. You are cautious about opening up, but once you trust someone, you often surprise them with wit, wonderment, and a playfully wild imagination.

29ᵗʰ Degree of Virgo

If this is your sun sign, you are dexterous, diligent, and usually hopeful as you weave your way through your path of life and social endeavors. You strive to maintain a pleasant demeanor and amicable manner of interacting with other people. Your diversity of knowledge and education can be an asset as you mix and mingle with those from many classes and ethnic backgrounds. Your sometimes excessive idealism can naïvely lead you to ventures with people of questionable intent and motive. Aside from those moments when you appear a bit spacey and seem to tap into the edge of the far-out, you are considered informed and well versed in matters.

NOTABLES WITH THIS DEGREE:

Henrich Cornelius Agrippa: alchemist, astrologer, occult author

Ray Charles: American singer, songwriter, composer

Michael Faraday: English chemist, physicist

Abdul Hamid II: Turkish sultan, diplomat

There is the karmic hint that you previously might have been involved in a utopian venture that included a large number of followers. Perhaps you were misled by those who had power behind the ostensible leadership. Maybe out of naiveté, the whole thing was poorly managed and brought about much loss and despair to all. There is a suggestion that you blamed yourself for the downfall, leaving a deep sense of guilt and responsibility. There might have been a spell of madness resulting from harsh self-judgment. You want to believe in humanity and are back once again to reach for the stars. However, you must learn to deal with human foibles and remain keenly aware of the treachery of this world.

There is a flair for the dramatic that goes with this number-sign combination, and you could find yourself entertaining others or in the public eye sometime during your life. When your deep sense of idealism is shaken, you can turn to the escape of drugs or other forms of addiction to help lessen the pain of disillusionment. For the most part, you are found in roles of mediation and as a go-between when there is misunderstanding or individual and group tension.

LIBRA

0 Degree of Libra

If this is your sun sign, there is much ambiguity and confusion associated with your life and the things that you do. It is often unclear just where you stand and what you stand for. You may be totally committed to something and unreserved in your effort and support of a cause or purpose in which you believe. More often than not, you vacillate between options and paradigms and get very little accomplished. It is up to you to make a choice or choose a course of action. Fate and circumstance will offer very little assistance in giving you a clue about your destiny.

There is the karmic hint that in another time and place, you were given important choices that influenced both your life's destiny and the fate of many others. There is the suggestion that you avoided making any commitments or decisions, thus taking the passive path of least resistance. You may have been conquered or overrun by opposition. You find yourself once again on an important stage of decision wherein rests the outcome that will determine the fate of many other souls. You are torn between the desire to render assistance and the fear of making wrong choices.

NOTABLES WITH THIS DEGREE:

Jacques Vallée: French venture capitalist, computer scientist, author, ufologist

Leah Dizon: American singer, model, entertainer

Phil Hartman: Canadian-American comedian, actor, screenwriter, graphic artist

John Marshall: U.S. Chief Justice, pioneer of establishing the American constitution

You possess many assets of human personality, and there are several courses you could choose, taking into account the varied potentials that lie within your being. Life is diverse and rarely boring unless you choose to avoid the richness and challenge of taking advantage of your many options, such as involving yourself in the dynamic of a group evolution. There are inspiring souls who come and go in your life, rendering a clue as to just how much you might get done if you stay focused on your inner purpose. There is much for you to see and do in this world at this time.

1ˢᵗ Degree of Libra

If this is your sun sign, you may be more direct and willing to take initiative than many of your Libra contemporaries. Where others dodge, you plunge. When others bite their tongues, you speak out. When others hesitate, you are willing to take the first step toward resolving the condition at hand. Many times, you even surprise yourself at the boldness and directness you implement to get reactions and results. At best, you do this with the well-known ease and diplomatic touch that Libras are noted for having. Such an approach can get you far in your quest to accomplish things in life.

NOTABLES WITH THIS DEGREE:

Barbara Walters: American broadcast journalist, author, television personality

Dmitri Shostakovich: Russian, pianist

Frederick William II: King of Prussia

Joseph Patrick Kennedy II: American politician, social activist

There is a karmic clue that in another setting of consciousness, you were paralyzed with the fear of speaking out or making significant decisions. Your hesitation and indecisiveness may have led to the loss or suffering of other souls. You have been savaged with guilt and suffering in many lifetimes. This is a time to find the right balance of courage and confidence to face decisions and challenges directly and truthfully. Eventually you will find a group of people with whom you can do this with ease. You will be appreciated for your gentle method of leadership and compassionate approach to tough issues.

You enjoy the fun and fanciful side of life, and at your best, you bring merriment and harmony to the environment around you. Your aesthetic touch is appreciated by others, and many will ask for your advice regarding things like dress, makeup, décor, and etiquette. At best, you are in tune with the times and a great consultant about trends and cycles of commerce and social intercourse. There will be many of you attracted to careers related to entertainment and communication. You are usually trusted and appreciated as a friend and an associate in whatever endeavor you may choose.

2nd Degree of Libra

If this is your sun sign, it is similar to having a double dose of Libra characteristics. This number-sign combination accentuates the tact and subtle softness that the Libra is known to possess. You may come across with a smooth, sophisticated, and possibly suave exterior demeanor. You know how to maneuver your way through the sticky wickets of negotiation and difficult confrontations. There is the karmic hint of past indiscretions and callous acts of behavior toward others. You can be a master manipulator and seducer. You are learning to appreciate the choices and life decisions others make for themselves and to be respectful of those who you deem to be less savvy and gifted of mind.

You may be known for your subtle taste and appreciation of rare objects of art and history. This penchant for finery could lead you into the field of collections or dealing in the exchange of rare artifacts from around the world. You move in circles of influential people, and you are a natural at networking with those who can get you the right goods. Your gift of expression could lead you into the public arena. There is usually careful attention to appearance and a keen sense of social taste. While you may joke behind the scenes, your public image is especially noteworthy to you.

Your smooth social skills can belie your strength and a strong, willful drive for recognition and achievement. Once your sights are set, you can be most persistent in reaching your objective. You just may take a little more time and require more attention to the choreography of diplomacy than the more direct personalities. You are particularly skilled at accruing power and influence through partnerships and alliances that can be of benefit to both partners. You look for the best in others and seek to bring out the best.

3rd Degree of Libra

If this is your sun sign, you are, at your best, gifted with a natural charm and simple eloquence that allows you to express the most obtuse topics with simplicity and ease. Your own inner sense of comfort allows others to be comfortable around you. This is the number-sign combination of the consummate host or hostess. At best, you like yourself. This creates an atmosphere in which other people can find a place to be more accepting of themselves. Such an environment lends itself to creating a space that makes it easier for people to accept others who are different or who perhaps appear threatening. When you have found harmony within yourself, you will be one of the best at creating harmony in the turbulent world around you.

NOTABLES WITH THIS DEGREE:

Marcello Mastroianni: Italian actor

Martin Heidegger: German philosopher, existentialist

Ammachi: Hindu spiritual leader, guru

George Gershwin: American composer, lyricist, pianist

There is a karmic hint that it has not always been this way in the sojourn of your soul through the lessons of this planet. There is the karmic suggestion that there have been other times in your evolutionary journey when you were abrupt, indifferent, and probably cruel. Your vanity and position in society may have caused you to believe in your superiority over others. Perhaps you were academically trained and a bit pompous about your learning and influence. You are learning to find a balance in expressing yourself directly and honestly with consideration for the feelings and beliefs of those to whom you communicate. Many of you are eloquent and gifted spokespeople.

You will be found where beauty, grace, aesthetics, and creativity are taking place. Your presence can be particularly healing in times of social chaos, catastrophe, and upheaval. Your voice stands out because of its harmonious ring and the vibration that you project. Many of you are naturals at the arts and in the area of entertainment and media. As a public speaker, you can be calming, persuasive, and convincing.

4th Degree of Libra

If this is your sun sign, you cloak a concerned and determined persistence to get things done your way. Your Libra personality traits of patience, soft-spoken tact, and carefully executed manners works well while you mix among people and maneuver your way through the web of social and political intrigue. This might be in your local community club or in the office of government. Wherever you find yourself, you are determined and certain of getting what you want out of the opportunities of life that present themselves. Your ambition can be formidable and your drive to accomplish endless.

NOTABLES WITH THIS DEGREE:

Serena Williams: American professional tennis player

Brigitte Bardot: French actress, singer, model

Alexei Mordashov: Russian business oligarch, self-made billionaire

Girolamo Cardano: Italian astrologer, philosopher, mathematician, physician

There is the karmic hint that in another time and setting, you may well have used your position and preeminence to force unwanted changes on unsuspecting groups of people. Once committed to a belief, you could be ruthless and cold while carrying out campaigns that served your own interests. Even now, it can be tempting to use your means and minions to manipulate the public for personal gains. Such tactics can be toxic and counterproductive to the intended soul growth of the population. Your conscience seeks to find alignment with the universal destiny of humanity rather than forcing your personal ideology of evolution.

You are attracted to the idea of building a better basis to the daily functioning of bureaucracy. You naturally grasp the excesses and opening for abuse the public service and governments innately manifest. The path opens an opportunity for you to take the higher road of service and step beyond personal ego as you find yourself dealing with the issues of the day. There is a likeable and disarming Libra persona that can be most charming and convincing when things are on the line. Your choices can be benign and for the betterment of humankind, or they can take you down the road of containment and purposeful design of social behavior.

5th Degree of Libra

If this is your sun sign, it will be difficult to tie you down and convince you to stay in one place or with one person for very long. While in your own mind you diligently maintain the Libra trait of loyalty, it is easy for you to convince yourself of your loyalty to whomever you may be with in the moment. If there are many in your life at the moment, you just think of yourself as spreading the loyalty all around. Some of those in your circle will probably not agree. Even your smooth Libra moves may not get you safely out of some of the emotional tight spots.

NOTABLES WITH THIS DEGREE:

Silvio Berlusconi: Italian Prime Minister, entrepreneur, media mogul

Hilary Duff: American actress, singer-songwriter, producer, author

Confucius: Chinese philosopher, teacher, politician

There is the karmic hint that in previous soul evolutions you took issues of intimacy and personal trust rather lightly. Perhaps you sold yourself out easily to those who made the most alluring personal offers. Perhaps you coveted what another person aligned with and feigned friendship in order to share the goods without earning the right to have such thorough, righteous deeds. Your zone of ethics and morality can get pretty gray as you work your way through the human plots of interaction. You seek to get back in balance with your true core self and realigned with the spiritual path that seems to have eluded you for some time.

There is a charm and bon vivant attitude associated with many of you who have this number-sign combination. At best, all of the diplomatic skills and soft approach of the Libra personality can apply. You charm the socks off of the world, and you get your way by speaking softly — carrying a soft stick. You love life, and there will be many who want to love you. At best, you are blessed with the good life and move effortlessly amid the many moods and tantrums of the daily social whirl.

6th Degree of Libra

If this is your sun sign, you can be vain, vigilant, virginal, and vulnerable. There is a patient and accepting way about you that makes it easy for people to turn to you for counsel and comfort. At best, you radiate a softness of touch and openness of heart. This makes you likeable and sought after for your healing presence. There is, however, a downside to your openness. You love to render assistance to the needy, and that can lead to an issue of vulnerability. This can be the number-sign combination of a saint or a helpless codependent. If out of harmony, you are a high-risk candidate for being codependent and a compulsive giver who has lost touch with your identity.

NOTABLES WITH THIS DEGREE:

Wilhelmina E. Drucker: Dutch feminist, social activist, politician, writer

William Wrigley Jr.: American chewing gum industrialist

Henry Fox: British Secretary of War, eighteenth-century politician

Patricia Neway: American operatic soprano, musical stage actress

When in the compulsive counselor role, you fail to see your own worth and personal needs. Thus, you get your boost of ego from the effort you put into rendering assistance to others. There is the karmic hint of having previously suffered very deep emotional wounds from the rejection or betrayal of an intimate lover or close confidant. There is a deeply rooted distrust for everyone, so rather than letting someone get close to you, you are always ready to distract the perceived emotional threat by offering yourself to aid whoever is at hand. That way, you do not have to deal directly with what you are truly feeling. This time around, you seek to find the balance between being of service to others and learning to service your own healthy wants and needs with equal or greater attention.

You have a flair for the arts and the creative side of industry or whatever area of interest your life takes you to. There is an air of refinement that follows you, and you are tasteful and often appropriate in dress and social décor. Your innate softness and tendency to be at ease puts those around you at ease as well. This allows for a warm, personable exchange of conversation about the intimate matters of life. At your best, you are gracious and blessed.

7th Degree of Libra

If this is your sun sign, you take the time to look under more rocks than many of your Libra family members. You may just find the treasure of knowledge that the universe provides. You have a little less time for the social circuit than some of your contemporaries, preferring rather to seek the deeper wisdoms of life and go beyond the superficial values of the society around you. This may cause some of your associates to think you have become something of a snob. It is not that you judge others as much as it is simply in your nature to want a closer sense of connection to the universal life stream.

NOTABLES WITH THIS DEGREE:

Jalal al-Din Muhammad Rumi: Persian poet, jurist, theologian, Sufi

Truman Capote: American novelist, nonfiction author

Annie Besant: British theosophist, author, women›s rights activist

When ego takes over, you may speak out with harsh criticism about the superficial and vacant lifestyle of the modern world. There is a karmic hint that in a past journey, you passed over an opportunity to connect with higher cosmic wisdom and chose the temporary pleasures and pampering of a prestigious position within your culture. You seek to find your lost connection to Source and to inspire others to implement the living laws of the universe into the social process. Your natural diplomatic acumen serves you well, and you encourage others through inspiration rather than exasperation.

You enjoy the studied and scholarly approach, except when academic arrogance blinds the accomplished from seeing the greater dimension of universal mind. But not all is mental and intellectual in your way of living. You do, after all, follow the Libra instincts of balance in all areas of your lifestyle. There is the aesthetic part of your personality that helps to keep you balanced between the mental, artistic, spiritual, and physical components that are essential to healthy daily living. You eat well and exercise regularly, which keeps the physical temple tuned and ready to receive the more refined messages from above.

8th Degree of Libra

If this is your sun sign, you might have been the first one who practiced "speak softly, but carry a big stick." The mild-mannered Libra personality can distract from your immense capacity to confront and deliberate the complex web of power and authority. Whether you are in your home, office, or in front of millions, you wield power and delicately maneuver amid the world of self-interests, political skullduggery, and the confused collective consciousness of the public. In most cases, you are perceived favorably by the society around you, and this adds to your capacity to persuade and direct.

NOTABLES WITH THIS DEGREE:

Mahatma Gandhi: Indian religious leader, social activist

Jimmy Carter: American president, humanitarian, Nobel Prize laureate

Sean O'Donnell: Irish parapsychologist, psychic

Isaac Bonewits: American singer, author of Neo-Paganism and magic

There is a karmic hint of having misused power in earlier evolutions of your soul journey on this planet. Perhaps you destroyed much and hurt many. Or possibly many suffered because of your edicts and dictums. Your desire is for humanity to live in peace and get along with each other without the violence and destruction that has been such a big part of Earth's history since earliest times. The irony is that sometimes you get others angry and violent in response to your peacefulness. You weave your way through a delicate plot of political intrigue and power plays. Those who know you might remember you for your constant negotiating and mediating among those who were in disharmony with each other.

There is an intellectual and artistic side of you that delves into the finer aspirations of humanity and encourages self-expression and the celebration of life. You may study religion or philosophy of society and sociology. You are curious about how people get along and would like to see them do it in win-win strategies rather than mean-spirited competition. For the most part, your disposition is cordial and caring, and you have a lighthearted sense of humor that easily discharges tension and potential aggressiveness.

9th Degree of Libra

If this is your sun sign, you have the potential to take the elegance and refinement of the Libra to new heights. You are highly idealistic and wish to see the best in people as you go through the interactions of life. There is an almost ethereal quality about this number-sign combination that makes some people envious and most people curious about just what causes your magic. This almost-pixie quality gives you a wonderful childlike freshness of innocence and mischievous fun. The other side of this combination can be disturbing and misleading.

NOTABLES WITH THIS DEGREE:

Groucho Marx: American movie and television actor, comedian

Gore Vidal: American novelist, screenwriter, essayist

Tiffany Chin: Asian-American Olympic figure skating champion

Yohji Yamamoto: Japanese fashion designer

There is the karmic hint of having been delusional and perhaps downright dishonest in another sequence of your soul journey on this planet. Perhaps you were a con artist or conducted purposeful fraud when dealing with others. You might have been employed by someone else, or you may have simply chosen to do so out of disgust and disregard for yourself and for others. You desperately seek to be truthful and straightforward in your discourse with others; however, this can also reveal a compulsive need to be excessively detached and idealistic. Compulsive idealism often hides the dark and deceptive side of your own self.

At best, your compassion and caring nature can light up the most skeptical of resisters. There is a gentle quality about you that disarms even the angry and hostile. Your tranquil and healing nature may take you to a setting where healing and forgiveness take place. Many of you will incline toward entertainment and myriad avenues of artistic development. There is a light and playful side of you that allows you to embrace many possible encounters of the unusual kind. You are giving and loyal, but you need to be cautious that you are not being used by the devious or debauching type.

10th Degree of Libra

If this is your sun sign, you find yourself fascinated with things that are new, fashionable, and functional. You are a bit of an idealist and worry that society often falls far short of what it could be. That goes for people also. You may live through a string of disappointments when their behavior does not live up to your high expectations. You just wish that people would honor the code of respectful conduct and consideration of others. You fancy a world that is orderly and takes into consideration the needs of all of its inhabitants. This does not necessarily mean that you only support

NOTABLES WITH THIS DEGREE:

Jean-François Millet: French naturalist and realism painter, Barbizon art school founder

Stefan Persson: Swedish billionaire business mogul, H&R chairperson

Susan Sarandon: American actress, social activist

status quo. On the contrary, your forward-thinking mind is always considering how things can improve and develop into yet a more glorious kingdom.

There is the karmic hint that somewhere and sometime, you were part of the decline and decay of a noble and grand civilization. Perhaps you spoke out against those who were letting it go. Perhaps you lost your life for doing so. Then you could have been a part of the principal parties who let it go, thus wreaking punishment on the whistleblowers who saw through your ruse. You are ever aware of the least slip in culture, and you seek to keep things functioning in an irreproachable manner.

Your insight and keenly aware perspective of life make you a sought-after authority for certain kinds of knowledge about group dynamics and the collective consciousness. People enjoy the exchange of repartee because you are always prepared and conduct your debate with grace and respect for your challenger. You support orderly evolution of society and may be right at the front of innovation and the implementation of new policies and protocols of development.

11ᵗʰ Degree of Libra

If this is your sun sign, you may appear more undecided about choices in life or demonstrate an amazing ability to find synthesis and synergy while others flounder with the dizziness of dichotomies. You see a common thread where others see only opposition and degrees of difference. You grasp a sense of wholeness where others see disparity and polarization of opinion and perception. Or you could become hopelessly confused and upset at the entire state of discord and the static resulting from the multitudinous perspectives of looking at life generated by all of the cultures of humankind.

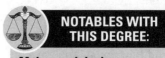

NOTABLES WITH THIS DEGREE:

Mahamandaleshwar Swami Nityananda: Indian spiritual leader, teacher

Rutherford B. Hayes: American president, military general

Chester A. Arthur: American president, attorney

There is a karmic hint that during another soul journey, you may have been pulled apart by the weight of differing viewpoints when controversy arose. Perhaps you were tortured or abused for taking a stance that was not popular with the predominant thinking of the day. Perhaps your soul destiny was to represent and defend a new doctrine of truth that was being introduced to humanity. Perhaps you buckled and caved in opposition to leaving your followers to suffer at the hands of a controlling regime. You have gotten yourself confused between right and wrong, or between enlightened and enslaved. You split hairs and become frozen when decision time approaches. Now is the time to reconnect to your center. You have that wonderful ability to see unity in duality and can serve to reunite people when struggles occur.

Your sense of taste is delicious, and you are able to mix and match colors and codes that others would never think about trying. You know how to find out-of-the-way places and out-of-this-world fashions and fixtures for your décor. Your intuitive reach takes you to lofty heights and can assimilate information into a form of communication that opens the heart and lifts the muddled mind to metaphysical realms of delight. There is an ethereal dash to your disposition that makes you a treat to have around when it comes to light-hearted social fare or intense theoretical debates about the future of humanity and the fate of worlds.

12th Degree of Libra

If this is your sun sign, you can be terrific, tempting, and taunting. There is a gracious and disarming persona that is characteristic of the Libra personality. You use this charming exterior to maneuver and manipulate people and opportunities your way. Those who are on your side appreciate your cunning and skill. Those you have opposed can be resentful and angry. This number-sign combination can be harsher than the usual easy-going Libra and very rapidly turn cold to the needs of other people and particularly what you see as their weaknesses. Although you are known to reward those you perceive to be loyal, you can be indifferent and even ruthless to those you feel have turned against you or wronged you.

NOTABLES WITH THIS DEGREE:

Alice Walton: American billionaire Wal-Mart heiress

Ren Cassin: French juror, law professor, judge, Nobel Prize laureate, social activist

There is a karmic hint that part of you feels that somewhere along your journey of growth, you did not receive the acknowledgment or recognition that you deserved. Perhaps someone less talented or deserving was given a position or honor that you felt should have been yours. Your ego still relentlessly stalks the arena of life, seeking to increase your notoriety, influence, and ultimately recognition. Along with recognition comes power and the opportunity to get the things you desperately long to have. You easily step on many toes to have your way. There will be a chance to be a positive source of empowerment and encouragement to people less fortunate than you.

As with many Libra personalities, you are capable of demonstrating good taste in dress, décor, and the selection of the material goods you acquire. However, you may lack the tact and tenderness of many of your Libra contemporaries, which can lead to a pretentious display of personal grandeur. You enjoy mixing with the elite and influential. It is easy to measure your success by the magnitude and might of those with whom you associate rather than developing a healthy internal connection to your true self. You can rise to great heights of achievement and have the opportunity to assist many others to reach their own wishes and goals.

13th Degree of Libra

If this is your sun sign, there is a rather notice-able stiffness and formality that is not charac-teristic of the Libra temperament. You appear to be unwilling to reveal a soft side of your personality that encourages patience, kind-ness, and forgiveness. It is easy to be hardened by life experience rather than enlightened. You are learning to lighten up and allow for spontaneity and joy within and around you. You want to believe in the human spirit, but at the same time, you do not trust others to meet the standards you have set. There can be control issues and difficulty letting go of responsibility by giving it to others.

NOTABLES WITH THIS DEGREE:

Jeff Mayo: English astrologer, educator, author

Stephen Arroyo: American author, astrologer

Vladimir Putin: Russian Prime Minister, diplomat

Simon Cowell: English television producer, reality show judge

Paul Hogan: Australian actor, comedian

You see many avenues of getting to the desired result, and this ability can make you a sought-after consultant and advisor. There is a karmic suggestion that your indecisiveness led to the loss of life for many people in another time frame. If you can keep ego out of things, you can present possibilities to humanity that may have a wide-ranging impact in offering more freedom and the expression of the uniqueness of our race. It is easy for you to hold on to the past and fear the death and transformation of both personality and institutions.

You find yourself in situations where things are falling apart, and you experience a sense of urgency about putting them back together again. You are troubled by the decay and decline of institutions and infrastructures that have served their time and place. Your keen political and social assets come into play when others collapse under the strain of chaos and destruction. Under your amiable Libra exterior is a determined, strong-willed personality that is not reluctant to grasp the reins of power when they are dangled right in front of your eyes.

14th Degree of Libra

If this is your sun sign, there is an essence about your personality that is decidedly present but at the same time seemingly intangible and difficult to define. Your natural Libra grace and disarming charm fit together well with this numerical component. You possess an extra source of compassion for the plight of humanity and other life forms thriving on this planet. There is a mysterious additional dimension of awareness that can be used well for healing the troubled and weary masses. This could occur through touch, talk, or other alternative forms of the healing arts. Your charismatic nature serves well in whatever course of life you choose to pursue.

NOTABLES WITH THIS DEGREE:

Eddie Rickenbacker: American fighter pilot ace, racecar driver, auto designer

Gus Hall: American union organizer, leader of U.S. Communist party

César Milstein: English biochemist, Nobel Prize laureate, antibody researcher

Kristanna Loken: American actress, model

You are very sensitive to the suffering of others, and there is a karmic suggestion at some time in your evolutionary journey of having created stress and suffering for many. This may have been through severe confinement, abuse, or — in extreme cases — the use of torture. You have a very present comprehension of the natural universal laws of balance and harmony. There is a keen desire to share this innate grasp of the natural laws with humanity. At the same time, your distrust can rear its troubling head since you are keenly aware of the human tendency to misuse simple and powerful information.

Although there is the suggestion of a kind of ethereal quality with this number-sign combination, you are quite capable of grasping the obvious and getting things done in an efficient and timely manner. When placed in a role of leadership, you are likely to be patient and considerate of others while dispensing direct and clear commands as to what needs to be done and precisely how you want it done. Among the Libra clan, you are more of a doer than just a talker and speculator.

15th Degree of Libra

If this is your sun sign, you are ardent and involved in matters of life, and you take a much more active role in society than other Libras. There is a kind of gambling spirit about you that makes you alluring and mysteriously intriguing. Your will endure some tribulations and harsh challenges in life, but you are equipped with a kind of armor that seems rather tough by Libra standards. There is the karmic suggestion of previous patterns of abrasiveness and indifference toward the suffering of others. You have set up a personality that is strong but tempered by the lightheartedness and patience of the Libra scales. With time, you mellow out and learn to be more compassionate about the foibles of humanity and yourself.

NOTABLES WITH THIS DEGREE:

Thomas Moore: American spiritual author, Jungian psychotherapist

Sigourney Weaver: American actress

Matt Damon: American actor, screenwriter, producer, activist, philanthropist

Miguel de Cervantes: Spanish novelist, poet, playwright

You may come across as a little more assertive than many of your other Libra brethren. There is a strong presence about this number-sign combination that catches the eye of the public and allows you to get attention when you want to make a point. In a woman's chart, this suggests the presence of a public persona of animus. You are concerned with righting the wrongs, and correcting the abuses that you witness around you. You can be particularly irate about cruelty and mistreatment of God's creatures.

This combination hints at much travel and variation of lifestyles. You are rebellious inside and might spend some time attracted to alternative subcultures or countercultural movements. There is a bit of a bohemian inside of you, and you could find yourself uneasy having to constantly behave in the prim-and-proper manner that society often encourages. You are strong of mind and can be independent in thinking, loving to debate and dissect theories about humankind and the universe.

16ᵗʰ Degree of Libra

If this is your sun sign, you are boisterous, buoyant, belligerent, and sometimes bad. Hey, that doesn't sound like a Libra! You can confound some of your more discreet and delicate Libra family with your display of such shenanigans. Your bluntness and direct approach to issues can earn you respect when handled with consideration for others. At times, you simply offend and step on sensitive toes with your demeanor. Before your life is over, you will likely have stirred up a few fires of tension and at times controversy. Being in touch with your highest self may result in the social questioning of the issues that you have presented. Positive social change can then follow. If done out of ego, you are more likely to attract public ire and negative reactions.

NOTABLES WITH THIS DEGREE:

John Lennon: English musician, songwriter, actor, political activist

William L. Alden: American journalist, humorist, author, diplomat

Ilan Halimi: French-Jewish man killed by Muslim gang, resulting in social outrage

Charles X: King of France and Navarre, Count of Artois

There is a karmic hint that in another time and life setting, you might have been a renegade and social outcast who sat on the outside looking in with anger and castigation. This is a number-sign combination of the proverbial rebel without a cause, although you most likely believe that you are staunchly defending your position. There is often anger toward humanity, the universe, and God. You sit at the precipice of enlightenment or possibly tragedy. You can take a giant step in the elevation of consciousness if you so choose. There is a restless portion of your soul that longs to get back in touch with your divine self. It is not so easy to let go of your rebellion.

You search for the higher truths of living, and there is an investigative quality about this combination. Once you get on the scent of a deep and arcane mystery, you can become a very good detective in whatever profession or pursuit you have chosen. Expect drama, excitement, and uncertainty. Anyone who wants to go on a journey with you should be prepared for the same.

17th Degree of Libra

If this is your sun sign, you may be more driven than your other Libra contemporaries. Whereas the Libra tendency is to think about relationships and other people, this number-sign combination suggests a more outspoken and self-oriented personality. You can mask your intentions behind that sweet Libra smile and try to convince others of your altruism, but it is not as easy to disguise your intentions from others as you might want to think. Your innate sense of personal value lets you rationalize that if you were going to do it, you would be the best at helping others. And sometimes you are right.

NOTABLES WITH THIS DEGREE:

Harold A. McDougall: American astrologer, author

Giuseppe Verdi: Italian romantic, operatic composer

Takeshi Kaneshiro: Taiwanese actor, model, singer

Naike Rivelli: Italian actress, model

There is a karmic hint of previous vanity and a royalty-like attitude. You have been a prima donna and possibly a persona who was worshiped or given great social status by your peers. It is difficult to let go of that feeling of importance. There is a healthy sense of self, and then there is the dysfunctional obsession with oneself. You struggle to find that balance. This degree of Libra is prone to evaluate circumstances in ideal terms rather than as they are. You want what you think is best, but you might overlook basic emotional aspects relevant to the people involved. This can lead to misunderstandings and hurt feelings.

On the bright side, you are dynamic and perhaps emit a more determined manner of getting things done than other Libras. You may lack some of the finesse and patience of some of your Libra brethren, but you still possess the charm to get through some of the tough moments. Many with this combination enjoy rigorous physical activity and can find it a useful outlet for venting pent-up frustration and internal stress.

18th Degree of Libra

If this is your sun sign, you may not be quite as cheerful and outgoing as many of your Libra contemporaries. There is an element of suspicion and a tendency toward caution about you that is noticeable to those who know you well. This trait does not entirely dampen your typically optimistic Libra outlook toward things. You do want to see the best in people and in the things they do. Your natural sense of harmony and aesthetic balance is noticeable in a fundamental nuts-and-bolts kind of way. That is, you may be involved in an environment of machinery, industrial development, or technology. No matter how harsh and demanding the environment may be, you have a soft touch and knack for making it more hospitable and ergonomically pleasant.

NOTABLES WITH THIS DEGREE:

Luciano Pavarotti: Italian operatic tenor, charity patron

Carlos the Jackal: Venezuelan anarchist, revolutionary

Eleanor Roosevelt: longest-serving First Lady of the United States, active political leader

El Greco: Spanish sculptor, architect, painter

Mohan Koparkar: Indian astrologer, author, mechanical engineer

There is the karmic hint that in another soul passage on this planet, you were so concerned with the details and micromatters of what you were doing that you did not realize the negative consequences of your task. Perhaps you were an isolated bureaucrat in a huge undertaking that had gone very wrong. Perhaps you feel guilty about disastrous results that took place. You are hesitant to trust anyone, especially within the chain of command of large organizations. You are learning to reestablish your sense of discernment and reading integrity within the heart of others and even more so within yourself.

There is a strong idealistic streak that runs through your veins. You may find yourself becoming part of a group of utopian thinkers or visionaries. Those of you with troubled aspects and an abusive background may even lean toward ideas of anarchy. You enjoy doers and achievers and learning about the path they have taken to be successful. This number-sign combination often includes inspired artists whose work taps into archetypes that delicately but effectively touch the hearts of awakening humankind.

19ᵗʰ Degree of Libra

If this is your sun sign, you want to make the world brighter and more colorful whether it is in the mundane world or in a spiritual manner of inspiring inner beauty. You are sensitive to a wide range of awareness, and this grasp of archetypes allows you to bring something grand and different into the world. When you do things, it is with a broad spectrum in mind and usually on a large scale. You possess knowledge of many avenues of thought and areas of proficiency. This makes it difficult for you to concentrate or settle down into just a single field of interest.

NOTABLES WITH THIS DEGREE:

Sacha Baron Cohen: English actor, comedian, writer

Margaret Thatcher: British Prime Minister

Stacey Kiebler: actress, model, professional wrestler

Dave Aaron: American UFO researcher, owner of largest UFO video inventory

Aleister Crowley: English occultist, astrologer, hedonist, ceremonial magician, social critic

There is a karmic hint at having previously been part of inhibiting or taking the life away from a large number of people. You are driven to give something to humanity and want to reach as many people as possible. Perhaps you do it through money or products or perhaps by teaching or administering others. Power will frequently be part of your play, and you enjoy being in control. Many of you will search through reams of studies in an attempt to solve the mysteries of life and spirit.

You are a bit of an enigma and float through life with an air of determination that is the envy of many. You may appear vacillating and unsure, but that is only while you are trying to make up your mind. Once done, you move with authority and surprising competence. You can be dashing and daring and then move quietly into the background, only to rise again when the occasion suits you. There is a quality of refinement that gives you a kind of mystique. This makes others curious to know more about this ethereal person who moves in and out of life with subtlety and often behind-the-scene posturing.

20th Degree of Libra

If this is your sun sign, you fluctuate between a wide range of experiences and episodes in your life that may sometimes raise the collective's eyebrows. There is a keen sense of public opinion associated with this number-sign combination, and you may find yourself caught up in a swirl of attention on your life sojourn. Such public scrutiny may not always be in your best interest, as you can be capable of stepping on the public's toes with your antics and exploits. As a public spokesperson, you can be brilliant and admired in one moment and, in the next moment, find yourself saying or doing the most awkward of things.

NOTABLES WITH THIS DEGREE:

Dwight D. Eisenhower: American president, five-star WWII general

Mary Greer: American author, divination practitioner

Shelley Ackerman: American actress, singer, writer, astrologer

Nancy Kerrigan: American Olympic figure skater

There is the karmic hint that in another time and setting, you were in a position of power that caused you to be indifferent to public opinion because of the control that you had over the masses. Perhaps you went too far with your personal exploitations to the point of upheaval and possibly rebellion against you. You still possess much of the pride of power, and on an unconscious level, you think you can get away with anything you want. You are learning once again to be respectful of others both in the personal and collective sense. The intentions of your heart are good, and if you are true to your heart, not your impulses, your life can be one of much impact and influence to the good of humanity.

This combination can stretch the indecisive and wishy-washy Libra nature to its limits. You just do not know where you are and what you stand for. But by working with the lessons of this combination, you can be an excellent negotiator of goodwill. Fate might place you in situations to bring about peace and reconciliation between two opposing entities that have substantial impact on world stability.

21ˢᵗ Degree of Libra

If this is your sun sign, there is a tendency to be outspoken and imaginative in your speech and self-expression. You are likely to get a reaction to your expressed opinions and points of view. You can be most gracious and well received but with adverse aspects. There is also the possibility of going too far and stirring up quite a bit of fanfare. The directness of this number-sign combination can overpower some of the Libra qualities of restraint, delicacy, and tact. You can get right to the point, which touches people directly in their emotional soft spots. This results in very immediate and strongly emotional reactions to your words and deeds.

NOTABLES WITH THIS DEGREE:

Sarah Ferguson: Duchess of York, spokesperson, screenwriter, film producer, philanthropist

Penny Marshall: American actress, producer, director

Ralph Lauren: American fashion designer, business mogul

Dino Buzzati: Italian novelist, painter, poet

There is the karmic suggestion of previous irresponsibility and lack of sensitivity toward others. Perhaps you lived a previous life behind a double standard of doing in private what, in fact, you were speaking against in public. You are learning to be more caring and compassionate toward those who are equally disposed toward what they believe and do. Perhaps most importantly, you are learning to be compassionate and accepting of yourself. There is much inner conflict between your own interests and how you are expected to behave socially. Manners, etiquette, and social mores will be brought to your attention often before your life is complete.

This is a refreshing combination that encourages friendships, fun, and freedom. You will see much and do much, and there will be many tales to tell your grandchildren once you reach your latter years. If anything, it will be difficult for you to focus on any one interest or direction in life, because so many things excite and enthrall you. You enjoy being around fashion, fine food, and other fineries of life. While your trusting nature can lead to some bad choices of associates, in the end, you receive much from family, close friends, and worthy colleagues.

22nd Degree of Libra

If this is your sun sign, you pack a lot of power disguised within that soft and mild-mannered Libra personality pattern. At its best, this number-sign combination can heighten your natural Libra diplomatic acumen, allowing you to sometimes catch your adversaries off-guard because they do not expect such underlying strength of character. This can work to your advantage in tough times, and you could very well find yourself around potent people who are able to effect change at the drop of a hat. This combination suggests a person with a strong and durable body with the stamina to sustain demanding loads of pressure and policy-making procedures.

Although you may want to pull away from the crowd and maintain a quiet and solitary existence, the likelihood is that you will, at some point in your life, be called on to assert yourself in some group effort. There is the karmic hint of having been in other life settings where you were less tactful and perhaps even belligerent in your attitude. You may have stepped on too many toes and tangled yourself in some politics of rancor and revenge. You have keen insight and can use your present disposition in a manner that can point out where weakness may exist and make the necessary changes, but you can do it without having to ruffle the feathers of those with whom you debate. You may find it easier to win allies rather than to stir up the wrath of old enemies.

You could be called in to handle complex technical matters or simply teach a talented troupe of dancers how to improve. You have a good grasp of mechanics, the natural laws of engineering, and nature. Some of this may be school learned, but most just comes from the wisdom and intuition of evolution. Behind your apparent flexible exterior is a very determined and focused life purpose and belief system.

NOTABLES WITH THIS DEGREE:

Friedrich Nietzsche: German author, philosopher, cultural critic, composer

Louis Pierre Althusser: French Marxist philosopher, author

Robert Atkins: American physician, cardiologist, diet guru

Arthur Miller: American playwright, author, essayist

Tim Robbins: American actor, director, producer, screenwriter, social activist

23rd Degree of Libra

If this is your sun sign, you are widely diverse and sometimes just plain wild. There is an almost precocious interest in life, and you revel in observing and representing the multitudinous mannerisms of humanity. There is a proclivity toward mimicry, impersonation, and comedic parody as you are acutely observant of human nature and love to represent it in your expression. Other, less robust people wonder where you find all of your zest for living and wish they could find it. You can pull off the absurd in a fashion that receives laughter when anyone else doing the same thing would likely be criticized or condemned. There is an almost childlike magical quality that you radiate when you are at your best.

NOTABLES WITH THIS DEGREE:

John Mayer: American singer-songwriter, producer, musician

Pascal Sevran: French TV host, author, producer

Kimi Räikkönen: Finnish race driver, Formula One competitor

Hema Malini: Indian actress, director, producer, charity patroness

There is a karmic suggestion of having taken behavior to an unacceptable social level in another time and setting. You probably offended someone of power or authority who brought the wrath of criticism and probably punishment onto you. You find yourself struggling between wanting acceptance and flaunting authority. You operate on the fringe of the brilliantly original or just plain absurd. You enjoy being unpredictable and catching people off-guard with your personal antics. Because of your boundless imagination and flair for the different, your presence will not go unnoticed by others.

You are just plain fun to be with, and you attract a lot of admirers who want to soak up some of your pleasure and fun. At best, you enjoy this and enjoy being the host or hostess to people of all kinds of backgrounds and different social persuasions. You create an atmosphere that encourages those around you to be comfortable and curious about exploring their own innate, unused personality potential. There is not much in life that goes by without you giving it a try.

24ᵗʰ Degree of Libra

If this is your sun sign, you may find yourself called on to perform on the stage of life even though there is a strong streak of shyness that runs in your veins. Whether or not you do make the stage, you will find yourself in many dramatic moments. Some of these could become public and bring considerable attention to you and yours. There is a part of you that almost seeks to have a public hearing in order to air your views. Conversely, there is often considerable anxiety about the possibility of being held to the court of public opinion. You are very loyal to your friends, feelings, and emotional ties. Under extremes, your emotionalism can be your undoing.

NOTABLES WITH THIS DEGREE:

EmInEm: American rapper, singer-songwriter, producer, actor

Melina Mercouri: Greek actress, singer, politician

Ricardo Salinas Pliego: Mexican media billionaire

Jean-Claude van Damme: Belgian martial artist, actor, director

There is a karmic hint that in a previous sojourn of the soul that you indulged in an environment of impersonal delight in the criticism, contempt, and constraint of others. Perhaps you held a high office of intellectual importance from which you scorned the stupid masses with arrogant impunity. Perhaps you were in a position to administer strict etiquette and social protocol in a harsh and impersonal manner. The maintenance of social norms was more important than the natural expression of human feelings. You alternate between surges of spontaneous emanations from the soul and an urge to control yourself for fear of public reaction.

If you do not create solid emotional boundaries and honor your true feelings, you have the inclination to get into sticky, codependent relationships. There is a natural artistic flair with this number-sign combination, and even if you do not become a professional of some sort, most of you with find some form of outlet for that part of your personality. You are loyal, witty, and full of jests, and you tease when comfortable with someone. Many of you with this combination are attracted to caregiving and alternative healing professions.

25th Degree of Libra

If this is your sun sign, you are likely to be a little more careful and conservative than some of your Libra family members. You can be mentally thorough and conscientious in acquiring information that is useful to your purposes of advancement. What appears to others as indecision on your part can disguise a process of very careful and deliberate analysis and review. You are meticulous and deliberate when other Libras might be carefree and unassuming. Such caution does not necessarily distract you from attaining the spoils of life. On the contrary, you may end up acquiring more because of your fussy ways.

In fact, this number-sign combination may result in disrupting the usually easy-going patience of the kind-hearted Libra. You can be prone to fits and outbursts of impatience, and you may become more cynical or harsh than others of your Libra clan. There is the karmic hint of having been a part of social upheaval and the victim of misplaced ideals in another sequence of your soul journey. You can be stubbornly controlling in one moment but in the next moment display some childish act of rebelliousness. You seek to find a balance between your intellectual mind and your heart-felt beliefs. You long to return to that place of peace with your inner core.

You can be both disarmingly charming and mentally headstrong in getting your way. You collect facts, figures, and any information that you believe will be of aid to you in the future when you have to make your point. This can make you a great storyteller and, when called on, a good personal motivator. There is a paradox of conflicting powers dancing within your being, and the choice of Libra makes the process of putting your displaced Humpty Dumpty energies back together once again.

NOTABLES WITH THIS DEGREE:

Peter Max: German-born American graphic artist, illustrator, human and animal rights activist

Dannii Minogue: Australian actress, singer-songwriter, fashion designer

Lee Harvey Oswald: American sniper who allegedly assassinated JFK, political defector

Martina Navratilova: Czech-American professional tennis player

26th Degree of Libra

If this is your sun sign, you can be irresistible, irreverent, and sometimes seemingly irrational in your joyous pursuit of living. This number-sign combination can add to the already vacillating and uncertain Libra personality. Depending on the aspects and transits, you are torn between dexterity, ambiguity, and hopeless indecision. You have the dexterity of a great athlete or perhaps musician but also the makings of a garish porn star or out-of-control addict. Self-discipline can be a struggle, but when you find it, you can reach mountain-high levels of achievements.

There is a karmic hint of having dabbled deeply in the dark, bizarre, and remote strangeness of human nature in other times and settings. You navigate between the fine lines of beauty and the bizarre or between the saintly and the shocking. There is a deep potential for success with the healing arts and a strong desire to bring out the best qualities of human nature rather than being victimized by the dark and dysfunctional. Many of you may be attracted to legal professions or areas of justice that work with the abused and mistreated.

You will find yourself wrestling between the public image you think people want from you and who you really are. At its best, this gives a sense of refinement and sensitivity to the better path of life experience. You will draw attention wherever you go. Power, money, and legal issues surround you as you travel through the wily wickets of life's choices. There is a definite formula for success written into this combination, and many of you rise to the top of your chosen endeavors. There is the likelihood of popularity. It is difficult not to be in the limelight at some time during your Earth sojourn.

NOTABLES WITH THIS DEGREE:

Mickey Mantle: American professional baseball player

Sylvia Browne: American author, controversial psychic, spiritual medium

John Edward: American psychic medium, author, television personality

Snoop Dogg: American rapper, record producer, singer-songwriter, actor

27ᵗʰ Degree of Libra

If this is your sun sign, you are refined, subtle, and a radiant font of lightness for the world around you. When poorly aspected, some of the luster may come off and send you into some of the more hidden and bizarre attributes of the human personality. You inherently do not seek power or influence, but you may find yourself thrust into the position of leadership and responsibility. Your idealism makes it difficult to cope with the realities of corruption and chaos in our modern times. Perhaps out of tragedy or violence, you are thrown into a cynical and angry course of action that leads you into a role as one who will restore things to how they once were.

NOTABLES WITH THIS DEGREE:

Liliane Bettencourt: French billionaire socialite, cosmetic business mogul

William Zabka: American actor, screenwriter, director, producer

Sir Christopher Wren: English architect, designer, astronomer

William the Conqueror: English King, military leader

There is a karmic suggestion that you were once disposed to change through violence and anarchy. You tore apart the opposing political and ideological structure with ruthless abandon. You presently struggle against such violent urges within yourself and society, and your desire is to bring about a more harmonious and less-confronting system of world government. Many of you search for a more spiritual and metaphysical source of inspiration in your foundation of belief. Your trust in the temporal nature of humankind is at best skeptical; thus it is easier to hope that the spiritual nature may someday shine through the dross side of your mundane personality.

Your refined sensitivities make it easy for you to be around a whole range of personality types and social subcultures. Your nonthreatening manner allows you to solicit a softer side of the stubborn people you meet. This gives you a knack for diplomacy and arbitration. Such a role comes naturally to most of you with this number-sign combination. An air of optimism coupled with a warm smile is a winning combination that can open many doors toward your success.

28th Degree of Libra

If this is your sun sign, you are deft, dextrous, and (more often than not) dazzling when you commit yourself thoroughly to getting something done right. Your attention to detail and timing allows you to prepare for and perform well in situations in which others cannot reach such levels. You are very aware of the conventions of the day, and you might spoof or mock them when they seem to get in the way of individuality and self-expression. You ponder the role of the individual in society and the effect of society on the individual. This number-sign combination may find you a little more aggressive than some of your Libra contemporaries. It helps you to overcome some of the indecisive characteristics of most Libras.

NOTABLES WITH THIS DEGREE:

Paul Brunton: British mystic, esoteric teacher, philosopher

Deepak Chopra: Indian-American holistic physician

Natalee Holloway: American student who vanished while on a high school graduation trip to Aruba

Samuel Taylor Coleridge: English poet, literary critic, philosopher

There is the karmic suggestion of having been a troublemaker and disrupter of the social process in other times and life arenas. Perhaps you held contempt for the law or social structure. Your interference, in effect, impeded the progress of many others. Now you find yourself wanting public approval, and you work hard so that you will do your best when called on to perform in the public arena. Matters of law and protocol are important to those who have this combination. Once you work through the unconscious blocks, you become a dynamic and tireless proponent of social improvement and personal growth.

You may find yourself in some capacity in which you use your skills in mediating, negotiating, or promoting public relations. Perhaps you will travel among diplomatic circles where you strive to solve the differences between antagonistic individuals or groups of people. Legal issues are also of interest and play a significant part in your life. You are a respected member of your community and recognized for the manner in which you calmly serve and attend to the needs of the less fortunate.

29ᵗʰ Degree of Libra

If this is your sun sign, you are considered affable, witty, and wonderful by many. Although outwardly engaging and entertaining, you hide a very private side of your personality that is not revealed to many people other than the very trusted. And trust is an issue with you. Your sensitivity to the opinion of others causes you at times to withdraw but at other times to strike out vigorously against those who would intrude into your personal life. You wish to see the best of human nature and aspire to contribute to the learning and advancement of society. Your curiosity is limitless, and you love the world of gadgets and inventions that reflect the aspiring nature of human experimentation.

NOTABLES WITH THIS DEGREE:

Jeff Goldblum: American actor

Timothy Leary: American author, psychologist, LSD researcher

Johnny Carson: American talk show host, comedian

Weird Al Yankovic: American singer-songwriter, musician, satirist, comedian

Lynette Fromme: American member of Manson gang, attempted assassin

You are somewhat of a utopian, and when you see less than a perfect world, you can be scathing and condescending toward those who are out of control or responsible for abuse. There is the karmic suggestion that you have participated in anarchy and the upheaval of previous cultures. Perhaps you were in disagreement with the behavior of the ruling class. Perhaps you were the ruling force and prevented any attempt at changing your controlled environment. Perhaps you were disenchanted when the rebelling contingency did not bring any improvement or benefit to the destroyed kingdom.

The sensitive nature of this number-sign combination leads many with this combination into poetry or another of the fine arts. If you incline toward the intellectual side, abstract philosophy and transcendental thought catch your attention. If you are scientifically motivated, most likely you are driven by work that you believe will bring about a more perfect world. You are refined and appreciate style and aesthetic considerations in your dress and home décor. You mingle with informed and academically trained people who are actively engaged in the community and world around them.

SCORPIO

0 Degree of Scorpio

If this is your sun sign, you can be frustrating, funny, and at times buried in fantasy. It may take you a little longer than some of your contemporaries to get a bead on just what it is you want to do with your life. During your search, you may go through some pretty dark and depressing times. It is not easy for Scorpios who feel lost and without purpose. You may compensate with satirical humor and funny fits of philosophy about why life is unjust and fate is fickle. Some of you with this number-sign combination may escape into flights of fantasy and perhaps fallacy.

NOTABLES WITH THIS DEGREE:

Roman Abramovich: Russian billionaire, business tycoon, private investor

Kevin Cline: American actor

Michael Crichton: American author, screenwriter, producer, director

Once you do become focused and centered on a purposeful life direction, you are powerful and potent in accomplishing your intended goals. There is the karmic hint that in another time and setting your imagination and passionate, creative consciousness ran into the stubborn wall of collective thought and conventional conservatism. You may have had very noteworthy ideas or projects unjustly denied by those who were threatened and became afraid that change would loosen their position of influence in the community. Perhaps you were ridiculed or told lies to undermine and embarrass your efforts.

You can be distrusting and at times cynical about those who hold authority. You may become attracted to people or groups who espouse the overthrow of inept or corrupt leaders and functionaries. More likely, you will turn your efforts to the determined direction of proving your point through demonstration rather than just supposition. Whatever your course of action, you will leave an impact on place and people. Your open mind and curious soul enchant many and will find you surrounded by colorful, clever, and creative souls. You stir up the stew of originality and inspire others to honor their own independent thought and course of action.

1st Degree of Scorpio

If this is your sun sign, you are outspoken, energetic, and ready at the drop of a hat to explore the unusual and the unknown. You can easily become impatient and temperamental with things that are boring or do not go well. It is not easy to place any label on you since you are constantly finding new interests and creating a new persona. You may appear lighter and less serious than many of your Scorpio contemporaries, but underneath, there still remains the intense, brooding Scorpio personality. That also includes the penchant, probing curiosity to get to the heart of matters.

You enjoy the limelight and recognition for being the first to achieve something. This may bring you fame or, in some cases, infamy. There is a karmic hint that in another time and setting, you may have been part of a big lie or fraud. Perhaps you were an unwitting participant because of your naïve belief in the perpetrator. Maybe you were an instigator attempting to gain notoriety and fame. You will benefit by being thorough with facts before presenting anything to the public. Be careful to know more about associates before giving them your trust.

It is difficult to find a Scorpio without some kind of sexual issue. You could be someone at the edge of experimenting with the exotic and more-heightened forms of sexual experience. While most of you keep this information within a tight circle, there is a greater chance of some form of scandal when aspects are unfavorable. This is a favorable number-sign combination for those who enjoy appearing on the stage or in front of the public in some manner. Whatever your course in life, it will be hard not to notice you as you traverse your way through the path of personal experience.

2ⁿᵈ Degree of Scorpio

If this is your sun sign, you are bestowed with some softening of the well-recognized Scorpio harshness and tendency toward scathing outbursts. This number-sign combination does not necessarily eliminate the possibility of such behavior, but it does suggest a more mild temperament and patient demeanor. The Scorpio strength is not diminished, just channeled into a more acquiescent, external manner of social interaction. This can enhance your negotiating skills and help you accomplish your goals of acceptance and social impact. You can be wily and willful in your way of going about getting what you want. When that goes to the extreme, your intent and actions can become criminal in nature.

NOTABLES WITH THIS DEGREE:

Hillary Rodham Clinton: U.S. Secretary of State, First Lady of the United States, New York Senator

John Cleese: English actor, comedian, screenwriter, producer

François Mitterrand: president of France, socialist politician

Pablo Picasso: Spanish painter, sculptor, printmaker, stage designer

There is the karmic hint that in another time and setting, you were rebellious and devastatingly outspoken in your attack on those in power, who you believe were guilty of injustice or misapplication in their positions of power and influence. Right or wrong, you may have made enemies and adversaries at every turn. You seek to stay true to your beliefs and codes of righteous conduct, but you are learning to be less self-righteous in your assessment of others' foibles. It is difficult to see the same qualities within yourself that you rail against when recognized in others.

The flexibility of the 2 combined with the Scorpio power can result in above-average athletic ability. You will likely be active in physical exercise and sports, and many of you could reach acclaimed heights or athletic achievement. Your endless energy allows you to take on the relentless task of tackling active issues of civic and institutional matters. You are not above putting on a most impressive act in order to make a point. In fact, many of you could find yourselves on the stage in entertainment or politics.

3rd Degree of Scorpio

If this is your sun sign, you are sexy, saucy, sensual, and sometimes salaciously entertaining in your zesty pursuit of life's pleasures. Ever-present sexual innuendo lurks under your humor and thoughts. Repressed negative sexual encounters from childhood may shade your attitude toward your creative abilities and sexual relations in the real world. This can lead to a more reclusive and restrained side of your personality coming into the foreground. Most of the time, your Scorpio daring will slip through the cracks of consciousness and reveal itself throughout your life.

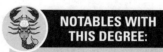

NOTABLES WITH THIS DEGREE:

Dylan Thomas: British writer, poet

Robert Chaney: American spiritualist, esoteric religious leader

Michael Harding: English astrologer, psychotherapist

Marla Maples: American actress, television personality, socialite

There is the karmic suggestion of another time and place where your creative potential got out of control and led to harm or injury to many. You are both constantly attracted, and at times, equally fearful of the power of human creativity on all levels. Your obsession with sex and the transformative process has taken you into the depths of depravity and most likely toward the heights of spiritual enlightenment. It may also lead you into some form of brilliant discovery related to the transmutation of mind or matter — or both.

Whatever your shortcomings or conquests of consciousness, the world will notice your passage through life. It will be difficult to miss your presence. That is because you are wired to make an impact and leave an impression on those you encounter. This number-sign combination is often found with those who are in the field of communications, arts, media, sales, or wherever a spokesperson is needed to get a specific message across to the masses. You will meet many and trust few. Your inherent Scorpio nature keeps you cautious and likely to let only a few select people into your close circle of intimate associates. The relationships that last will be those of major impact, and you will share timely secrets of humanity and the workings of the universe itself.

4th Degree of Scorpio

If this is your sun sign, you are a force in action. This number-sign combination gives focus and purpose to an already intense Scorpio personality. You feel you were born to do something and accomplish some purposeful goal. Your life will not be content until you feel you are on the path of getting that purpose accomplished. You are willing to set aside other conveniences and relationships while you seek to strike your fortune and fame. You might not be world famous, but you will most likely leave an impact on the social circle in which you work and live.

You establish a work ethic that would make many shudder, but once the work is done for the day, baby, you know how to play! Secretive Scorpios like to hide much of their playful doings from the family and public eye — not that it is necessarily wrong. It's just none of their business.

NOTABLES WITH THIS DEGREE:

Julia Roberts: actress and promoter

J. A. Jance: American mystery and horror author

Teddy Roosevelt: American president, historian

Roberto Benigni: Italian actor, comedian, screenwriter, director

James Cook: British explorer, navigator, cartographer, Royal Navy captain

Jill Dearman: American writing coach, editor, astrologer

There is a karmic suggestion of excessive behavior in a past time and place, and this haunting memory can lead you to be a bit overcontrolling when trying to deal with possible addictions or compulsive behaviors. That may be one rap you hear more often than you want: the fact that you can be very controlling about what you do and with those who do it with you. Those who you really care for are able to tell you this. And you will listen to those you trust and care for when they do hit on the truth. You don't have to let your Scorpio guard down, but there is a healthy way to monitor feelings and actions within you. Your search to get to the bottom of your behavior has no limit once you are bitten by the bug of self-awareness and personal growth.

5th Degree of Scorpio

If this is your sun sign, you are willing to be a little different from others, flaunting your eccentricities or differences to the public. This can bring attention and possible fame, or it could lead to much ridicule and outcry. While not all of you may go to this extreme, there is a rebellious and independent nature associated with this number-sign combination. You are curious about life matters and the human experience. The Scorpio interest in sexuality is enhanced here. You could end up doing research into sexuality, even if it is just your own unique form of personal investigation through experimentation.

There is the karmic hint of having gotten involved in psychologically manipulating others through substances or other forms of invasive control. You struggle between inordinate attempts at self-control only to slide into temptation and indulgence of nonproductive behaviors. You will likely be attracted to some kind of recovery program or support group that helps those who have been out of control. Others are particularly interested in sexual abuse and lending assistance to people who are recovering from misapplication of the human sex drive.

You are lively, lovely, and full of tales and adventures of life. Your striking appearance and dynamic style of presentation capture attention and interest from the public. You have tried a lot of things and are usually open to considering something different and new, but all may not be play and experimentation. You have much wisdom and valuable learning to give back to others. You are excellent as a teacher or in positions that assist other people at becoming more adept at living. Once settled into your life direction, you are powerful and probably prominent in the roles of leadership and existential learning.

NOTABLES WITH THIS DEGREE:

Bill Gates: American computer software magnate, investor, programmer, social activist

S. Robson Walton: American billionaire, Wal-Mart chairperson and heir

Vera Stanley Alder: English painter, mystic, self-growth author

Daphne Zuniga: American actress, environmental activist

Rufus Sewell: English actor

6th Degree of Scorpio

If this is your sun sign, you manifest a slightly less harsh persona than many of your Scorpio contemporaries. Your innate connection to the emotional pool of the collective consciousness allows you to get a good read on public opinion and the events of your times. This can be of considerable value for you in business or career ventures. You would be comfortable in areas of service and rendering assistance to struggling populations. Many of you will perform your tasks as entertainers, exercising theatrics and drama to get your point of view across to others.

NOTABLES WITH THIS DEGREE:

William F. Halsey Jr.: U.S. Navy admiral

Bill Mauldin: author, actor, two-time Pulitzer Prize winning editorial cartoonist

John Adams: American president, first American vice president

Grace Slick: American singer-songwriter, model

Most of you with this number-sign combination feel like you carry some kind of burden or excessive amount of weight on your shoulders. There is the karmic suggestion of having been calloused and indifferent to the strife and struggle of other people in another time and setting. There is a deep sense of guilt that haunts you even though your scruffy Scorpio personality attempts to disclaim such. You dislike emotional blackmail and manipulation, but you are unaware most of the time how much of it you do. You are learning to become less of a user and more of a supporter in your interaction with others this time around. This is a time of moving from selfish to selfless.

Whatever you choose to do, your presence is felt, and it is difficult for others to ignore your input. You have put a lot of thought and contemplation into the major issues of life and often have very worthwhile insights to share from your experience. You are almost like an artist in the way you prepare and present what you have to share. This makes it even more tantalizing for others to give their time and attention to your presentations. You enjoy being with other people of resolve and deep convictions.

7th Degree of Scorpio

If this is your sun sign, your personality is about as similar to Scorpio as it can get. The 7 is analytical and probing. There is also the intuitive side of the 7 that goes beyond the limitation of logic and into the expanded dimensions that surpass the interest of those among the mass consciousness who are not yet awakened. You are like a cosmic Sherlock Holmes, and it frustrates you if you think you have left any stone unturned, no matter what the mystery.

NOTABLES WITH THIS DEGREE:

Teresa Hamilton: American author, Vedic astrologer

Dan Rather: American journalist, news anchor, magazine editor

Eva Marcille: American actress, model

Bud Spencer: Italian actor, filmmaker, lawyer, professional swimmer

There is a repressed quality about this combination, and the other side of the coin yields a kind of funky and perhaps rebellious or antisocial element to your personality. You probably enjoy facts and fiction more than real-life encounters. You might possess a dramatic flair that gets you into the entertainment industry in some fashion. A karmic hint suggests that in another life sojourn, you were emotionally injured by betrayal or abuse in some form. Perhaps you experienced love unrequited. You chose to shut down your feelings and protect yourself with a kind of mental armor that sorts everything out before it gets directly close to your heart. As your search continues, you will not only connect to truth but once again to your heart.

Your depth, daring, and sometimes disarming personality make you a magnet for fun seekers and those who like to step outside of the socially prescribed norms. You can be caustic, crude, and crazy, but in the end, your deep concern for human welfare peaks out from behind the cynical armor. Your mind is active and often profound in its conclusions. This is an archetypal jackpot for the investigator, researcher, and quizzical type who looks for the meaning and motive behind life and its perplexities.

8th Degree of Scorpio

If this is your sun sign, you have extraordinary insight into motivation and machinations of human consciousness. Power is the name and control is the game. You distrust human excess and believe in a world that is regulated and maintained in predictable order. The rules do not seem to apply to you, however, as you are inclined to partake of many libertine delights. As with all Scorpios, sex is a prominent issue with you and partners. You are fascinated about the relations between sex, power, creativity, and the dynamics of energy flow. Many entertainers are found with this number-sign combination, and it lends itself to an increased probability of success on stage or in the entertainment arena.

NOTABLES WITH THIS DEGREE:

Aishwarya Rai: Indian Bollywood actress, model

Charles Koch: American billionaire business mogul, philanthropist, engineer

Cheiro: Irish astrologer, palmist, occultist, clairvoyant

There is a karmic hint of having been in control of large masses of people in another time and place. There is part of you that wishes to liberate humankind from the fears and insecurities that allow them to be so easily manipulated as a group. At the same time, there is a certain sense of omnipotence that comes with being in control and having authority over the many. You will wrestle with these issues throughout much of your life in the home, office, or even on an international scale.

People with this combination are often found in roles of responsibility and leadership. You can be a masterful manager or supervisor, and you will often be found in administrative roles in large organizations. You usually fare well with money and financial matters. If you are not busy making money for yourself, you could be found advising others about the best way to make gains in the marketplace. You see trends coming far ahead of many financial experts, which can give you the edge at making quick profits. You are an enigma and a mysterious personality that creates allure and fascination.

9th Degree of Scorpio

If this is your sun sign, you may often find yourself peeking into possibilities and potentials that mere mortals would never conceive. You are a dreamer who beholds visions that can inspire the advancement of humanity, resulting in the transformation of the planet. It is not an easy task for you to stay grounded because your consciousness grasps the fringes of reality and senses so many subplanes of awareness. For some of you, this may come in the scary form of what is not working with the human condition. You become frustrated with the superficiality that pervades so much of human social discourse.

NOTABLES WITH THIS DEGREE:

Shahrukh Khan: Indian actor, producer, television host

Burt Lancaster: American actor, producer

k. d. lang: Canadian singer-songwriter

Larry Flynt: American publisher of adult magazine, *Hustler*, political aspirant

There is a karmic hint that in another life setting, you were instrumental in contributing to the development of some form of advanced civilization or kingdom that was on the verge of huge strides in the understanding and application of higher laws of science, religion, technology, and spirituality. Perhaps egos got in the way and the group was misled into misuse or abuse of knowledge. Perhaps the dark forces permeated the group and brought about compromise and corruption of the efforts. You are distrusting of and often downright reactionary toward those who are lax in the pursuit of truth. You have only harsh criticism for those who ignore the universal laws and scoff at inner truth.

You seek reconciliation with your own inner core and always strive to lead a righteous existence. You would benefit from slowing down once in a while and learning to play in the simple and forthright manner of an innocent child. Your seriousness can sometimes get in the way of your truth. This can cause someone who might be interested to back off from the pressure you apply in your efforts to enlighten others.

10th Degree of Scorpio

If this is your sun sign, you are daring, dapper, and ready to do almost anything. Your pioneering spirit shows in nearly all that you do. Not content with things as they are, you look for the new, different, and unusual. It is part of your nature to want to be the best and at the forefront of successful ventures. You work hard to achieve success and recognition. There is pride with this number-sign combination that can readily turn into a form of hubris. Be cautious about overinflating your worth while not seeing equal value in other people and what they do.

There is a karmic hint at having previously been in a position of creative or innovative success. Perhaps you were some form of national hero or legendary figure within a culture. You expect to be treated like a king and gain the favors of those who adore you.

NOTABLES WITH THIS DEGREE:

Marie Antoinette: controversial Queen of France

Warren G. Harding: American president, Ohio Senator, journalist

Aga Khan III: First president of League of Muslims, president of the League of Nations, social activist

Meiji Mitsuhito: Emperor of Japan during the industrialization period

James K. Polk: American president, lawyer

You can become bitter and critical when you do not receive the adulation that you expect. You are learning to be humble and appreciative of all people, no matter how magnificent or limited their personalities might be. You can be a wonderful role model and leader if you learn to set aside ego and become at ease with your true self.

You could have difficulty making a choice about where to focus your life since you have multiple aptitudes. There are so many things that you could do and want to do. Your personal magnetism is strong, and it is easy to attract others into your life. You may have to be selective and careful not to be taken in by hangers-on and those who want to live off your success. There is a likelihood of travel and contact with other cultures as you pass through the many stages of your life.

11th Degree of Scorpio

If this is your sun sign, your grasp of the world around you is far-reaching and filled with a depth of insight that most searching souls rarely obtain. The already-penetrating Scorpio mind is enhanced with this number-sign combination, giving you an expanded intuitive range along with the established substantive Scorpio intellect. You struggle with some issues of dualism. The skeptical Scorpio matched with the idealistic 11 makes for some interesting aspects in the reconciliation of dichotomous self-debate. This can be used to uplift and enlighten or to add further confusion and debate to an already extremely confused global population.

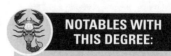

NOTABLES WITH THIS DEGREE:

Roseanne Barr: American actress, comedienne, director, writer, producer

Walter Cronkite: American broadcast journalist, television anchorman, political activist

Afef Jnifen: Tunisian model, actress

There is a karmic clue that somewhere in another sojourn of the soul, you had to face the responsibility of having access to extended knowledge possessed only by a select few. There is added responsibility with the use of such knowledge, especially when the application affects the lives of many other souls. Perhaps you disagreed with the powerbrokers of the time about what information to give and when. Maybe you saw misapplication of knowledge and watched the needless suffering of others because of its misuse. Possibly you tried to warn others and suffered humiliation.

You can be hesitant to speak out publicly about deep inner wisdom that you hold close to your heart and soul. You distrust the whims of the masses and are concerned with how the public processes information. This combination can soften the Scorpio sting somewhat, which may be to your advantage when working with the politics of a group or an organization. When you want to, you can be most mesmerizing and convincing in getting your way, convincing others of what you have to say. You are capable of accumulating and storing vast amounts of information that can be used to present a very detailed and precise rebuttal to an argument or debate.

12th Degree of Scorpio

If this is your sun sign, you have a way of getting yourself into situations that can put you under an additional load of stress and strain. You are capable of some very unpredictable antics that will keep those who know you on their toes whenever you are around. This manner of behavior can be charming and challenging to some, but it is mostly frustrating to those who truly care about you. You can be an excellent problem solver, and you are a survivor by nature. These survival instincts can turn into real assets when giving guidance and advice to others, since you have learned very valuable lessons about getting through tough situations under pressure.

NOTABLES WITH THIS DEGREE:

Sir George Trevelyan: British author, founder of the New Age movement

Vivian Leigh: British actress

Joel McCrea: American actor, outdoorsman, real-estate mogul

Eike Batista: Brazilian billionaire, oil tycoon

There is the karmic hint that during another life sojourn, you could very well have been a people pleaser who was willing to give up your own identity and beliefs to others in order to survive and get along. Perhaps you lost your own way and purpose, selling out to the pressures of others. Maybe you lacked personal conviction when disturbed by the actions of someone who disappointed and deceived you. You have had trouble trusting others and your own judgment. You are learning once again to find your own center of purpose and to live according to your inner wisdom.

Your sometimes "oh golly, shucks" persona may fool some of the people some of the time. However, your false humility only gets you so far. As you stand up and live in a way that is true to yourself, you find an entirely new circle of friends and competent souls surround you. You are mischievous and wacky at times, but your spoofs on current people and events reflect a very learned and well-thought-out conceptualization of human nature. When you do communicate on a public scale, it is done with pinpoint purpose and the intent of being as accurate as possible.

13th Degree of Scorpio

If this is your sun sign, you will somehow find yourself intimately involved in the questions of life and death and the cycles of being on this planet, which offers an immense assortment of options and directions for living. You ponder the grandeur of creation and the micro-detail of existence in your search to unravel the mystery of being human and being here. This relentless search could take you into areas of speculation and such obscure theories that you could experience ridicule and rejection by the ill informed.

NOTABLES WITH THIS DEGREE:

Dusty Bunker: American author, astrologer, numerologist

Ana Ivanovic: Serbian professional tennis player

Maria Shriver: American journalist, author, television announcer

Desiderius Erasmus: Dutch humanist, theologian

There is a karmic clue of having been caught in situations in prior lives in which you compromised inner convictions of truth in order to be accepted and gain recognition within your community. Perhaps you had suffered some inflic-tion of pain and torture and gave in to your tormentors. Perhaps something seduced you into giving up eternal values for the temporary lusts of power and the body. Perhaps you tried to mediate between two groups who had opposing ecclesiastical and philosophical viewpoints. If you attempted to find a compro-mise, you were scorned and rejected by both. You will once again be called on to stand up for your deepest convictions in a time when the collective trend is opposed or threatened by such truths.

You live on the edge and will encounter more thrilling moments in your life experience than many would experience over a millennia of evolutions. Your poignant views and passionate personality can make you very persuasive and convincing when you are at your best. You are fortunate to meet wise and wonderful souls from around the globe. You network with many enlightened and aware lightworkers who also see the higher light emerging into the human life stream. These contacts lead to important breakthroughs in understanding higher human consciousness.

14th Degree of Scorpio

If this is your sun sign, you are blessed with a kind of charismatic presence that adds to the impact you have on those you meet. This somewhat amplifies your already-potent Scorpio life force. Your curiosity about subtle forces and the paranormal will open vistas of dimensional breakthrough and new worlds of awareness. You have a strong spiritual nature that searches to better understand the relationship between humanity and its creator. Your fascination with the mysteries of life brings you into contact with many unusual and unconventional personalities. For some of you with this number-sign combination, there is an increased likelihood of contact with life forms of other dimensions and worlds.

NOTABLES WITH THIS DEGREE:

Billy Graham: American-Christian minister, evangelist

Marie Curie: French-Polish chemist, physicist

Joan Sutherland: Australian opera singer

Alain Delon: French-Swiss actor

You will likely administer comfort and care in some form to others for a good part of your life. There is the karmic suggestion that in another life, you were given rare and special gifts that were taken lightly and misapplied. You now find yourself knowing that there is a special part of your consciousness that you would like to develop, but it may not be easy to do so. This is a natural combination for the physician, and the admonishment is, of course, first you must pay attention and "heal thyself." Many with this combination are gifted with spiritual qualities of a special nature. You might render healing through words, medicine, alternative methods, spiritual practices, or any number of other ways, but service will be your calling.

Your domineering Scorpio personality may hide the compassion and caring nature that is deep within you. You have many potential talents, and it might be hard to specialize in one area of service. It is not that you are totally impersonal; however, you find the principles and theories of things sometimes more fascinating than the human equation. You are full of vigor and passion, and you can be highly entertaining and humorous in your personal interactions. People aggregate around you because of your fascinating viewpoints on life and human nature.

15th Degree of Scorpio

If this is your sun sign, it suggests a kind of clash of qualities that can be both baffling and beguiling: There is a good-guy feeling that radiates from this number-sign combination, along with an undertone of shady characteristics lurking just below. You are tough, tenacious, and tightfisted about many of the issues in your life. You are a determined individual who will go after your desired goals with a vengeance. You may find yourself attracted to health care or some aspect of medical research. This can come about due to the advent of health issues in your own life or in the life of someone very close to you.

NOTABLES WITH THIS DEGREE:

Raja Rao: Indian spiritual author

Rupert Allason: English politician, military historian, novelist

Leon Trotsky: Russian political leader, Marxist revolutionary and theorist

Johnny Rivers: American singer-songwriter, producer, musician

There is the karmic suggestion of having been involved in some pretty nefarious activities in another time and place. This could include illegal activities that defied social laws. Or it could have been the intentional misuse of natural laws for your own gain and glory. The unresolved issues linger in your present persona and can be the source of mixed messages that you project to the public. You have an innate sense of public opinion and know how to manipulate it to your own advantage or work collectively to enlighten and awaken the masses from their stupor.

Your lighter side is concerned with the well-being of humanity, and you might be drawn toward the education or information fields. Your dramatic nature could cause you to be attracted to some form of entertainment as an outlet for excessive energy stored within your personality. You are shrewd, swift, and decisive in your professional actions and dealings. You are not averse to having luxurious items around you that make a statement about your accomplishments and success.

16th Degree of Scorpio

If this is your sun sign, no matter how mundane the task at hand, you have an air of expectation and anticipation of something extraordinary that is going to happen before your life is over. There is a sense that somehow you are destined to become an integral part of whatever that happening should be. You search for and long to know what that could be, and you become increasingly ecstatic as the events and purpose fall into place. You give much attention to fate, kismet, and destiny, as well as the machinations the universe goes through in its distribution of justice.

NOTABLES WITH THIS DEGREE:

Carl Sagan: American astronomer, astrophysicist, author

Angel Thompson: American astrologer, poet, author

Spiro Agnew: U.S. Vice President, Governor of Maryland

Hedy Lamarr: Austro-American actress, communications technology innovator

There is a karmic hint of having been involved in another setting where something went dreadfully wrong and caused considerable grieving from the population. You carry over guilt from the feeling of somehow having contributed to the miscue. You can become troubled with a nagging concern that something terrible is going to happen. Deep down, you desire to right any injustice and make good in a situation of crisis and conscience. There is a strong possibility that such an opportunity will present itself in this life sojourn.

There is the potential in this number-sign combination for quirkiness and eccentric tendencies. You will seek to find a very select subculture in which you can express some of your more unconventional areas of interest. You have an innate sense of knowledge and potential wisdom, and many of you will complement these natural proclivities with academic and intellectual training. This combination of intuitive access and specialized learning can become most valuable when training others to cope with challenging and complicated situations of adversity and possible disaster. You know what to do and how to do it in the moment of panic and collapse. Others will respect and respond to your leadership and take-charge confidence.

17ᵗʰ Degree of Scorpio

If this is your sun sign, you might very well reveal the softer side of the Scorpio personality a little more easily than others. This number-sign combination, at its best, adds some patience, mellowing the famous Scorpio sting when it comes to language and interpersonal communication. You see a thread of hope when others only see despair. You uncover a touch of good while others are focused on the dark and threatening. You are able to weave your way through the often disorganized and blatantly dark side of the social system. A touch of the chivalry extended in the legends of the knights and damsels of old is present in this combination.

NOTABLES WITH THIS DEGREE:

Tina Kandeláki: American-born Russian journalist, television host, actress, politician

Niki Karimi: Iranian actress, director, screenwriter

Bruno Peyron: French yachtsman, sailor, set world record around-the-world sail

MacKenzie Phillips: American actress, singer

There is a karmic hint of having played the part of taking away promising hopes from a lot of people. Maybe you offered to rescue a group of desperate people. Perhaps that rescue failed. Possibly you placed your belief in someone who offered to get you and others out of a repressive situation, and it failed. There is a deep issue regarding trust associated with this combination. You are learning to trust your own inner wisdom and then share that with the right people at the right time. Timing and discernment are key ingredients of the lesson here. It is important to know who to trust and when.

The discipline of accumulating knowledge is important to you, and there are many scholars among you who are now teaching and conducting research that seeks to open the doors of human endeavor and allow for expanded pathways to a better dawn. You can easily attract money when in tune with your purpose, and you enjoy the refinements of living that come with material success. There will be chances for many of you to hob knob with powerful and influential people. When called on, you can be a most effective spokesperson and leader of those who are muddled and confused.

NUMEROLOGY OF ASTROLOGY

18th Degree of Scorpio

If this is your sun sign, your life will be fraught with many twists and turns along your path. You aspire to the noble and kindhearted, but you are constantly reminded of the devious and twisted aspects of human nature. There is a desire for perfection associated with this number-sign combination but, at the same time, many disappointments when people fall far short of such highly placed expectations. You are inclined to take action against the forces of wrong and evil, and you have the necessary drive to attract followers who are moved by your conviction and courage.

NOTABLES WITH THIS DEGREE:

Leonardo DiCaprio: American actor, producer, activist

Fyodor Dostoyevsky: Russian novelist, philosopher

Kurt Vonnegut: American author

Fuzzy Zoeller: American professional golfer

There are things that go on behind your back and those who plot against you because of your strong opinions and firm stand. The karmic pattern hints at a previous issue of power in another time and place. You may come under siege by those who are in power or hold an authoritative position at an influential institution. This combination of numbers and inherent Scorpio traits indicate there will be lingering undercurrents of sexual discomfort and doubt. You will have to face issues regarding the role of women in society, including feminine sexual empowerment and expression.

There are many temptations of flesh and fame that come with this combination. Power and the seduction of luxury can become distractions to the more pure and purposeful path your soul has chosen to take during this lifetime. Your adventurous spirit and willingness to attack adversity head-on attract many admirers. This adds to a strong and commanding personality that strengthens your skill at weaving your way through the hedgerows of political maneuvering. Once you have come and gone, you will have left many changes in the lives of the people you have encountered.

19th Degree of Scorpio

If this is your sun sign, you fluctuate within a wide range of human potential and possibilities. There is a kind of rarefied purity suggested by this number-sign combination that can lift you to the highest elevations of awareness, allowing you to fly with the angels and into the deepest spiritual corners of the cosmos. You take on the challenge of trying to meet the standards of unconditional love. Like the rest of humanity, you find yourself coming up short. You aren't there yet. But you do provide many with some guidelines and clues to an unabashed, loving consciousness.

NOTABLES WITH THIS DEGREE:

George Patton: U.S. Army general

Demi Moore: American actress, producer, director, songwriter, model

Calista Flockhart: American actress

Grace Kelly: American actress, Princess of Monaco

Charles Manson: American cult leader, murder mastermind

But all is not rosy, Scorpio. There is always the other side of human behavior, and yours is no exception. There is a karmic hint of having been indifferent and misleading to others in another time and place. You may have manipulated a misplaced idealism or the human quest for utopia in such a way as to gain power over the masses. There can be deep-rooted guilt for having disrupted normal social, emotional development because of self-serving motives, the need to control, or some other nefarious reason. Many of you are working through this karma by using your energy to uplift and inspire the optimism and hopes of those who may feel downtrodden or socially unable to get a chance at growth.

You are free spirited and undaunted in the quest to solve the mysteries of life and the universe. Metaphysical speculations can take up as much of your mental time as thinking about sex — well, maybe not that much! Your striking appearance and strong personal magnetism make you a magnet for attracting a crowd and getting attention from someone in particular. You can be found when reformation is in the air. You take keen note of the social developments happening in the world around you. Many of you will have a direct impact on those developments.

20th Degree of Scorpio

If this is your sun sign, there are a lot of behavioral options at your fingertips, and it can sometimes be difficult knowing just who you are and what you stand for in the public and personal arenas of life. This number-sign combination gives deep insight into the universal nature of humanity, revealing a somewhat cosmic and ethereal perspective. This leads many to misunderstand you, leaving you perplexed about what you are really trying to say or accomplish. Your viewpoint is generally more liberal and utopian in its intent. You lean toward tolerance except when ego enters into the fray. When that happens, you can be scathing and judgmental toward those with whom you have disagreements.

NOTABLES WITH THIS DEGREE:

Whoopi Goldberg: American comedienne, singer-songwriter, author, political activist

Ryan Gosling: Canadian actor, director, writer, musician, mouseketeer

Robert Louis Stevenson: Scottish novelist, poet, travel writer

There is the karmic hint that in another time sequence, you have been extremely critical and unyielding in your attitude toward others. Your caustic tongue and arrogant sense of power created much dissension and anger in the surrounding kingdom. You are learning to soften your criticism and become more accurate with your facts and figures before taking a stand on important public issues. You secretly crave power while denouncing those who have it and use it to your displeasure.

This combination can soften the severe and direct Scorpio disposition. It is a more mystical and intuitive combination than a hardnosed, down-to-earth one. It is not easy for you to stay grounded, and you may be viewed as unstable and unpredictable, especially if you become distraught with all the ugliness you see in the work around you. Then it is easy to slip away into a world of drugs or other escapist indulgence. You are multigifted and might find it hard to just stay centered in any one area of personal interest.

21ˢᵗ Degree of Scorpio

If this is your sun sign, you are outspoken, complicated, and at times cantankerous. There are many crosscurrents of consciousness associated with this number-sign combination that make for potential conflicts within self and paradoxical behaviors. You are studious and strong, and you are determined to get to the crux of matters. It is very likely that your childhood experiences are influenced heavily by social beliefs and conventions of the day. You struggle to fit in with social norms but also rebel at the restraints and absurd demands expected from the con-

NOTABLES WITH THIS DEGREE:

Condoleezza Rice: U.S. Secretary of State, author, activist

Jean Seberg: American actress, civil rights activist

Ayaan Hirsi Ali: Somali-Dutch-American feminist, atheist activist, controversial Dutch author, filmmaker

ventional thought of the time. You speak out in disagreement with convention but are often caught by the weight of tradition and social expectation.

There is the karmic suggestion that in another time and setting, you were in the position to speak out for the need for change, but your station, title, or ego might have prevented you from doing what your heart knew was right. You waffle between standing up to opposition and then crumbling under the weight of authority and tradition. You will have a chance to take a stand on issues at a very crucial point in social development and your own destiny.

You can be the most colorful character, and when you are at your best, people enjoy being around your for your studied insight on issues and your candid flair for amusement and whim. It is not easy for you to be at ease in any role of authority or responsibility for the needs of the myriad interests represented by the people around you. Once you find yourself connected to your inner truth and to what you truly stand for within your heart and soul, you will be able to stand up firmly and represent your views with respect, receiving a pleasant response.

22ⁿᵈ Degree of Scorpio

If this is your sun sign, you are dynamic, driven, and frequently dubious about people and events that take place around you. There is a sense that you have something to accomplish, but it may take you until late into your life to figure out just what that might be. A number of you are late bloomers and come into your own after many of your contemporaries have already established and proven themselves. You understand well the hidden motives that underlie much of human behavior, but you may not know as much about your own. This can lead to distrust and conflict in the art of getting along since you might be running from yourself while projecting your issues onto others.

NOTABLES WITH THIS DEGREE:

Erwin Rommel: German military general

Beverly d' Angelo: American actress, singer

Prince Charles: Prince of Wales, author, spokesperson

Burgess Meredith: American actor, director

You find work that provides for your needs, and it would seem that those basic needs are met. Even though you are taken care of, there is a gnawing in the soul that there is something more that you are here to do. There is a karmic suggestion that in another sequence of your soul journey, you made a commitment or were given the task of fulfilling a specific type of work. For some reason, you did not get that accomplished, and the failure to do so still haunts your spiritual progress. You will search for inner work that brings contentment to your soul and closure to your unfulfilled task.

While others may find you a bit too serious and dedicated to duty, you can be a most fascinating person. Your depth of insight and wide range of human experience allow you to draw from multiple levels of experience when sharing stories and life experiences with others. A magnetic quality draws you to other people who are accomplished and successful at what they do. You could very well become a part of a team that makes far-reaching accomplishments.

23rd Degree of Scorpio

If this is your sun sign, you are not ready to be held down on the farm. You are extraordinarily inquisitive about things, and in many cases, you go to extremes to investigate a potentially wild adventure. Life is waiting, and you go after it with a lust for living that few can match. There is a willingness to try almost anything and go almost anywhere. This can result in immensely valuable growth for your personality and soul. It can also lead you into an abyss of indulgence and out-of-control abusive behaviors. Sex, drugs, or alcohol could be your undoing, tragically calling many of you to your grave prematurely. That does not have to happen, and with a close Scorpio examination of your life circumstances, you will have an excellent opportunity to work through some long-running and deeply embedded karma.

NOTABLES WITH THIS DEGREE:

René Guénon: French author, activist

Terence McKenna: American author, philosopher, consciousness theorist, futurist

Marg Helgenberger: American actress, breast cancer spokesperson

Gemma Atkinson: English actress, glamour model

There is the hint of having taken many people down a spiral of despair and escapist indulgence. Perhaps you held power and influence within a gathering of souls who lived off other people and drained the resources of all you conquered. You are used to getting what you want and unfortunately have to struggle in this lifetime to learn boundaries and to set limits. You may very well experiment right on the edge of expanding consciousness, but you could choose to take shortcuts to get to a higher place of awareness. More often than not, the shorter the cut, the greater the tumble you will end up experiencing.

You are mischievous, masterful, and mindful of how individual and social behavior works. You can manipulate the environment or help those close to you awaken. No matter what course you choose, you will be noticed and leave an impact anywhere you have been. Your playful nature allows you to inspire those who are more inhibited and repressed to take a step out of fear and into healthy experiences.

24th Degree of Scorpio

If this is your sun sign, you share a very complex relationship with yourself and with others. You are very connected to the underlying issues of the collective consciousness and bounce in and out of this collective pool often. You are particularly aware of what creates taboos and repressed anxieties. It is tempting to step over some of these lines of acceptance to explore the outer bounds of human experience. Your own unconsciousness is troubled and confused by the many conflicting crosscurrents of opinion that pass through your thoughts.

You are intrigued by and in touch with public taboos to do with sex and sensuality. You might be known for pushing the parameters of sexual experimentation while turning your back on public opinion and the attitude of the day. There is the karmic hint of having callously breached public standards in another time and setting. You may have brought instability and dissension to a community or group of people. You are torn between pushing for change against moral or behavioral standards and wanting acclaim for altering the status quo and putting forth your own set of conduct.

It is not easy for you to settle into a traditional type of relationship. However, once you do find the right partner, you can be surprisingly loyal and considerate. While priding yourself at being free from the restraints of conventional living, you end up becoming predictable and repetitive in the way you conduct your relationship. Once you have worked through your dysfunctional patterns, you can be an exceptional instructor or coach helping others to face and resolve the age-old hold that dysfunction has on the human race. Wherever you go, you will leave an impression on those you meet because of your distinct personality traits and individual path of proceeding through your daily interaction with others.

NOTABLES WITH THIS DEGREE:

Sophie Marceau: French actress, director, screenwriter, author

Martin Scorsese: American director, screenwriter, producer, actor, film historian

Maggie Gyllenhaal: American actress, social and political activist

Lauren Hutton: American supermodel, movie actress

25th Degree of Scorpio

If this is your sun sign, you are different, demonstrative, and sometimes defiant. It is not easy to stick this Scorpio blend into any one basket. If someone tries to describe you, you will purposely act differently. You would like to think that you do not conform, and you would like to think you are socially independent. The ever-strange irony is that in your defiance, you are controlled by that very society with which you have issues. Your studies and research provide you with much illuminating information and data from which you make often-accurate assessments and predictions regarding events around you. You can be affable and open when it is necessary to get the information or perspective you need to accomplish your aims.

NOTABLES WITH THIS DEGREE:

Danny DeVito: American actor, comedian, producer, director

Linda Evans: American actress, alternative healing activist

Mahinda Rajapaksa: Sri Lanka president, military leader, lawyer

Yram: French author, occultist, out-of-body exponent

There is a karmic hint of considerable conflict in past lives with social issues and the manner in which public figures live their lives. You are sensitive to abuse and excess. Perhaps you were in a very public position and chose a lavish and exploitive lifestyle for which you were rebuked or loathed. Maybe you saw the abuse of office by social leaders, and now you feel guilty for not having done more to prevent such behavior. You are learning to overcome your own addictions and excesses of behavior. In turn, you seek to support those who live wholesome lifestyles and contribute to a more stable, ethical, and morally based community.

Many of you are multitalented and excel in physical, mental, and spiritual interests. Your contact with other cultures allows you to learn many subtle lessons about human behavior that enables you to improve your own character. You enjoy nature and outdoor activities. Although your life may constantly put you into social contact and the business of routine mundane and material affairs, you deeply crave meditative time and contemplative moments that put you in touch with the divine and cosmic attributes of your being.

26th Degree of Scorpio

If this is your sun sign, you may struggle in the early years of your life to fit in with the standards and norms that society has established. Early on, you recognize the potential for abuse by those who have power. You may have been a victim of abuse by someone in a role of authority. You could be active in demonstrations or perhaps groups that espouse reform of institutions that have become mired in misuse and mismanagement of human or public resources. You grow into a more empathetic and patient personality than many of your Scorpio contemporaries. Your ability to articulate the emotional sentiment of the masses can result in earning you the position of spokesperson for a large assemblage of discontented souls.

NOTABLES WITH THIS DEGREE:

Larry King: American radio and television talk show host

Ted Turner: American business magnate, founder of CNN, social activist

Jody Foster: American actress, film director, producer

James Garfield: American president, lawyer

Indira Gandhi: Prime Minister of India

There is the karmic hint of past abuse of authority on your own part in another setting and sequence of your soul journey. It may have been an ecclesiastical, an academic, or a political position that involved administering the rules and regulations of the institution or organization that you represented. Perhaps you had to carry out corrupted orders against your beliefs and will. Maybe you delighted in having authority over others and seeing them suffer and yield to your overbearing ways. At present, you could find yourself going out of the way to avoid any role of authority for fear you may do injustice or harm others.

At best, you possess a deep sympathy and concern for life that results in an attitude of responsibility others admire. You are well versed in what you do and are discreet with sensitive information. This earns you trust and respect. Your negotiating skills allow you to cut to the heart of matters quickly and respectfully in regard to the concerns and worries of both sides.

27th Degree of Scorpio

If this is your sun sign, as with all Scorpios, you ponder life deeply and thoroughly. You are perplexed by the many ironies, paradoxes, and uncertainties the social fabric of humanity manifests. Your relationship to this world is complex and filled with mixed emotions as to what you want and how you are going to get it. You have a high degree of idealism starting out in life. This can lead you into a visionary life that becomes focused on the rejuvenation of humanity. Or for some of you who turn cynical and disillusioned, it can be a world of under-the-table dealings and unholy pacts that create confusion, fear, and perhaps, in the end, only chaos.

NOTABLES WITH THIS DEGREE:

Meg Ryan: American actress, producer, activist

Milton Black: Australian astrologer, author

Stephen Hill: American astrologer, author

Martin Luther: German monk, Catholic priest, professor of theology, central figure of the Reformation

There is the karmic suggestion that in another life setting, you held very idealistic and utopian dreams for the world and the human kingdom. Perhaps you supported a political sect that espoused such ideals. Perhaps those high hopes were sold out by someone in a leadership role that threw the party into disillusionment and disrespect from the general populace. Perhaps you saw high aspirations turned into a deceptive tool that ended up bringing your group under the control of another leader's more Draconian methods. Perhaps you saw the deception occurring and chose not to speak out. Now you have confusion and guilt about your role in social change. You seek the right people and the right social stratagems that you feel will elevate the human condition.

This is the number-sign combination of poets, visionary thinkers, inspired academicians, and transcendental artists. You mix and mingle among unconventional and sometimes disillusioned subcultures. A seductive, ethereal quality makes you mysterious and fascinatingly convincing when you speak about your visions and hopes for the future of the human race.

28th Degree of Scorpio

If this is your sun sign, you want to be noticed. You want to have an impact. This combination lends itself to the diplomacy of power and opinion. You are attuned to, although often not in agreement with, the thinking of the times. You dream of transformation and seek to provide others with the tools to further awaken into the stream of pure consciousness. You are sensitive to the abuse of power and quick to speak out when recognizing it among public leaders. There is a karmic hint of having mishandled a public event in another time and place. This leaves you with fear of criticism and public scrutiny. You must be careful to see that sometimes what you cry out about the most is also a big part of your own behavior. It is easy to talk the talk, but it is also well known that it is more difficult to walk the walk.

NOTABLES WITH THIS DEGREE:

Dick Durbin: U.S. senator, senate majority whip

Björk: Icelandic singer-songwriter, producer, actress

Lynn Buess: American numerologist, author, speaker, innovative wellness guide

Robert F. Kennedy: U.S. senator, Attorney General, politician

Kelly Gallagher: American model, interior designer, Playboy Playmate

This number-sign combination can diminish the Scorpio directness a bit so that others may not be able to see just how much of an influence you have on a given situation. You seek to bring emotional release to those who remain repressed and victimized by their refusal to see the dark side of their own behavior. This pattern of service can get you mixed into the frying pan of another's victimhood and misguided ideals. Rather that rescuing dysfunctional souls, you can find yourself engulfed by their discordant behavior.

This combination suggests mental and intuitive creativity. You are often ahead of the public in your perception of newer, universal, archetypal energies entering the planet. Your enthusiasm to share your vision can lead to disappointment when the many just do not share your vision or care enough to give up material securities for the spiritual benefits you reveal. Your search for higher truths may threaten those who hold positions of power in the temporal world. Some discretion and caution is urged where and when you speak out about the shortcomings of the mighty.

29th Degree of Scorpio

If this is your sun sign, you can be a bit of a utopian but also remain acutely aware of the pitfalls of social evolution. You speak out boldly for change, and you can become overly zealous, perhaps even fanatical, in your support of those you believe can make the changes that you desire. That could be especially true if the one who can initiate change is you. This number-sign combination offers some diplomatic savvy, and you can soften some of your Scorpio directness

NOTABLES WITH THIS DEGREE:

Billie Jean King: American world tennis champion

Lynn Buess: American author, alternative healer, therapist, numerologist

Ralph Meeker: American actor

when absolutely necessary. However, you will not give up your conviction; rather, you will find another way of presenting the issue in order to convince your detractors.

There is an aspect of personality that makes you stand tall among your peers and leads you to better understand the social nature of your fellow humans. You are curious and critical, and you are not above offering comments on the current events that take sway in the world around you. There is the karmic suggestion of having misguided and misled others in another time and place because of excessive idealism. You have a strong desire to see society work, but you are ever wary of its flaws and shortcomings. It is not as easy to see the same within yourself. With dogged Scorpio determination, you face your adversaries and disclaimers with pride, self-righteousness, and conviction. You thrive on challenge and experience great pride in victory.

This combination adds some refinement to the sometimes-rough Scorpio personality, and there is a likelihood of interest in poetry or writing. You are keen about history and social trends. When time allows, you may explore transcendental philosophies or existential thoughts. In the end, you find that these high-minded and noble treatises are not so easy to implement in the harsh world of human reality. Your adherence to the ideal and dreams of perfection make it difficult to find satisfaction with the constant shortcomings of humankind.

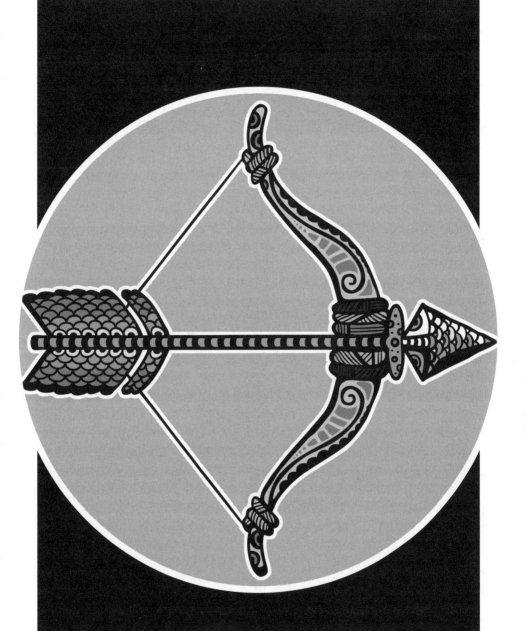

SAGITTARIUS

0 Degree of Sagittarius

If this is your sun sign, you have some extra zing and special verve that causes you to stand out from the crowd. There is a refreshing openness about this number-sign combination that catches people off-guard and allows them to be candid and straightforward in your presence. If you become too overrun by others' attention, there can be just enough barb on that wagging tongue of yours to keep those who approach at a safer distance. But for the most part, you strive for a diplomatic approach and benefit from the limelight that may come your way during your lifetime. Your openness to new things usually means you can be found at the forefront of change, challenging the status quo. Because you see yourself as unbiased and universal in your attitude toward life, you may not be aware when what you say or do might be offensive or distasteful to someone else.

NOTABLES WITH THIS DEGREE:

Scarlett Johansson: American actress, model, singer

Alexandra Rosenfeld: French beauty queen, social activist

Kelly Brook: English model, actress, swimwear designer

Maria Flávia de Monsaraz: Spanish astrologer, educator

There is a karmic hint that in another time and situation, you held an attitude of careless disregard for certain groups of people. You may have spoken out in a calloused manner, causing substantial negative reaction and commotion. Because of your bias, you could not see the offense and overlooked the consequences of your actions until they came back on you in a harsh and punitive manner. You try to be universal in attitude in this go around, but you sometimes still cover up some deep-seated prejudices that find a way to jump up and bite you by surprise.

You are capable of doing many things and have an interest in many areas of life, so it may not be easy to simply settle into one path or interest. Many of you may find yourselves doing one thing while spending a good deal of time wishing it were something else. It might seem to you that there is always greener pasture just around the bend that might yet offer a more exotic or exciting new twist of fate to an already adventurous life.

1ˢᵗ Degree of Sagittarius

If this is your sun sign, you are vibrant and dynamic. You are determined to express yourself in an almost hectic schedule of performance. It will be difficult to keep you from taking the initiative or lead role when it comes to performing or getting something done. Your knack for self-expression is well recognized by those around you. There is a natural sort of naïveté about your personality. This quality puts people at ease and makes it easier for them to accept what you have to say. There is little hesitation in wanting to speak and communicate, and you will likely be found in a profession that gives you this natural outlet for self-expression. Many of you feel driven to make your point and to be noticed by others.

NOTABLES WITH THIS DEGREE:

Franklin Pierce: American president, lawyer

Miley Cyrus: American actress, singer-songwriter

Billy the Kid: American gunman, Old-West outlaw

Asafa Powell: Jamaican world-class sprinte

There is a karmic suggestion that you may have been a leader or spokesperson in another time and situation. Someone may have distorted your message in order to control the masses. You are determined that people clearly understand your intent in this lifetime, and you are overly sensitive to misrepresentation and distortion of your actions or intent. You watch the shift of public moods with a wary eye.

Your interests are varied and may take you into some form of religious or spiritual study. Metaphysical thought and speculation about the origin and evolution of human consciousness are never far from your awareness. Whatever interests you, pursue it. There will always be an extra ear to give a listen because you project so much enthusiasm and passion into what you believe. Your directness and straightforward manner of communication can be refreshing in this age. Once you do find your real inner truth, you will be like a magnet that attracts avid listeners and believers of your message.

2nd Degree of Sagittarius

If this is your sun sign, it sometimes gives a meek and mild manner to what can be a very strong and forceful soul. You foray into the delights of religion and the philosophies of life. You seek principles of harmony, yet you might find yourself amid intense debates. Direct, outspoken, and without guile, your openness may cause discomfort to those who have much to hide and protect. You delight in weighty discussions and debates about the nature of God and humanity. More important, perhaps, is your interest in the rules and directives that become guidelines to people's behavior.

NOTABLES WITH THIS DEGREE:

Katherine Heigl: American actress, film producer

Ted Bundy: American serial killer

Lucky Luciano: Italian-born American mobster, father of modern organized crime

Baruch Spinoza: Jewish-Dutch philosopher, rationalist

Those of you with this number-sign combination can be outspoken and critical of social issues with which you have disagreement. At the same time, your manner at home can be cordial, cooperative, and compassionate. While your life may be simple, your mind is likely to wander into some of the most complex and perhaps controversial issues of the day. You seek to unravel the dichotomies of religion and philosophical ideas. Your curiosity can take you far into the reaches of the mind and manner of humankind. Your sensitivity to personal ethics and consideration of those near you garner you much admiration and appreciation from family and friends.

There is a karmic suggestion of having trodden on many toes in another time and place. While considerate of others, you still are not immune to taking a firm stand on your principles. Your physical appearance and mannerisms more often than not have a fragility and element of softness to them. Your manner is quick and concise. When your humor erupts, it can catch everyone off guard and throw them into fits of delight due to your keen insight and grasp of the unique. Your propensity toward thoughtfulness is much appreciated and adds to the positive regard in which many hold you.

3rd Degree of Sagittarius

If this is your sun sign, it will be difficult to keep you from sounding out your opinions and thoughts. This is a quintessential number-sign combination that adds a flourish to the already existing Sagittarius traits. Many of you will find your place in fields that involve media, sales, or other forms of communication fields. Your zeal and enthusiasm are like a tonic for those who want to speak out but are not as easily inclined to do so. There are some cautions that come with this combination. It is easy for you to be so zealous that you overstep courtesy and common sense, disturbing social amicability.

NOTABLES WITH THIS DEGREE:

Tina Turner: American singer, dancer, actress, author

Elwood Babbitt: American author, clairvoyant, medium

Zachary Taylor: American president, military leader

Bô Yin Râ: German philosopher, spiritual initiate, painter

There is a karmic suggestion that you have spoken out indiscriminately in another time and place. Such indiscretion got you into a lot of trouble. Even now, your directness can be threatening and offensive to those who are more repressed and draped in denial. This time around, you will learn about developing a style of presentation that speaks your truth without having to stir up negative reactions from those you want to reach the most. At its best, this combination suggests a person with a gilded tongue and the ability to charismatically touch the hearts of the masses.

You enjoy nature, the outdoors, and very possibly sporting events that let you be outside and free to excel in your physical abilities and prowess. You have a bountiful energy to set free in environments of merriment and joy with harmonious associates. Your flights of thought and philosophical wandering can take you into heightened states of spiritual reverie and mystical delight. You are stifled by the boring and routine and will be best suited to working with people who possess imaginative and forward-thinking natures.

4ᵗʰ Degree of Sagittarius

If this is your sun sign, you might be seen as a little more restrained than some of your Sagittarius contemporaries. The conservative 4 can reign in the free-flying and optimistic aspects that are so characteristically yours. At its best, the wait-and-prepare posture typical of the 4 can be a true blessing. By becoming rightfully prepared for the moment, it can just add luster and additional pizzazz when everything falls into place and brings a desired success. You may take a little longer to get there, but the dividends at the end can be greater.

NOTABLES WITH THIS DEGREE:

Jimi Hendrix: American musician, songwriter

Vera Fischer: Brazilian actress, beauty queen

Anders Celsius: Swedish astronomer, scientist, set temperature standards

There is the karmic hint that in another time and place you acted on total impulse without considering any implications about the outcome of your behavior. There is the suggestion you may have stepped on someone else's toes or spoken out glibly concerning something that another person was trying to hide or did not wish to reveal. Or you may have simply overstepped any acceptable boundaries as set by the community in which you dwelled. You are learning about where and when to express yourself in order to get the best possible results for personal and collective growth.

You come out with the most clever witticisms and insights at just the right moment to offset the tension and underlying elements of uneasiness among the group at hand. Those with this number-sign combination have the capacity to store information and then share it in the right setting. This quality makes you a valued and sought-after consultant. You take a little more time than some of the other Sagittarius clan to think through philosophical and psychological theories. Once you do reach a conclusion, it is likely to be appropriate and accurate within the context of the time and place you function.

5th Degree of Sagittarius

If this is your sun sign, make way for the mayhem, the magic, and the marvelous that will follow you through an exciting course of living. You move though events like a whirlwind of learning, drawing everything you can into your funnel of fun, fancy and formidability. Your daunting quest to live life to its fullest can be infectious and helps to get more passively oriented souls into the spirit of living rather than refining their skills as couch potatoes of consciousness. Just be careful that you don't move so fast that you forget to absorb any meaning or knowledge from your experiences.

NOTABLES WITH THIS DEGREE:

Caroline Kennedy: American author, lawyer, ambassador to Japan

Bruce Lee: Hong Kong–American actor, martial arts expert

Stefan Zweig: Austrian novelist, playwright, journalist, biographer

Rachida Dati: French politician, Minister of Justice

Anna Nicole Smith: American model, actress, sex symbol

There is the karmic hint of sometime long ago in your evolution having pushed the limits of experience within a restrained or controlled community. You may have been shunned or punished for stirring up behavior unacceptable to the etiquette of the time. Because of this, perhaps now you are afraid of reprisals or experience guilt from having caused suffering to those you influenced. There is the suggestion of several subsequent life experiences of extreme withdrawal from human activity. You may have become a monk, nun, or recluse of same kind in order to avoid getting into excessive activity. Now you seek a balance in which you can live on both the outer level and inner level of the soul and higher self. You seek to realign consciously with the cosmic dance that you once followed so well.

You will travel, talk, and get in touch with people from all cultures and classes of life. Your lightness of heart and optimistic attitude are fetching and fascinating to many people. The number-sign combination of wisdom and experience makes many of you inspirational communicators and effective teachers. You spread the word of spiritual, scientific, philosophical, or psychological advancement to seeking souls throughout the world.

6th Degree of Sagittarius

If this is your sun sign, you can be magical, mundane, and in many cases, magnificent in the way you play your role on the ongoing stage of human endeavor. From average to sublime, your behavior manages to stand out with an extra spark of personality, making you an intriguing soul. You have an innate sense of compassion for those you endear. Those who know you receive the goodness and benefit from your comforting touch. Some of that usual Sagittarius enthusiasm and ever-hopeful disposition is quietly tempered by this number-sign combination. You have a deep concern for the unfulfilled needs of humanity and take to heart the suffering that you see around you. You do not understand the motive or rationale of those who would purposely deceive and abuse others.

NOTABLES WITH THIS DEGREE:

William Blake: English poet, visionary, painter, printmaker

Ylenia Carrisi: Italian television personality

Rexella Van Impe: American religious spokesperson, television ministry co-host

Andrew McCarthy: American actor, producer, screenwriter, travel writer

Alfonso XII: King of Spain

There is the karmic hint of having been a part of deceiving and perhaps injuring others in another time and setting. You can use your Sagittarian naïveté and ever-optimistic persona as a screen to separate yourself from deep and disturbing emotional conflicts within. This can lead to a compulsive need to help others while at the same time causing you to run away from the same troubling issues within your own being. There is a dark side of past abuse that lingers in your unconscious, and you have come here to release the negative influence of that past in order to once again more truly let the unabashed light shine from within.

Your inquiring mind and restless soul will most likely eventually lead you into some form of service and healing-related endeavor. You could well be involved in developing new instruments or methods of improving the healing process of the human body, mind, and soul. There is an artistic side of this combination, and you are appreciative of aesthetics and maybe drawn to one or more of a myriad art forms.

7th Degree of Sagittarius

If this is your sun sign, you have chosen a path that will lead you to uncovering both the shocking and the sublime. Your inquisitive Sagittarius mind wants wisdom that works. You will not settle for endless intellectual discussions and debates that go nowhere and lead to nothing. You are likely to be at the forefront of investigative efforts of an academic, scientific, social, or commercial venture. Your lively spirit and sense of adventure can make this journey both fun and revealing. You do not like intellectual snobbishness, and you hold strong convictions that knowledge should be turned into beneficial products and processes that in the end serve to uplift the human experience.

NOTABLES WITH THIS DEGREE:

Mark Twain: American author, humorist

Louisa May Alcott: American novelist, teacher

Elmo Zumwalt: American naval admiral

Winston Churchill: British politician, Prime Minister of the UK, author, Nobel Prize laureate

There is the karmic hint that in another life setting, you were involved with the misuse of advanced knowledge that was distorted and used to enslave others and provide mastery of the few over the many. Perhaps it was an authority figure who dictated dogma over dealing with the issues of life freely. Maybe something that you discovered was misused by others. You distrust people with power. Rather, you search for the most efficient ways for finding the empowerment of self.

Your ability to appreciate and integrate the intellectual left brain and the intuitive right brain allows you to enter expanded realms of thought. Many of you who develop this further will at some time want to teach others how to open the door to the paranormal and transcendental. This number-sign combination also has a practical and down-to-earth side; you just want to enjoy nature and physical activities that work to integrate all levels of the body, mind, and spirit. You are valued for your grasp of issues and the entertaining manner in which you can reveal very weighty topics.

8th Degree of Sagittarius

If this is your sun sign, you can be more self-controlled and serious than many of your Sagittarius contemporaries. There is an air of convincing authority about you that allows you to command attention when you need it the most. You are more inclined toward being realistic rather than overly optimistic like the traditional Sagittarius personality. Perhaps you feel like the reins on your experience are held in tighter than you might like. There can be a strong issue with morality, and you can be outspoken about those you feel overstep the boundaries of righteous behavior.

NOTABLES WITH THIS DEGREE:

Olga Worrall: American psychic, author, healer

Magali Amadei: French model, actress

Abbie Hoffman: American radical social and civil activist

Vaira Vike-Freiberga: first female president of Latvia

There is the karmic hint that in another Earth sojourn, you could well have been blasphemous and belittling toward those who were devout in their faith and righteous in their lifestyle. Perhaps you purposely made it a point to seduce and dissuade those types of follower away from their devotion. Your amoral or immoral position on life was the ultimate guideline to whatever indulgent behavior you chose. You are still uneasy with strict directives that inhibit life experience. You seek to find reconciliation with spiritual bylaws that come straight from the heart rather than someone else's book.

There may be a period during your life of outlandish, extreme behavior of indulgence and excess. The normal restraints can give way to old unconscious desires coming from the past. You may suddenly realize this is not what you want and turn to a more inner-directed life of simplicity and restraint. Once centered within, your external world is full of meaningful and intense life interactions. As you resolve the lessons of this number-sign combination, you can be very convincing and effective when helping direct others to teachings and inner experiences to help them connect with the truth that comes directly from the heart and the soul.

9th Degree of Sagittarius

If this is your sun sign, your generosity as well as your high expectations of others can go off the charts. This number-sign combination highlights the natural tendency of Sagittarius to be open hearted and well intentioned. You may reach out to a stranger with unconditional love and get your pocket picked. You see the higher potential of humankind and want so much for it to manifest in this world. Unfortunately, not everyone is ready to live in the idealistic environment you know to be within reach. At the same time, you can make a noticeable contribution to the elevation of human consciousness by staying true to the inspiration that comes from within your higher self.

NOTABLES WITH THIS DEGREE:

Earlyne Chaney: American spiritualist, esoteric religious teacher

Jeff Green: American author, astrologer

Bette Midler: American actress, comedienne, singer

Woody Allen: American director, screenwriter, actor, comedian, musician, author

There is the karmic hint of misplaced trust carried over from experience in another time and setting. Perhaps you were part of a society that aspired to live a utopian dream of selfless community living. Maybe you were misled by someone who spoke of high spiritual ethics but secretly participated in hidden vices and fraudulent activity. You want to trust and believe in the best, but you are haunted by memories of previous deceptions and lies. When deception rears its ugly head, the place to start looking for the source is within your own self. You must clear out your own dark side if you are to see accurately into the heart and soul of another.

Your vision is far-reaching and is witness to hauntingly beautiful images of archetypal vibrations coming in from a higher dimension of consciousness. If you are an artist, you seek to integrate these impressions into your art form. If you are more scientific or academic by disposition, you are on the threshold of taking a quantum leap of insight or innovation. You can be a delightful entertainer and storyteller because of the way you tell your tales with slightly unexpected twists and turns.

10th Degree of Sagittarius

If this is your sun sign, this is a number-sign combination that often results in a most outspoken personality. You can reach many and have a large influence on the world. Just how you do that depends on your willingness to resolve dysfunctional issues in order to perform at your highest level. Many promoters, salespersons, media representatives, entertainers, and politicians have this combination. You have a grand flair for invention and recognizing novel and unconventional ways to get things done. Your fiery nature and unyielding will lead you into situations of high drama and intrigue. You can step on the toes of people in high places when you become misled or betrayed.

NOTABLES WITH THIS DEGREE:

Benny Hinn: Israeli author, televangelist

Bernard de Montréal: Canadian author, pioneer of evolutionary psychology

Britney Spears: American singer-songwriter, dancer, actress

Terry Cole-Whittaker: American new-thought minister, consultant, motivational speaker

Caroline Myss: American author, mystic, medical intuitive

You possess an abundance of energy and can capture the attention of others with your array of entertaining qualities. You are curious and fascinated by the glamour and intoxication of the fast lane. You can become quite enamored with your image and playing to your audience. You have a kind of sparkling magnetism that causes you to draw attention. Many performers have this combination. There is the karmic hint that in another time, you were emotionally overbearing and willfully controlling of a large population. You can be impetuous and offensive to the public when your penchant for indulgence takes you too far.

This combination suggests travel, adventure, and a variety of experiences in numerous ports of call. You are infatuated with life and hunger for more knowledge about what is beyond. When awakened, you become devoted to spirituality and metaphysical exploration. You seek to blend spirit with matter and may enjoy martial arts or yoga-like exercises that help to mingle the yin of the gods with the yang of humanity. You can easily live in the clouds, but you are learning that to be human means to live on this plane of matter.

11ᵗʰ Degree of Sagittarius

If this is your sun sign, you most likely radiate a little extra spark and walk with a little extra spring compared to some of the other Sagittarius number-sign combinations. You exercise a special savvy in the way you present your thoughts and beliefs. While you still radiate that Sagittarius optimism along with those gregarious traits that endear you to so many, you have an extra sensitivity to the nuances of social blending. This allows you to read other people quickly and know how to present yourself in a manner that interacts smoothly and brings out information that others might not share as easily if they were with someone else.

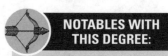

NOTABLES WITH THIS DEGREE:

Katarina Witt: German Olympic figure skater, model

Brendan Fraser: Canadian-American actor

Fauziah Latiff: Malaysian actress, singer

Franz Klammer: Austrian Olympic skier

There is a karmic clue here that in another time and setting, you may have used inside information to control someone or perhaps defeat an enemy. For example, you might have been a spy or undercover agent. Such a position could have been used for good or malfeasance. You have worked in the crevices of the dark side and know its nature well. You have a chance to use your esoteric understanding to uplift mass consciousness, or you could slide into the role of manipulator and use others for your benefit. You may choose to be a kind of New Age detective, bringing out the best in others by rooting out the dark nature that gets in their way.

There is a capacity for clear thinking and penetration into some of the sparkling and brilliant new archetypes of color, sounds, and symbols that now permeate the planet from the higher reaches of cosmic consciousness. Despite seeing its dark side so clearly, you are forever optimistic about the evolution of humanity because you also see the higher potential, believing fervently that humanity will soon reach its divine purpose and higher potential.

12th Degree of Sagittarius

If this is your sun sign, this number-sign combination adds to the already outspoken and inspirational qualities of the Sagittarius personality. It will be difficult to keep you from speaking out through song, speech, or any other form of media. There is suffering and struggle with this combination, and your life will reflect sensitivity to those who sacrifice and go through great odds to get the things they want out of life. You project pathos and pain well. Should you receive the calling to perform on stage, you will most likely do tragedy very well. For those of you who do not reach the stage, your dramatic reaction to events leaves you noteworthy in people's memories.

NOTABLES WITH THIS DEGREE:

Walt Disney: American animator, producer, screenwriter, director, business magnate

Eva Joly: Norwegian-born French magistrate, social reformer

Benjamin Creme: Scottish artist, author, esoteric speaker

Marisa Tomei: American actress

You are colorful and energetic, and you possess the capacity to explore and do many things. There is a more guarded quality to this combination that distinguishes it from the usual open and gregarious Sagittarius personality. There is a karmic suggestion that you have been deeply hurt and betrayed in another time and place. Therefore, there is a reserved part of you that takes time to warm up. You are learning once more to be free of spirit and able to trust yourself and others. You excel as a teacher in special education programs or in positions where you can give others the confidence to overcome their own personal shortcomings.

There is a strong sense of justice, morality, and the desire to see the universal principles of harmony and balance reflected in the everyday lives of humanity. Your spirit of adventure can take you to many lands and expose you to many ideas of life and how to live it. You wish to see people free from the limitations of social repression and from the restrictions of their own insecurities. Your idealism draws you to charismatic leaders and movements that seek to bring perfection to this troubled world.

13ᵗʰ Degree of Sagittarius

If this is your sun sign, you live with a kind of fatalistic attitude toward life and the events that happen to you and around you. This can motivate you to seek your own destiny, or it may leave you passive and reactive to whatever life places in your path. You may believe that any real effort to get ahead will probably come to no avail. This can lead to reckless abandon as you tempt fate by taking uncalled-for risks. For many of you with this number-sign combination, it is easy to assume a kind of happy-go-lucky persona. This allows you to interact with others in a manner that requires little commitment and keeps you from getting into demanding attachments.

NOTABLES WITH THIS DEGREE:

Robert Hand: American author, astrologer, academician

Gary Allan: American musician, singer

Martin van Buren: American president, American Vice President, U.S. Secretary of State

Little Richard: American recording artist, singer, songwriter, musician

There is the karmic hint of having avoided responsibility and thoughtfulness in another time and place. You may have been ruthless and uncaring in the pursuit of whatever it is you wanted. You find yourself at odds with authority, and when under pressure, you can resign yourself to childish rebellion and immature responses to circumstances. You are learning to grow up and have an adult response to the pressures and challenges you face. You have the determination and tools to accomplish much in life, and it is up to you how much you are willing to give in order to get what you want while applying the dynamic universal laws of mastery and mind.

You are capable of much charm and childlike playfulness. In the right time and context, this makes you a wonderful playmate and companion when it comes to working off pressure and stress. Taken too far, these very same qualities lead to immature and irresponsible activity and indulgence. In one way or another, you will manage to find yourself at the center of attention. You do a most bedazzling dance that can lead to wonderment or worry from others.

14th Degree of Sagittarius

If this is your sun sign, your quest for living can take you through some dazzling hoops of consciousness along the way through life. You radiate a transcendent quality when you begin to sense your true source of wisdom and empowerment. At your best, you radiate an aura of faith and trust in the eternal truths that you seek to live by. When you fall short, your sense of compassion and hope softens your tendency toward criticism and complaint. Your zest for living introduces you to an expanded range of experiences that drown you with a wonderment of universal design.

NOTABLES WITH THIS DEGREE:

Alberto Contador: Spanish world-class bicyclist, Tour de France winner

Dave Brubeck: American jazz pianist, improvisational musician

Dulce María: Mexican actress, singer-songwriter

Eli Wallach: American stage and screen actor

It hasn't always been that way. There is the karmic hint of previous lifetimes when your passions and possessiveness of creation caused you to grasp, judge, and harshly hold on to objects of accumulation. At times, jealousy and rage caused you to turn against those close to you and attach those who threatened you. When you are ego-centered, you see things as being your own. When you are cosmically centered, you see things as they are. You are learning to see things and accept people as they are. This awareness allows you to understand universal supply and the sharing of divine bountifulness.

Those with this number-sign combination are active, ardent, and always looking over the horizon for new and exciting adventures. Physical activity is important to you, and you may choose to excel in some area of sport or competitive athletics. You wonder at the design and construction of things, and you possess an element of engineering mentality. You are not opposed to having a good time, and you can often be at the helm of some frolicking good parties or assemblies of friends for high-spirited occasions. Special occasions can include rituals of soaring into transcendent realms of light and truth in your quest to know more of divine design.

15th Degree of Sagittarius

If this is your sun sign, you have a baffling quality of behavior that both mystifies and captivates. This adds mystery to a sun sign already known for unpredictability and paradoxical temperament. You can switch from saint to sinner, benign to unmerciful, or charming to scheming in the twinkle of an eye. There is a touch of cynicism that you couch in humor and rivulets of mental parrying that confuse just what it is you are really trying to say. Perhaps your internal conflicts also get in the way of you knowing just what you mean.

NOTABLES WITH THIS DEGREE:

Larry Bird: American professional basketball player and coach

Jim Morrison: American singer-songwriter, poet

Gregg Allman: American singer-songwriter, musician

Noam Chomsky: American philosopher, political activist, linguistics theoretician

You are both alluring and put-offish in the same moment. Many will find you engaging, curiously drawn to further understand your unique and mysterious personality. Maybe it is because you have been bequeathed with so many contradictory character traits that people are curious to know more about you. In the process, they might secretly wish to find out more about their own selves that has eluded their personal quests for self-understanding.

There is a karmic hint of being both a con and a cherub in another time and place. You return now with a desire to integrate and acknowledge seemingly irreconcilable facets of personality. This process may be as baffling to you as it can be to those who know you. You remain devilishly delightful in the way you present the story of repentance and release, making you popular as a communicator when it comes to the art of motivation. You have a valuable story to tell about the chronicles of personal growth, and many of you will be drawn to positions that allow you to teach and assist others who struggle on their own paths of personal integration.

16th Degree of Sagittarius

If this is your sun sign, do not be surprised when at some time in your life you catch the attention of a lot of people. There is a determination and drive associated with this number-sign combination that causes you to be relentless and sure once you are on track to what you want to achieve. With favorable aspects, the chances are good for reaching the top in what you do. There will be many dramatic twists and turns along the way, however; and all will not be a bed of roses. You will find yourself amid controversy at some time during your life, and you may be the one who generates it. This combination might be seen in the position of spokesperson for the downtrodden and less fortunate.

NOTABLES WITH THIS DEGREE:

Donny Osmond: American singer, musician, dancer, actor, author

Judi Dench: English actress

Elisabeth Schwarzkopf: Austrian-British soprano opera singer, recitalist

Sammy Davis Jr.: African-American dancer, singer, musician, comedian, actor

Your inquisitiveness about human nature can lead you into studies of religion, psychology, or philosophy. Some of you will choose to act out your convictions rather than engage in prolonged studies. There is the karmic hint of having become dogmatically attached in another time and place to some spiritual or theocratic system of thought. Perhaps you tried too hard to convert others to your beliefs, or maybe you were in the position to coerce people into following your way of life. You will be placed into a position of choosing between following a dogma or living true to what is existentially valid in the moment.

People with this combination often have a way of leaping to gigantic conclusions that eventually find their way to becoming true. You may frequently ask yourself where the information is coming from, since it often surprises even you. There will be many events during your life that cause you to ponder and question the process of fate and circumstances.

17ᵗʰ Degree of Sagittarius

If this is your sun sign, you are quite capable of shining the light so brightly that no one can resist your tales of truth and deeds of daring. You illuminate dark places, shining a spotlight on areas previously left uncovered. There is great joy in the revelation of new truth. Reactions may not always be rosy. When the light shines brightly, this number-sign combination can reveal the dark, dangerous, and demonic as well as the divine. When you stir up the shadow side of others, they will fight you and resist you to the fullest extent of their maligned powers.

NOTABLES WITH THIS DEGREE:

Kirk Douglas: American actor, producer, author

Maharaj Ji: Indian spiritual leader, meditation teacher

Teri Hatcher: American actress, author, NFL cheerleader

Sonia Gandhi: Italian-born Indian politician, social activist

There is a karmic hint of having delved into the dark arts in other life sojourns of your soul. If you hide from your own dark side, the negative forces can do you in; the riddance of those forces might be your intended path. If you have reached a state of reconciliation with your own dark side, you can become most effective at assisting others in doing the same. You are here to spread the joyful news of good tidings right when the world appears to be in one of its darkest moments of despair and doom.

You are learned and level headed, and you long to tell the story of humanity as it is. You are frustrated with the prevarication of those who control the media and institutions of learning that skew history to fit their own selfish agenda. You dance to the rhythm of the cosmos, listen to the songs of the angels, and await the day that the world is reunited with its plan of highest purpose. You are active in keeping your mind, body, and soul alert and prepared to take on the challenges of converting the world from the pit of darkness back into a beacon of light throughout this sector of creation.

18ᵗʰ Degree of Sagittarius

If this is your sun sign, you may struggle to keep on the optimistic high note of life as per most of your Sagittarius family. Those with this number-sign combination are observant of human nature and enjoy witnessing the back and forth of human power play. Where many of your contemporaries see roses, you are very quick to identify the good, the bad, and the ugly. There is an old saying that there is a little larceny in everyone, and you have the lingering feeling that it could lurk somewhere within you. This may be true even if you have not done anything to warrant those feelings.

NOTABLES WITH THIS DEGREE:

Bhagwan Shree Rajneesh: Indian guru, spiritual theorist, oil and gas billionaire

John Malkovich: American actor, producer, director, fashion designer

There is a karmic hint that in another life setting, you could have hidden from earlier transgressions and unacceptable misconduct. You did everything you could to maintain the proper code of social behavior but were nagged by the guilt of conduct for which you found it hard to forgive yourself. Your Sagittarian nature wants to be carefree and full of positive life force. As you uncover and release the negative influences of the past, you will experience a shift in consciousness of a dramatic and profound nature. You could then lead, inspire, and help elevate the awareness of those who seek enlightenment but are also hooked and bound to their negative pasts.

People are attracted to your high spirits and willingness to reach for the stars. It is not always so easy for you to keep your feet planted on the ground as you ponder the celestial wonders. You could be asked to lead when you would most like to wander, or you might be asked to take on a burden of responsibility when you would rather be prancing about with a poetic rhythm of mental and emotional celebration. Once you have found your calling, you can be most convincing and accomplish much.

19th Degree of Sagittarius

If this is your sun sign, your imagination soars to the noble and romantic, but your real life may be full of tragic pitfalls and compromises. You set a high standard of ideals for yourself, but slip into the less than sublime as reality overtakes your desired aspirations. You are colorful, convincing, and clearly persuasive about what you want to have. You can be entertaining and delightful in one breath and then turn surly and sour with the slightest upset to your ego. You are sometimes drawn to people for what they can get you rather than for who they are.

NOTABLES WITH THIS DEGREE:

Frank Sinatra: American singer, actor

Karl Renz: German author, musician, visual artist

Brenda Lee: American singer

Viswanathan Anand: Indian chess grand master

There is a karmic hint at the previous misuse of power and influence to get your selfish needs fulfilled rather than considering the best for others. Guilt haunts you throughout much of your life, and you may try to assuage this through generous gifts to charity and people who support you. You can be sidetracked by power plays and influenced by those who manipulate your ideals for their own gain. There is a detachment in the way you treat personal relationships as you try to overcome a distrust of closeness and intimacy in this life.

There is a high charge of energy often associated with this number-sign combination, and you may very well radiate a special aura of prominence and charisma. You are hesitant to trust, but when you finally accept someone, you are generous and embracing. There will be a few guarded souls in your inner circle but not much of an all-inclusive reach into the social climate of sharing and interaction. You are independent, aloof, and always looking for the perfect partner or mate in your personal and commercial endeavors. At its best, there is an inspiring quality in this combination that encourages transformation and elevation of human aspirations.

20th Degree of Sagittarius

If this is your sun sign, you tiptoe through life in a delicate dance of diplomatic maneuvers that delight your supporters and disturb those who would try to misrepresent you in the social arena. Your air of optimism brings hope to those who are disenchanted with the world, seeing little hope of social reform or human behavior. On the other hand, when you discover corruption that has gone undetected, you can become as cynical as the best of them. You very much want to see governments and institutions run with integrity and forthrightness. Many with this number-sign combination will find themselves right at home within the challenges and events of institutional politics.

NOTABLES WITH THIS DEGREE:

Dionne Warwick: American singer, actress, TV show host, U.S. Ambassador of Health

Marc Ravalomanana: president of Madagascar, politician

Curd Jürgens: German-Austrian actor

Portia Simpson-Miller: first female president of Jamaica, political activist

There is a karmic hint that you have been the perpetrator of deceit and social manipulation in another time and place. You seek to right the wrongs that deep in your heart you feel guilty about having committed. There is an air of reformist about you that motivates others to get things corrected. The transformation of humankind is something you aspire to assist with. You are very much interested in your own evolution and the development of your consciousness. You move through some very impressive social circles and hobnob with those who will take part in altering history.

There is an air of refinement and, some would say, dignity about you. You care about fine things and appreciate quality in craftsmanship. Your wit and charming manner make you a hit at parties and social occasions. Your sensitivity to others' hardship and suffering make you a natural in areas of service that aspire to atone for injustices of human behavior. Sometimes people may find you to be naïve and gullible; however, you are quite astute about the underhandedness of human nature and quite capable of ferreting out the mendacities and hidden games that people play.

21ˢᵗ Degree of Sagittarius

If this is your sun sign, you are a constant source of radiant energy and enthusiasm in the pursuit of living life to its fullest. At your best, you glimmer in the sunlight and shine like a jewel. Many of you will be attracted to some form of communication or an artful form of self-expression. You are natural, articulate speakers. Sometimes you can aim too high and are shot down by those who are more inclined toward skepticism or cynicism. It is hard to keep you down for long, though, and your perpetual optimism will have you back at things within a short time.

A hidden part of you fears to speak out and let your light shine brightly. There is the karmic hint that in another time and place you were highly vocal and outspoken about errors in the ways of those who had been given the responsibility of stewardship over the many. Perhaps you lost your life or were severely punished for speaking out against wrongdoings, even though what you observed and what you said were true. That part of you still can cause you to hesitate at moments when it is time to step up and identify what is going wrong.

You are learning to give without being taken advantage of. There are those who would feed off your light and drain your energy rather than sharing with you in an even exchange. It is important to learn not to burn your bright wick at both ends but to direct it purposefully. Those with this number-sign combination will likely find themselves traveling and oftentimes find restoration out in the open among the many settings of nature. Your faith and personal drive is inspiring to many, and others admire you for your staying power and continued optimism.

NOTABLES WITH THIS DEGREE:

Sanjay Gandhi: Indian politician, automobile executive

Dick Van Dyke: American actor, comedian, dancer, writer, producer

Aga Khan IV: Imam of Nizari Ismailism, racehorse owner/breeder

Mary Todd Lincoln: First Lady of the United States

22nd Degree of Sagittarius

If this is your sun sign, your sometimes scattered and swashbuckling Sagittarius personality can become rather firmly planted on the ground as if by some divinely orchestrated intent. This number-sign combination brings out focus, direction, and intent to the inspired and optimistic Sagittarius personality. You may very well know early on what you want to do and how you are going to do it long before many of your contemporaries have a clue about their lives. If your chart has poor aspects, there could be a delay in your revelation. In such a case, you might spend a good part of your life among the clueless.

There is the karmic hint that you previously participated in an experiment to establish a utopian-style environment on planet Earth. Your vision was clear, but perhaps you relied more on inspiration than perspiration. You might not have thought out the day-to-day details of construction and administration. Maybe you chose to work with enthusiastic but unqualified people in an attempt at perfection. Possibly you were undermined by those who prospered from failure. You are here to learn that what you want to achieve takes careful preparation at every stage of development. You want to be sure to attract qualified associates. You can make dreams come true, and it is possible to see your vision become reality.

You need time to pull in and connect with your inner self. You very likely alternate from being outgoing and engaging in public events to suddenly retreating from the outer world as if in search of something more fulfilling to the soul. It is important to keep searching, but the answer most likely will come directly from quiet contemplation. You have had trouble finding reliable and trustworthy people in past endeavors, but there will be an opportunity to find your spiritual family and get important things done in the spirit of fun and sharing.

NOTABLES WITH THIS DEGREE:

Eben Alexander: American neurosurgeon, author of near-death experiences

John Paulson: American hedge fund manager, investor, philanthropist

Nero: Roman emperor

Pope Julius II: Catholic Pope, aggressive foreign policy maker and builder

L. L. Zamenhof: Polish doctor, linguist, inventor of Esperanto language

23rd Degree of Sagittarius

If this is your sun sign, you are fun, funky, and decidedly full of life. Your zest for living is contagious, and when you are at your best, people flock around you to experience a little portion of that exuberance. You enjoy many avenues and outlets of curiosity and possess endless energy. Your pace of living can be exhausting to many. There is a bit of a caution about overdoing things to the point of putting your physical and emotional health under stress. This should not stop you, however, from the healthy and vibrant pursuit of maximum vitality.

There is the karmic hint that in another time and moment you were swept away by theories and teachings of pure theoretical reasoning and intellectual speculation. Once you realized these concepts did not really work in the daily world, you may have plunged into a world of escapist addictions and indulgence. You can be attracted to exploiting others' weaknesses for personal gain. You will consequently find yourself more attracted to down-to-earth, functional philosophies of living rather than the dry and detached academic philosophies that remain above most people's heads, having little day-to-day value.

This is a classic number-sign combination of travel, exploration, and investigation into numerous realms of social, metaphysical, and esoteric strategies for living. You are mellow, mild, and unmeddling when socializing with others. This puts people at ease, allowing them to be open with you in return. Your curiosity and whim for the unknown keep you at the edge of new thinking and part of the pioneering people you find around you. You mix among many diverse cultures and meet the most varied and unusual people in your journeys in this world and into the realms of higher consciousness. For many of you, the greatest peace comes from settling into a comfortable spiritual place of experiencing the living truth.

NOTABLES WITH THIS DEGREE:

Lynne Palmer: American actress, astrologer, author

Margaret Mead: American cultural anthropologist, researched human sexuality

Gustave Eiffel: French architect, structural engineer, designed Eiffel Tower

Maruschka Detmers: Dutch actress

Najoua Belyzel: French singer

24th Degree of Sagittarius

If this is your sun sign, you tread your way through life somewhat more quietly than many of your Sagittarius contemporaries. You have learned how to speak softly but carry a determined stick. This number-sign combination gives you the perseverance to stay with an issue until you have settled it or completed it to your satisfaction. You are keen about the social welfare of others and keep a close eye on the social developments that are of interest to you. You may be drawn to issues such as animal rights or other circumstances where abuse is the issue. When called on, you can work with infinite detail and bring a complicated project to closure with thoroughness and professionalism.

NOTABLES WITH THIS DEGREE:

Jane Austen: English author of romantic fiction

Wassily Kandinsky: Russian painter, printer, art theorist

Ludwig van Beethoven: German composer, pianist

J. Paul Getty: Anglo-American oil tycoon, art collector

There is a karmic hint that you have been careless in another time period about the health and welfare of others. Perhaps you were addicted to the rush of conflict and aggression, or maybe you put others under more strain than their bodies and emotions could handle. You may be overly concerned about taking care of others while negligent of your own needs. It will require a little extra effort for you to maintain the daily tasks of maintaining your body and soul.

You are more cautious about taking risks and plunging into the unknown than some of your Sagittarius peers, but when you do plunge, more often than not, you come out of the situation with good results. You have a refined quality and may be drawn to the finer arts rather than less-cultured forms of entertainment and expression. Many of you will end up in situations where you can write or play a part recording statistics and data for important research and development that will have a large impact on the population. You enjoy the steady, serene, and sagacious.

25th Degree of Sagittarius

If this is your sun sign, you range from articulate and outspoken to barely audible and uncertain. There are several internal conflicts that affect the timing of your social clock. The Sagittarius part wants to speak out loudly and spread the word of human freedom and joy. There is a karmic hint of past-life conflicts with social order and leadership. Perhaps you were a rebel and suffered rancor or even death for your efforts. Maybe social opinion turned against you and made you a suffering martyr. The underlying result leaves you caught with mixed emotions about social mores and expected social behavior.

NOTABLES WITH THIS DEGREE:

Milla Jovovich: American model, singer, actress, fashion designer

James Van Praagh: American medium, author, movie consultant

Willy Brandt: Chancellor of West Germany, politician

Andrew Thomas: Australian-born American astronaut, aerospace engineer

You are an ardent student of history and the evolution of human consciousness on the planet. This number-sign combination can give an academic quality to your research methods and bring you great satisfaction in uncovering events and circumstances that have shaped the awakening of human awareness. You particularly appreciate theories that can be readily applied in a manner to bring about practical benefits to society. Pure speculation leaves you with a feeling of uselessness and frustration because you want to see results from the use of intellectual machinations.

You move in a flash from open and communicative to withdrawn and reclusive. It is hard to get a grasp of just what you stand for and who you are because you are so changeable. When open, you are effusive and excited about what you have learned or discovered. In this time, you are inspirational and motivating to others. You have a penchant for detail and must have specific proof before you are willing to accept another's claims or assumptions. When uncertain, you become hesitant and can rattle off all sorts of miscellaneous information just to appear knowledgeable and in control.

26ᵗʰ Degree of Sagittarius

If this is your sun sign, your imagination and search for reality takes you through a wide range of ideas and avenues in trying to capture the nature of your humanity. You are curious, confident, and constantly turning over stones to get a glimpse into some nuance of the human personality. This number-sign combination brings an element of managerial competency and organization to the zealous and impulsive Sagittarius personality. Along with your imagination is a keen sense of detail and knowing how to bring out the talent of those who work with you. This allows for innovation and success in the projects and endeavors you select to take part in.

NOTABLES WITH THIS DEGREE:

Brad Pitt: American actor, producer

Christina Aguilera: American singer-songwriter, dancer, producer, mentor

Paul Klee: German-Swiss artist, educator

Jonathan Cainer: British columnist, astrologer

Leonid Brejhnev: General Chariman of the Communist party, politician

If your chart has poor aspects, you can be belittling and abusive. Such behavior deters from the excellence you are capable of producing. There is a karmic suggestion that you have been publicly abusive and unfairly belittling of those who have opposed you. You are harsh with yourself and demanding about the performance of others. In the end, they usually give you their best, and you can feel good about what you have done. Your openness about life allows you to take in a full range of experiences. It is from this vast perspective that you single out certain issues to focus on. Because you see them in a broader light, you are able to touch the heart of social reaction and get the desired response.

This combination brings a sense of stability to the restless and sometimes impulsive Sagittarius personality. There is a potential within this combination to attract prosperity and the better things in life. Although the Sagittarius personality is independent and not easily tied down, this combination does encourage the nesting instinct, and you will be happy behind the white picket fence once you have found the right partner. Most likely, that partner brings mental stimulation and depth, along with the attributes of good looks and sensual appeal.

27ᵗʰ Degree of Sagittarius

If this is your sun sign, you may be a little more tactful, tidy, and timid than many of your outgoing Sagittarius brothers and sisters. Although that Sagittarius spark is there, you may hide it under a bushel until you fully understand just how bright it is and how you can best let your illumination radiate freely. At best, you are emotional, intuitive, and highly attuned to the archetypal energies of the universal feminine energies. Your consciousness is circular and inclusive, and the feminine qualities of embracing and nurturing can be seen in the activities that you perform. Much of this might still be unconscious and not so obvious to the sleeping world around you.

NOTABLES WITH THIS DEGREE:

Steven Spielberg: American director, screenwriter, producer

Alyssa Milano: American actress, producer, singer

John Milton: English poet, essayist, civil servant

Uri Geller: Israeli illusionist, magician, psychic

There is the karmic hint of periods of illumination gone awry in a previous spiral through the woven web of Earth's lessons. Perhaps you awakened the kundalini coil prematurely and spiraled out of control in a delirium of a drug-like stupor and psychedelic deluge of fantasies galore. Possibly, your intellectual rigidity and strongly based patriarchal training caused you to distrust the emanations of the soul and intimations of intuition. Maybe you wrongly used information gained from higher states of mind. You are learning once more to trust the higher mind and to ground its wisdom into daily forms of benefit to all.

You are a student of humankind, always looking for sources of information to clarify the real origin of this curious life form among the stars. It would not be out of character for those with this number-sign combination to contemplate the thought that perhaps their true core selves have come from some point far beyond terrestrial beginnings. Such thoughts are kept close to the vest and rarely shared with anyone. You do value those close friends and associates with whom you can speculate about theories of spiritual and scientific thinking, life throughout the universe, and the breakthroughs that would come from sharing information with other advanced civilizations.

28ᵗʰ Degree of Sagittarius

If this is your sun sign, you have the opportunity to stand out in your Sagittarius class. There is a strong desire with this number-sign combination to be someone and accomplish something. You are blessed with the social and personal skills to accomplish what you want through any number of avenues and tactics. Some of that Sagittarius straight-shooting style of speech may be modified with some smooth talk and subtle skills of diplomacy. This will serve you well as you maneuver your way through the web of power and intrigue on your climb to the top.

NOTABLES WITH THIS DEGREE:

Chris Evert: American world professional tennis player

Hu Jintao: President of People's Republic of China, Communist party leader

Infanta Elena: Duchess of Lugo

Leo X: Catholic Pope at time of the Protestant Reformation

There is the karmic suggestion that in another moment of your soul journey, you got caught up in an ideology that went wrong and resulted in the upheaval and disruption of lives. Perhaps you were part of an attempt at creating a utopian culture that turned dysfunctional and doomed. Maybe you sought freedom for the masses only to see the masses manipulated into another situation of control and servitude. You long to witness the administration of laws that reflect the laws of the universe and divine justice. You are tempted by the perks of power and toys of pleasure that come with money and influence. The soul seeks to find realignment with higher purpose and administration of the higher laws.

In you lighter moments, you likely enjoy the outlet of sports and vigorous athletic activity. Much of this ability comes naturally to you. More often than not with this number-sign combination, a touch of competition adds a little spice to the flavor of the contest. Your quest for knowledge and the accumulation of details, facts, and statistics provides you with information that is useful both in commerce and the daily art of social conviviality. You can be witty and urbane, and when necessary, you can change your social demeanor to fit the circle of associates around you.

29th Degree of Sagittarius

If this is your sun sign, you are highly idealistic and persistent in wanting to make the world perfect according to your standards. You can be charming and most fascinating when speaking about the world and events as you see them. However, there is also a kind of cold and detached quality that allows you to become indifferent toward those who challenge or disagree with you. Those of you with this number-sign combination espouse a philosophy of accounting for the collective good but are not immune to grabbing the best of the goodies for yourselves. With adverse aspects, you can essentially become out of touch with the real events around you by escaping into the hopes, aspirations, dreams, and idealistic aspirations you have for yourselves and society.

NOTABLES WITH THIS DEGREE:

Frank Zappa: American songwriter, musician, producer, and film director

Samuel L. Jackson: American actor, producer, civil rights activist

Benjamin Disraeli: British Prime Minister, writer, aristocrat

Phil Donahue: American talk show host, producer, author

There is the karmic hint of having been fanatically devoted to a belief system that justified any type of control or reprisal of those who might have disagreed with your view. Perhaps you were harsh and abusive to rebels. You are ardently supportive of systems that espouse improved conditions for the masses but can become vindictive against those who do not see your way of creating the best conditions for others. You are learning to get in touch with your own inner reality rather than attempting to find perfection out there in the exterior world.

You enjoy the trappings of honor and the display of achievement. Your search for public adulation can get in the way of just being natural and who you really are deep within the eternal core of self. You will be introduced to many cultural belief systems and people representing a multitude of concepts for social evolution. These encounters can open up your vision to more humane ways of dealing with the population or can lead you to become more provincial and smug in self-nurtured ideas about the betterment of humankind.

CAPRICORN

0 Degree of Capricorn

If this is your sun sign, you may climb mountains, move mountains, or buy a cabin in the foothills to sit and look at mountains. There is always ambiguity with the number 0 when it comes to finding your path or purpose in life, and with this number-sign combination, you may have more potential than most people. The question is where to focus the talent and how to use it. You might have so many choices that it seems impossible to choose. Perhaps you look to your parents or someone else to tell you what to do. Often you end up getting poor advice when you turn to seek advice from another person.

NOTABLES WITH THIS DEGREE:

Srinivasa Ramanujan: Indian mathematician, largely self-taught

Chet Baker: American jazz trumpeter, flugelhornist, singer

Silvia of Sweden: Queen of Sweden

Diane Sawyer: American television reporter, newscaster

You are at a turning point in your spiraling evolution, and it is up to you to make choices and do what your innermost conviction directs. There is the karmic suggestion that you reached a similar plateau in another time and situation. Perhaps you buckled under the pressure and took the easy way out. Maybe you became ego involved and messed up an opportunity to make huge progress in your evolutionary journey. This is the time to overcome old fears and resentments. You can accomplish much in your soul journey if you put yourself to the task.

You may feel you are unique, and most likely, you will stand out in the crowd because of unusual abilities or gifts of the soul. You prefer to be around new things that are in progress, and you are most comfortable with people who are also at the forefront of making things happen. You have an opportunity to see much of the world and to meet many people from different cultures and conditions of life on this planet. Your soul thirsts for truth and craves to find its direct path to the summit of consciousness.

1ˢᵗ Degree of Capricorn

If this is your sun sign, you are industrious, bold, and deliberate in your ambition to get things done. This enhances the Capricorn flair for achievement and gives an extra jolt of pizzazz to an already high-voltage capacity for success. You are confident and capable of taking on tasks that others have abandoned. You love to succeed where others find only resistance and defeat. Those with this number-

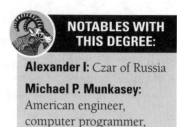

sign combination often have the capacity for discovering improved methods of management and efficiency. You know how to get things done properly, promptly, and when necessary, prodigiously. You will likely find yourself as the problem solver in your circle of friends and associates.

There is the karmic hint of having avoided leadership or decision making in another time and setting. Perhaps you played an important role in starting something that went woefully wrong and have since been hesitant to take initiative. You may feel compelled to tell people how to do things or constantly point out flaws in others. Life will put you in positions where you will be called on to demonstrate your ingenuity and originality. Once you are comfortable with yourself and your situation, you will do well and achieve much satisfaction.

Underneath what appears to be a rather cool and standoffish Capricorn temperament, you can be quite congenial and open. Your keen sense of observation leads you to clever and witty insights about the foibles and follies of human endeavor. You do enjoy spinning things with a touch of comedic humor. Many of you are naturals at mechanical and technical apparatus and often have the latest technological toy in your treasury of professional tools. You are particularly appreciated during crises because of your keen ability to make quick assessments and take appropriate action.

2nd Degree of Capricorn

If this is your sun sign, you are wary, wise, and capable of weaving your way through the political traps of commerce and community. While the Capricorn nature is to rise to the top and lead, with this number-sign combination, you may be more indecisive than some of your contemporaries. It is easy for you to get caught in the minute details of things and miss out on the importance of getting the big project completed. You might spread yourself thin due to your interest in so many projects and ideas.

Your social skills are crafted to get you what you want from others. When called on, you can spew forth charm and euphemistic praise. However, your fundamental nature is to be cautious and reserved. There is a karmic hint of times and places when you were indifferent to social opinion and in conflict with the collective viewpoint. There is a distrust of others' judgment and a tendency to go your way sometimes just to prove others wrong. You will confront many hurdles regarding public reaction and the whims of the collective unconscious.

You think in terms of what works efficiently and what can make an improvement in the flow of social intercourse. Others may see you as impersonal and insensitive. While you do want to produce the best, you can be more attached to the product than to the person who receives it. One of your life lessons is learning to be more considerate of what others think and feel. If you are appreciative rather than competitive in your interaction with others, you may find that it brings out the best results from those with whom you interact.

3rd Degree of Capricorn

If this is your sun sign, you are considerate, convincing, and careful in the manner that you express your emotions in public. This can be a very guarded number-sign combination, and trusting others may not be easy for you. Although you might put on an open public persona, you are more inclined to protect yourself and your feelings from external scrutiny. You are industrious and quite capable of getting ahead in life. Many of you will reach a high level of accomplishment in the area of interest that you choose. The charm of the combination of Capricorn drive and the number 3 opens many possible avenues to success.

NOTABLES WITH THIS DEGREE:

Helena Christensen: Danish supermodel, beauty queen, Victoria Secret's angel, photographer

Humphrey Bogart: American actor

Sissy Spacek: American actress, singer

Conrad Hilton: American hotelier

Despite the outward appearance of success, you may struggle and suffer internally with the emotional quibbling among the representatives of groups and institutions that carry on human endeavors. You run up against those who are untrustworthy and willing to compromise their integrity for some form of personal gain or recognition. Many of you can become cynical over time, trying to resist the corruption and abuse of special interest groups. There is a karmic hint that in another time and setting, you may have purposely taken a position against mass opinion, resulting in considerable humiliation or punishment. Perhaps you were trapped into taking a stance against your own beliefs. Maybe you sold yourself out to someone rather than being true to a cause.

Life will place you in situations in which you will have to be tenacious and determined if you are going to make the headway that you desire. The 3 vibrations add some charm and a potential soft touch that makes it easier for you to weave your way through the thorns of debate and the delays of human endeavors. You will have a few very close and trusted friends who support you and encourage you throughout most of your life.

4th Degree of Capricorn

If this is your sun sign, this number-sign combination gives you both the drive and the endurance to complete your appointed round. The tenacity of the 4 along with the upward mobility of the goat make for powerful potential to push your way to a point of prominence in whatever you choose. Your street sense and down-to-earth practicality are both huge weapons in your arsenal of achievement. Once focused, there is virtually nothing that can stop you. It can help to nurture your light side, as the seriousness of this combination can turn off potential associates and allies.

NOTABLES WITH THIS DEGREE:

Louis Pasteur: French chemist, microbiologist

Mother Meera: Indian healer, spiritual teacher

Barbara Mandrell: American singer, television entertainer

Tony Martin: American actor, singer

There is the karmic hint that in a previous life scenario, you had all the tools and necessary assets to be very successful. Perhaps you were involved in a venture in which many people depended on your acuity to complete a project on time and in the most efficient manner possible. Possibly, you did not stay with the project or did not take the time to do the required preparation. You feel the burden of unfinished business and are determined this time around to prepare and perform at your highest level.

All work and no play make Johnny dull. You will benefit greatly by developing your humor and a less heavy approach to managing and motivating people. Most likely, you are cultured, informed, and studious in your approach to life. While you may not be considered intellectual, your common sense know-how takes you a long way toward having the best of what life has to offer. You are not one to let the paradoxes, ironies, and twists of fate slip by unnoticed. Not wishing to be caught in such uncertainties, you are fully determined to chart your own course and be the captain of your own ship.

5ᵗʰ Degree of Capricorn

If this is your sun sign, this combination gives an additional openness to the cool Capricorn nature and suggests a softer and more engaging public persona. In addition, it suggests a more sensual and attractive magnetism than the normally more-reserved and staid Capricorns. You are full of life and ready to live. You tread where others fear to go and do what others only dream of doing. At times, this can be almost reckless, and you may find yourself in trouble at some point in your life for taking things a little too far. But all in all, this number-sign combination is a blend that allows for a most fulfilling life opportunity.

NOTABLES WITH THIS DEGREE:

Denzel Washington: American actor, director, producer

Gérard Depardieu: French actor, film maker

Salman Khan: Indian actor, producer, TV presenter

Marlene Dietrich: German-born American actress, singer, entertainer

Édouard de Rothschild: French business magnate

There is the karmic hint of indiscreet behavior in other times and places that may have created scandal that caused you loss of face or reputation. Perhaps you were careless with responsibility or misused an important position for unethical or moral reasons. You are riddled with conflicting feelings regarding the issues of personal freedom and social responsibility. You may be tempted more than your contemporaries with questionable offers from people of uncertain repute.

Your innate Capricorn tendency for organizational and leadership qualities go hand in hand with this combination to add a more personal style to your execution of authority. You have a more sensitive connection to the needs of those you lead rather than seeing your role in impersonal terms such as increasing production and profits. This is a good formula for a labor leader or person heading up human rights initiatives. You are familiar with the hard knocks of life and know what hardships many people have to go through just to meet the minimum needs of life. You seek avenues of effort that result in less adverse effects and more accomplishments.

6ᵗʰ Degree of Capricorn

If this is your sun sign, you may not appear to be as driven as some of the members of your Capricorn family. People with this number-sign combination are often inclined to be less aggressive and competitive than most of the other Capricorn combinations. You are rather inclined to assist others up the mountain rather than trying to beat them to the top. While you thoroughly recognize the tactics and ruses of the power game, you are less inclined to exploit this knowledge than many of the Capricorn clan. Some of those who know you might see this as a weakness that, if carried too far, turns you into a possible doormat personality. More often than not, your friends and associates who are more aware will respect your appropriate mix of compassion and competitiveness.

NOTABLES WITH THIS DEGREE:

Ratan Tata: Indian electronics tycoon

Maggie Smith: British actress

Nigel Kennedy: British violinist and violist

Tito Schipa: Italian opera singer

There is a karmic clue that in another life setting, you acquired considerable power and influence through scheming and plotting of dubious distinction. You made decisions that were abusive or punishing to those who threatened you or from whom you could acquire further property and influence. There was most likely the involvement of treachery and deception. You aspire to be honest with yourself and with others. Many of you will be drawn into the study of some form of psychology of the unconscious and the darker side of human nature. Your deepest desire is to mend, heal, and administer.

There is an artistic side to this combination, and if you do not actually pursue an artistic venture, you will most likely become some form of patron of the arts and creative souls. You are a loyal and considerate companion. Although it may not be easy for you to directly say what you feel, your deeds often speak louder than words, as you have a very thoughtful and, at times, generous nature.

7th Degree of Capricorn

If this is your sun sign, you often find yourself contemplating the larger picture of life as an ongoing universal progression rather than a minimal-time-allotted existence upon this orbiting rock. You leap into transcendental realities and bring back a plan for making your life in this physical world more meaningful and celestially productive. That is to say, your down-to-earth Capricorn personality demands that you have something to show for all of your quantum journeys. With this number-sign combination, you tend to be colorful, collected, and confident in the way you conduct your life. These traits attract many and endear you to other people who want to be productive and accomplish something by themselves.

NOTABLES WITH THIS DEGREE:

Andrew Johnson: American president, governor of Tennessee

Woodrow Wilson: American president, governor of New Jersey

Shizuka Arakawa: Japanese Olympic champion figure skater

Titus: Roman emperor

There can be conflict between your intellectual training and the innate sense of truth that feeds your intuition with some pretty unconventional and seemingly irrational possibilities. There is a karmic hint of having had access to elevated knowledge in other times and settings. Perhaps you misused advanced learning and caused harm to others. Maybe you were tormented and rejected for espousing ideas far outside of the conventions of the day. Possibly, your ideas were ahead of the times, and it was impossible to implement them, causing great confusion and disbelief from others.

Many of you prefer the comfort of discussion and debate with a small but close circle of friends and associates. If you are going to speculate, you prefer to have some fundamental benefit from excursions of the mind and soul. You may not trust the judgment of the masses, causing you to be hesitant about going public with your ideas and theories. In your element, you are widely recognized for your wit and worldly wisdom. You probe the outer limits of investigation and look under the tiniest of stones for clues that provide a greater answer to how and why we are here.

8ᵗʰ Degree of Capricorn

If this is your sun sign, whatever you choose to do will be done with an authority and thoroughness that makes it stand out to others. There is a commanding presence associated with this number-sign combination that can take the usually accomplished Capricorn personality to an additional height of achievement. You are determined, tough, and tenacious. Your flair for success and dynamic nature add to your aura as a sex symbol, and you have a well-recognized personality in your circle of associates. Power is the game and not to misuse it is to gain.

There is a karmic suggestion of previous misuse of power that can daunt your drive toward the top. The cool Capricorn temperament is prone to disregarding the feelings of others and going for the jugular of success. You are learning that you do not have to step on others toes to make your own way to the top. Success can be shared along the way with all of those who play a part in your plans. You would do well in motivational fields and areas of helping others to empower themselves. Your spiritual and philosophical beliefs end up being centered on results more than trysts of faith and hope.

This combination favors the good life and often brings the luxuries and spoils of triumph. Many of you will share your good fortune through philanthropic efforts and the support of self-help institutions. It might seem as if it is difficult for you to show warmth and intimacy, but with the right partner, you open yourself to sharing your deepest thoughts and visions for humanity and the life you wish to share with your chosen one. You sometimes give material things in a way of representing how much you care for someone. It is important to learn to give of yourself when your feelings are sincere.

NOTABLES WITH THIS DEGREE:

Tiger Woods: American professional golfer

Zhenzong: Chinese emperor of Song Dynasty

Billy Mitchell: U.S. Army general, advocate of air power

Matt Lauer: American television journalist, newscaster

Anne Cox Chambers: American media proprietor, billionaire business magnate

9th Degree of Capricorn

If this is your sun sign, you are dreamy and determined, and you long to find your place in the world. There can be a bit of a conflict between your inclination toward idealism and the Capricorn tendency toward down-to-earth practicality. If you can reconcile these differences, you can benefit from the best of both drives. This may be accomplished through some social cause, scientific innovation, medical breakthrough, educational reform, or form of entertainment, among many possibilities. You may compare yourself to an idealistic concept of your ideal mate. Or perhaps you try to meet someone else's impossible expectations. In this case, you will likely constantly find that you come up short.

NOTABLES WITH THIS DEGREE:

Elizabeth Arden: Canadian-American cosmetic industry giant, horseracing enthusiast

Christy Walton: billionaire Wal-Mart heiress

Anthony Hopkins: Welsh actor, composer

Val Kilmer: American actor

While you may give the appearance of being laid back and easygoing, it does not take anyone long to see that you have a strong personal drive to be acknowledged for your good work. You must stay busy and often feel guilty when you seem to lose time by wandering off in your thoughts to worlds of imagination and seeming folly. There is a karmic hint that you might have punished yourself for having repressed and possibly abused others in a past setting. The contrary conflict can be the desire to be free to dream while being trapped in some job or obligatory situation of exhausting limitation.

This number-sign combination enhances refinement and can add a seductive quality of delicacy of expression that makes intimate moments with your partner a special event. Your lofty themes attract the sentimental and the dreamers of the world. You can experience frustration with the limitations of your body, and this can lead to escapism through drugs or other stimulants such as alcohol. It just becomes so difficult for this body to reach the aspirations and mystical visions of the angels.

10ᵗʰ Degree of Capricorn

If this is your sun sign, you are dynamic, distant, and often decidedly determined to get things done right. With this number-sign combination, you may have many natural talents or potential possibilities for expressing yourself. It is difficult for you to single out one particular ability or interest. It may take you a little longer than some of your contemporaries to find your path in life. Once you do, however, you proceed with a determination that would rival any zealot. Your self-confidence and leadership qualities are well known, but if these are compromised, it can lead to flawed thinking, indecision, and a passive form of manipulation. You become underhanded rather than commanding.

NOTABLES WITH THIS DEGREE:

J. Edgar Hoover: American, first director of the U.S. Federal Bureau of Investigation

Isaac Asimov: American author, biochemist, columnist

Donna Summer: American singer-songwriter, activist

Noel Tyl: American astrologer, writer, opera singer

Ronald Perelman: American billionaire business magnate

You are concerned with the importance of social order and the maintenance of the protocols and procedures of law. You are aware of the freedom and fulfillment that comes from finding your place within the greater whole. You are sensitive to the forces that disrupt a well-functioning society. There is the karmic suggestion of having been in power or authority in another time and place. You watched as your society became compromised and collapsed, possibly in a spectacular manner. Perhaps much blame or public shame was inflicted on you. You dream of a utopian world and fear the decision-making process that can lead to social collapse.

The Capricorn personality is known for being distant, perhaps cold and unfeeling. From the outside, this appears true. From an inner perspective, there is much compassion and caring for others, but it is not easy for you to express forms of affection in words. You are more comfortable displaying your thoughtfulness in the actions and deeds that you perform for others. You see options and solutions that are ahead of the times, and you might live on the fringe of social changes that are evolving.

11ᵗʰ Degree of Capricorn

If this is your sun sign, you dream of a utopian world that is administered efficiently
and fairly for all of its citizens. However, you
find yourself in a dysfunctional world that
seems intent on rejecting the very universal
principles that you know in your heart will
work to the good of all life on every level of
existence. Your nature is to be efficient, thorough, and accomplished. You realize that
inner law must be applied in the outer world
if humanity is to have a utopia here in this
dimension. Perhaps it is not meant to be.
Even so, that need should not prevent you
from trying to do your part.

**NOTABLES WITH
THIS DEGREE:**

Jim Bakker: American
author, well-known
televangelist

Pierre Jovanovic: French-
Serbian author, editor,
known for works about
angels

Roger Miller: American
actor, singer-songwriter,
musician

Tia Carrere: American
actress, model, singer

There is the karmic hint that you may
have failed in another time and place to ful-
fill the implementation and completion of a far-ranging vision. The shortfall
resulted in public rejection and deadly anger. You somewhat grasp the micro-
cosm of applying the principles of creation, but your attention to detail can
cause you to miss the point of the entire experience. In your persistence for
correctness, you can easily miss out on the existential purpose of the life event
itself. You can be very emotional without knowing your feelings. You respond
in despair when, in fact, something broad and wonderful has taken place. You
may not see all of your dreams for humankind come true, but you can place
yourself in the right place and time to be a major role player in the planetary
transformation taking place.

Life will take you to the people and place you need to be to witness and
participate in a major project of human evolution. Your number-sign combination of vision and skills will be just the right part of the group puzzle that helps
to bring about results of tremendous importance. If you want to be at home
within that group, it is important to be at home within yourself. When you
look for it, the right guidance will come into your life.

12ᵗʰ Degree of Capricorn

If this is your sun sign, there is some confusion about your rightful role in society, and you struggle to find compatible friends and associates of faith. It is easy to look for answers in the external world while overlooking the truth that they exist within your own soul. There was likely a loss of someone or something very important to you in childhood that has left scars and emotional fear. You may overcompensate through your efforts to be successful and to be heard by the world. The strong personal drive associated with this number-sign combination indicate the possibility of becoming well known in the social world you choose. There is a karmic hint of having been sacrificed or martyred against your will. This leaves an element of distrust toward group psychology and crowd behavior.

NOTABLES WITH THIS DEGREE:

Mel Gibson: American actor, director, producer, screenwriter

J. R. R. Tolkien: English writer, poet, philologist

Victoria Principal: American actress, author, business entrepreneur

Gabrielle Carteris: American actress

You can be somewhat of a martyr and take up causes that may not be popular with the masses or powers that be. You respect those who stand up against tyranny, even when it is at the expense of their own lives. You speak out against hidden agendas and deception, but deep inside, you also fool yourself about character traits you have tried to deny. As you come out of hiding from yourself, you are anxious to share the process with the masses. There is a kind of global concern with this number-sign combination that keeps you abreast of events in the world. You want to see the best of humankind, but you seem to end up at the back end of the collective dark side.

As you mature into your life circumstances, you want to live well and partake in the variety of offerings this planet provides. You may well put your experiences into some form that allows you to share them with the many. You have the conviction and drive to overcome many obstacles in order to accomplish desired goals. Whatever the circumstances of your life, you will make yourself heard.

13th Degree of Capricorn

If this is your sun sign, you operate from a kind of fatalistic approach to life, and that part of you feels like much that we do may have been already scripted. This might make you feel a bit like actors on the stage going about doing what you do. Yet within that framework, there is a somewhat rebellious and creative part of you that likes to push limits and test the timeline of fate. Those with this number-sign combination are often of agile body and enjoy challenging physical activities, which may be an outlet for stress and possibly the career path you take. There is a natural charm that goes with this combination, but that may mask a very determined and competitive soul.

NOTABLES WITH THIS DEGREE:

Isaac Newton: English physicist, mathematician, astronomer, alchemist

Telma Lip: Brazilian actress, model

Julian Sands: English actor

Tigran Keosayan: Russian-Armenian actor, director, writer

There is a very harsh side to this combination, and you may step on some toes on your way up to the top. Your exterior persona brushes it off as a simple matter of fact; however, your dark ego can be calloused and indifferent when you are after something. There is a karmic hint that you may have brutally eliminated your foes in another time and place. Your present inclination is to try not to be judgmental. When you are placed in that situation, you strive to be fair, considerate, and honest. However, the old pattern arises under stress, and you can be underhanded and self-serving when your future is on the line.

At times, you lack the drive usually associated with the Capricorn personality. That is partly because you believe it is your fate to get there. Your flair for imaginative and alternative ways of doing things makes you an interesting partner and associate. There is a childlike quality many of you radiate that attracts friends and associates readily and easily. Your life will have much variety and fun as you traverse your course.

14th Degree of Capricorn

If this is your sun sign, there is a kind of ethereal aura that radiates from you like a beacon of light when you operate at or near your peak level of performance. Those of you with this number-sign combination may appear to lack empathy and sentiment when compared to many of your brothers and sisters on this planet. This is because of your no-nonsense approach to getting things done in life. While others dream, you do. While others wish, you earn the necessary credentials to get started. You have the gift to get what you need done efficiently and thoroughly. You might be seen as a little cold and indifferent by traditional standards of measurement. Although your exterior manner may appear impersonal, you have a big place in your heart filled with concern for the mismanagement and abuse of our planetary and human resources. Many of you will be found behind the scenes getting a lot done but receiving very little credit.

NOTABLES WITH THIS DEGREE:

Alan Watts: British writer, speaker, interpreter of Eastern philosophy for Westerners

Jeane Dixon: American author, astrologer

Konrad Adenauer: German chancellor, statesman

Carrie Ann Inaba: American dancer, choreographer, reality show judge

There is the karmic hint that you have been in previous life situations in which the virtues of humanity were subverted and misdirected for the selfish intentions of the controlling elements of leadership. You witnessed the misuse of resources and human dignity. Perhaps you were a part of the power elite who benefited from such abuse. There is a strong desire within you now to bring out the best within yourself and inspire others to reach for the best within themselves.

There is a daring and dashing innocence about you that charms the socks off your detractors. You can be most convincing when called on to persuade. You can be an ardent exponent of physical activity, and many of you are drawn into competitive athletics or vigorous physical tests of endurance. You travel and mingle among many cultures and ethnic variations of the human spectrum. These travels give you a rich basis of material for teaching and telling tales.

15th Degree of Capricorn

If this is your sun sign, there is a great energy of wisdom and flow of forces throughout the universe. You could be attracted to science, alchemy, or fields that involve transformation and synthesizing elements. This is a number-sign combination of industrialists and scientists who search to tame the forces that move planets and universes. You may make machines and implements that reshape lands. Or you may just be an ordinary person with a knack for the transmutation of nature's constituents.

You may find yourself frequently having to cope with the myriad issues regarding power and control in the daily process of human life. You may find yourself in a position of giving advice to others. It is a constant temptation not to use such a position in a manner that makes others subservient to you. The karmic suggestion is the likelihood of manipulating the black arts in another time and place. You are cautious to manifest truth and abundance only using the universal laws of harmony.

There is a pervasive drive within you to do what you can to render assistance to your fellow man. You are not one to easily share personal feelings, but while awakening, you can do so in a manner that empowers those with whom you share it. You are more concerned with destiny than petty personal matters. You glimpse the grand scheme of things and ponder the riddle of the universe with zeal. You delight in finding ways to communicate such deep topics in simple and inspiring ways that reach the hearts of the many. You find it unjust when power-seeking people keep such knowledge to themselves for private and political gain.

16th Degree of Capricorn

If this is your sun sign, you will be taken through the fickle follies of fate, fame, fortune, and fortitude. Depending on the aspects, things may not be quite so dramatic, but for many of you, several of the abovementioned may come true. There is a lot of energy stored up with this number-sign combination, and which way it goes is often a puzzle. The unexpected, for better or worse, can be just around the next bend. When you are at your highest, there can be a surprise stumble, and when you are feeling low, events may bring you the most sublime high.

There is the karmic hint that in another time and moment, you might have used your position to alter what might have rightfully happened to someone else. Maybe you were a king who passed over the rightful heir in order to gain more power by choosing someone less deserving. This possible scenario gives you a clue as to one possibility. Perhaps you feel guilty about being assigned to an important position for which you are unqualified, or maybe you have been undeservedly passed over for an assignment for which you would have been the best candidate. Your life will take many twists and turns until you settle your existential feet understandingly on the ground.

Those who have this combination often radiate a special aura and become easily recognized for their efforts. You can be determined and convincing when given the role of spokesperson or representative of a cause in which you earnestly believe. You are often found speaking out regarding the misuse of authority and the injustices of others that result from abuse by those who hold power. You have an ambiguous relationship with money, and it may come and go in large sums an unusual number of times before your life is over.

17ᵗʰ Degree of Capricorn

If this is your sun sign, you have an exuberance along with a stirring quality that reaches for the stars. You are full of vitality and want to share your optimistic outlook with all you meet. That does not mean your life will be without hard knocks. Quite the contrary, your pervading hope is likely underscored by recollections of terrible times and terrible events that haunt your karmic memory. You want to turn that around by spreading your message of hope and fortunate outcomes in life. This combination can attract material success and the comforts of a material world. Money can slip through your fingers when you become careless and generous to a fault.

Underneath these good-time feelings is a strong will and hardy drive toward accomplishment and the attainment of ambitions. You do not show your feelings easily in the daily exchange of personal interaction. Many of you seek an outlet such as stage, song, or sculpture to vent internal feelings you find difficult to express. Another frequent outlet is the subconscious focus on constructing products that will make life easier for the consumer. In this way, you get satisfaction from helping others indirectly. This is a number-sign combination for advancement in big business when other aspects support it.

Although it is easy for you to become a bit ostentatious and compulsive about appearances, there is a deeply spiritual side that seeks humbleness and peace of heart. You may not share your deepest thoughts about life with the public, but you are likely devoted to a teaching or philosophy that nurtures the soul as well as the body. You are one who knows that material success does not have to mean spiritual bankruptcy.

NOTABLES WITH THIS DEGREE:

Katie Couric: American journalist, author, talk show host

Arthur Ford: American psychic, spiritual medium, clairvoyant

Elvis Presley: American singer, musician, actor

Stephen Hawking: English theoretical physicist, author, cosmologist

David Bowie: English musician singer-songwriter, arranger, producer

Millard Fillmore: American president, lawyer, last member of Whig party

18th Degree of Capricorn

If this is your sun sign, you will find yourself treading more than your share of some pretty unconventional and unusual scenarios along your way through life. Your creative potential is vast, and it may be difficult for you to focus on just one of many avenues in which you could successfully perform. Your blazing insight and the outspoken manner in which you present your viewpoint can stir up controversy, and at times, adverse reaction. There is the karmic hint of having been involved in much misdirection and many webs of deceit in another time and place. Most of you relish the opportunity to debate and defend your beliefs, and like a warrior, you will leave a deep and convincing impression on those who come up against you.

NOTABLES WITH THIS DEGREE:

Domenico Modugno: Italian singer-songwriter, actor, politician

Lee Van Cleef Jr.: American actor

Dick Enberg: American sports announcer

You will find yourself in some pretty bizarre and unusual experiences. This number-sign combination tends to attract some dark and dysfunctional people, which brings out your own proclivities for the same. You may find yourself struggling with addictive issues and hidden obsessions that become troubling to your psyche. With this combination, there are usually repressed sexual issues that affect that particular part of your life in a dramatic fashion. Many of you will be attracted to professions or careers that focus on helping victims and people struggling with serious dysfunctional issues.

You leave no stone unturned in your quest to get to the bottom of understanding human nature. Your ability to put into words what are very complex theories gains you attention from those who have the same experience but are unable to articulate that subjective nature of what has transpired. You may soar up to the heavens and descend into the hells of consciousness as you follow your quest for enlightenment. Whatever you chose to do, you will do it with drama, daring, and a dose of danger.

19ᵗʰ Degree of Capricorn

If this is your sun sign, you are an adventurer and a leader, and you are often found at the forefront of change and revision. This combination gives a little more self-expression to the sometimes more stable and conventional Capricorn personality. You may take steps that are different and even defiant of the accepted social norms of your time. This is an excellent combination for pioneers in new business methods, technological innovation, research, and study into developing areas of medicine or science. You are a visionary and renovator of the norm.

There is the karmic suggestion that in another time and place, you were given an opportunity to manifest a beautiful vision that would have benefited many people. You did not follow through with your inspiration, and there was much suffering because of the lack of action. Your strength and conviction make it easy for others to join your cause. There is an indication of elevated religious or moral values, and it is common for you to speak out and react strongly toward those who disregard them. But with negative aspects, you may be just such a person. You can be critical of others while doing the same things that they are doing.

You frequently set unrealistically high standards of perfection for yourself and others. This can result in conflict when these standards are not met. The upside of this is that many of you will successfully develop something entirely new before your life is over. The grounded Capricorn with this combination may feel excessively restricted by physical limitations and seek to soar above it all. This can lead you into extreme sports or fringe activities. You are fiercely independent and self-contained. Potential lovers and associates may think you are too aloof to be available. More often than not, as much as you like your independence, you truly seek the company of a partner in order to give your life the settled and content trappings of security.

NOTABLES WITH THIS DEGREE:

Richard Nixon: American president, politician, statesman

Kate Middleton: Duchess of Cambridge

Joseph McMoneagle: American author, remote viewing pioneer

Joan Baez: American singer-songwriter, musician, activist

Linda Lovelace: American porn actress, later antipornography activist

20th Degree of Capricorn

If this is your sun sign, you are particularly sensitive to the dualities and dimensions of consciousness that include those beyond our normal range of sensitivity. There is a practicality to your vision that enables you to put your extended viewpoint into use and apply it to mundane tasks. Those who have this number-sign combination often display excellent grasp of the politics of the office place. The Capricorn sense of leadership combines well with the numerical grasp of the rules of society, allowing you to manage and maneuver your way through the labyrinth of institutional pitfalls and potential openings for huge leaps in advancement.

Some of you choose to live on the edge of social rules and norms and thrive in the give-and-take arenas of discussion and debate that arise from the dichotomies of our world. You may use your understanding to unite and integrate people. On the other hand, you may use your insight to fan the flames of discontent and controversy. There is a karmic hint of past prejudice and contempt for certain segments of society. Perhaps you were part of an intellectual elite or philosophical group that believed your views were far superior to the ignorant masses. You find it easy to be arrogant and egocentric concerning your value and importance. You seek to heal, mend, and guide others into enlightenment in a quest to release old patterns of hubris and cynicism. Wherever possible, you speak out against the dichotomy of duality and lend support to those who espouse harmony and unity.

You enjoy moving among the powerful and productive. There is an element of prosperity that applies with this combination, and you will likely find yourself enjoying a high standard of living. You may end up teaching the laws of prosperity and the roadmap to success. This would be a favorable combination for a motivational speaker.

NOTABLES WITH THIS DEGREE:

Albert Hoffman: Swiss scientist, known for developing LSD

George Foreman: American World Heavyweight boxing champion, Baptist minister, entrepreneur

William James: American philosopher, pioneer psychologist, physician

Mustafa Sandal: Turkish songwriter, musician, producer, dancer

21st Degree of Capricorn

If this is your sun sign, this combination gives kind of a chatty quality to the usually more reserved Capricorn personality. If you don't take yourself too seriously, this can bring candor and a witty sense of presentation that can make you a highly valued spokesperson for an organization or cause. The down side is that you can be arrogant and so sure of what you say that you become intolerant of others' valued perspectives, making it is easy to be pedantic and pompous to a fault. Under those circumstances, you create polarization and pandemonium rather than unity and inspiration.

Whatever your chosen path, it will not be easy to keep you from outwardly expressing your opinions and views. This is a good number-sign combination for teaching, lecturing, or expressing yourself through writing, art, or other outlets. This can be an excellent combination for motivators and people who lead and direct others. You like the perks of power and are not opposed to displaying the trophies that represent your position of prosperity and influence. You may challenge some of the notions that Capricorns are sure-footed, wary, and reliable. There is the karmic hint that in another life setting, you failed to fully develop special talents with which you were blessed. You may very well still possess such innate traits, but they are less obvious because of your outward thrust toward life.

Capricorns are grounded and deal well with the reality in front of them. This combination gives a little extra zing to your self-image. You are able to be more sensual and expressive of sexual and romantic energies than some of your other Capricorn family members. Your combination of success and the ability to express yourself well can make you a desired partner and mate. This can apply to short-term fun or long-term commitment.

NOTABLES WITH THIS DEGREE:

Maharishi Mahesh Yogi: Indian meditation and Eastern philosophy teacher

Kirstie Alley: American actress, comedienne

Swami Vivekananda: Indian Hindu monk, spiritual leader of vedanta and yoga philosophies

Siti Nurhaliza: Malaysian singer-songwriter, producer, entrepreneur

Rush Limbaugh: American radio talk show host, conservative political commentator

22nd Degree of Capricorn

If this is your sun sign, you are dedicated, determined, and sometimes depressed in your pursuit of the themes of your life. Your chosen career will be of much importance to you, and there is an underlying sense of having something important that you must get done before your life is over. You are perceived as quite serious and probably are much of the time. However, this can hide a very quick and subtle type of humor that may fly right by the less observant. The people with this number-sign combination are often well versed on many topics and astute observers of things going on around them.

NOTABLES WITH THIS DEGREE:

Horatio Alger Jr.: American author of early young adult fiction

Jeff Bezos: American billionaire technology entrepreneur

George Gurdjieff: Greek-Armenian mystic, spiritual teacher of sacred dances

Howard Stern: American radio and TV personality, media mogul, actor, author

You may take a lot of criticism and acrimony during your life. This may seem harsh to you. You feel you don't deserve such treatment, especially since you think of yourself as a humanitarian and try to get along with all people, honoring opportunity for all. There is a karmic hint at the likelihood of placing restrictions on others in another time and place. Perhaps you were controlling or overbearing. You try very hard to be fair, allowing others the chance for the good things of life. You may be acknowledged for your compassion and patience with stressful social issues of the day.

In your lighter moments, you can be most entertaining and appreciated for spinning great anecdotal yarns about personal adventures and other stories you have heard. There is a quality of loyalty that is very important to you, and you are likely to have a few very trusted and valued friends. This is very important, as there are also detractors who can bring frustration your way, so it is always a blessing to have a trusted inner circle of associates to turn to in times of dissent.

23rd Degree of Capricorn

If this is your sun sign, you may appear to be more rambunctious than many of your Capricorn contemporaries. This number-sign combination bears the possibility of greater instability and excessive behavior than many of the other more conservative Capricorn combinations. The upside is the possibility of greater flexibility and willingness to take things a little further than others might. You can be outspoken and active in an attempt to correct the wrongs that you see and stand up for the oppressed and abused. You are willing to take an unconventional path to get things done.

NOTABLES WITH THIS DEGREE:

Guy Williams: American actor, fashion model

Penelope Ann Miller: American actress

Harold Shipman: British physician, notorious serial killer

William Bendix: American radio and film actor, screenwriter

There is the karmic hint of having gone to extreme excess in another time and soul sequence. There may have been bloodshed or some loss to others that has left you with regrets and shame for past deeds. Perhaps you got out of control with an addiction to power or drugs or some other stimulant. You may have lost your ideals and given in to someone else's journey of lust for control. Now you seek to find the balance between freedom of expression and the proper restraint given the social and political climate of the moment. You are more willing to trust others now than in times past.

You blend well into the type of crowd with whom you enter discourse. This allows you to solicit information from the group that can be of immense value when seeking to unite those who have things in common. You are able to make yourself comfortable in almost any setting and show respect for other cultures and creeds. You are a good friend and delightful companion. Others seek you out for both enjoyment and serious matters of advice. Your organizational skills are very helpful as you develop effective networking capabilities and help stabilize groups entering the preliminary stages of development.

24th Degree of Capricorn

If this is your sun sign, you are likely to demonstrate more compassion and emotional sensitivity toward people than many of your Capricorn family. On the way to the top, you are capable of showing conscience and may be attracted to more service-oriented types of commerce rather than the highly charged competitive world of wheeling and dealing. Family and other domestic responsibilities can take up a good part of your life, and you are willing to put in the effort to be a good provider. You can be subtle and persevering in the art of negotiation and tend to wear down adversaries rather than overwhelm them through intimidation.

NOTABLES WITH THIS DEGREE:

Joan of Arc: French folk hero, Roman Catholic saint

Faye Dunaway: American actress

Albert Schweitzer: Alsatian theologian, musician, philosopher, physician

Yukio Mishima: Japanese author, playwright, noted for nihilistic themes

You may be more cautious than necessary and can miss "the moment" in your hesitation. There is the karmic hint that in other life sequences, you likely were overzealous and perhaps out of control when making decisions of a socioeconomic nature. Maybe your family or sponsor had deep pockets, and you were willing to take excessive risk with someone else's assets. Perhaps you were unprepared to take on the responsibilities of decision making that were given to you. You threw away valuable resources and came up short in promised results. Now you are more considerate of the impact your decisions will have on others and take time to think in terms of the benefits to all concerned.

This is a number-sign combination that is favorable toward those in medical, healing, and caring fields. You have a good eye for detail and the patience to stay with the challenge at hand until a favorable solution is found. You enjoy discussions with the learned and academically disciplined. Your humanitarian inclinations will often take you into areas of psychology, sociology, or philosophies relating to the role of the individual in the group consciousness.

25th Degree of Capricorn

If this is your sun sign, you are fascinated with social change and the transition of power within the politics and administration of governing. You enjoy strategy and trying to figure out the motives of those with whom you interact. It is fun to win the game, and you spend time studying the people who succeed. You will find yourself around philosophers and practitioners of politics, whether it is in a personal group or on a broad scale. You mix and mingle among people from all walks of life and social heritage.

There is the karmic hint that you have been involved in political treachery and power plays in other times and places. You are still intrigued by power and how it works behind the scenes unknown to the mystified masses. You can find yourself caught in compromise and conflict if you do not listen to the best within your soul. It can be easy to be seduced by someone who knows how to work the power process. Many psychologists and students of human nature have this number-sign combination since you are highly curious about where humanity is and how we got here.

You have a gregarious social side that you can turn on when you feel it is to your benefit. Your street sense serves you well under scrutiny. You want to be careful about exaggerating your credentials or experience because little transgressions of fabrication can come back to bite you in your behind at the most unpleasant moment. There is an always an element of arrogance underlying your personality, and when it does rear its head, you may find resistance and people turning away. Many with this combination are wonderful storytellers with spellbinding ways of describing life experience.

NOTABLES WITH THIS DEGREE:

Martin Luther King Jr.: American preacher, prominent social activist

Kate Moss: English supermodel, fashion designer

Fuad II: King of Egypt and the Sudan

Captain Beefheart: American musician, painter, bandleader

26th Degree of Capricorn

If this is your sun sign, you will feel pressure "to do something" with your life. Imminently aware of public opinion and social subtleties, you are always looking for a way to present the proper image and maneuver your way into positions that give you recognition and applause. The karmic pattern suggests past abuse of power, which can leave you with both a fear of and craving for authority. It is easy for you to be angered by social injustice, yet you can become easily overwhelmed by repressed anger when under stress. It may be difficult to face your own anger rather than project it out into the affairs of society.

NOTABLES WITH THIS DEGREE:

Cary Grant: English actor, entertainer

Michelle Obama: First Lady of the United States, lawyer, author

Newton M. Minow: American lawyer, chairman of the FCC

Jim Carrey: Canadian-American actor, comedian, producer

This number-sign combination adds intensity to the Capricorn nature, particularly as it applies to the politics of power. Typically, your personality is engaging, and you learn much from the day-to-day chitchat that is part of social interaction. At your best, you are a meticulous planner, but you can often go overboard in trying to control the habits and behaviors of those in your life. Your desire for order can be an asset when called on to take a leadership role.

While there is much power in this combination, you can be capable of gentle persuasion and approaching issues with a caring touch. You are a good observer of social rules but not always a follower. You find comfort in your home with family and intimate friends. It is there that you will let you hair down and be more natural. Your family naturally likes this and responds to you with appreciation. You are not always successful at choosing the right partner and may go through several trials before settling into a long-term commitment. When out of sorts, you are manipulative and emotionally dominating.

27ᵗʰ Degree of Capricorn

If this is your sun sign, you have a sensitivity and poetic quality that may not be readily available to the public. You have a rich inner life of spiritual and metaphysical contemplation. You would like to see the world live in more alignment with deep spiritual truths that you feel in your heart. Your intuition and anticipation of events is uncanny, and you may amaze your friends with the things you say and foresee. You find solace in the deeper philosophies of life, relishing those few occasions when you have the time to delve into the sacred mysteries of creation.

You keep many of your most personal feelings close to your chest. However, once you have been provoked, you can be an ardent spokesperson for the abused and oppressed, speaking with sensitivity about public and social issues. There is the karmic hint of previous alienation from society and the incompetence in government and bureaucracies. You could find yourself placed in a position in which you have to take a stand about a particular social issue. You are a bit of a perfectionist, and this proclivity toward detail can assist you in the process of reaching great heights of achievement. Idealism can get in the way of seeing things in a realistic manner.

This number-sign combination does not facilitate an easy expression of your true feelings, so you may find yourself acting out at times in an attempt to articulate what you truly feel. It is not easy for others to get close to you, even though you are caring and compassionate. You put your all into your cause, speaking in universal rather than personal terms. This is a combination that seeks perfection and utopian ideals, so you can find yourself frequently disillusioned with the foibles and follies of humanity.

NOTABLES WITH THIS DEGREE:

Muhammad Ali: American world heavyweight boxing champion, social activist

Benjamin Franklin: American politician, ambassador, inventor, printer, political theorist

Andy Kaufman: American comedian, actor

Seung-Hui Cho: Korean student who carried out mass killing on college campus

28th Degree of Capricorn

If this is your sun sign, you have a strong need to feel successful and acknowledged. At the same time, there is a presence of independence in this number-sign combination that does not want to comply with many of the conventional norms. This adds to the potency of the Capricorn drive for recognition and attainment. You are sensitive to public opinion and sense what the mood and need of the collective unconscious is manifesting. When out of balance, you can be taken under by the force of the tide of collective unconscious demands.

There is a karmic suggestion of past involvement with public scandal and abuse. You want approval from society, but at the same time, you have enormous anger toward that society for the abuse and injustice you feel you have been dealt. Often those with this combination demonstrate the capacity for management and organizational skills. You like to be in charge, and with favorable aspects, you can become very accomplished in the role of leadership. You particularly catch others off-guard when you go into the mischievous and playful side of your inner child. There will be many hurdles for you to jump, but your penchant for attainment takes you through them on the way to reaching your goals.

This combination gives a little more flexibility and fun to the somewhat more staid Capricorn image. Despite all of the talk about being self-sustained, you do crave the warmth and security of a compatible group around you. There are many with this combination in the realm of business, science, and political administration. Whether you find yourself in such a role, or in the arts and entertainment, you will be a force for change. You are always looking at a way to do things differently. This can bring you much recognition and perhaps some scorn because you disturb the status quo:

NOTABLES WITH THIS DEGREE:

Robert E. Lee: American military general, politician

Alan Milne: English playwright, author of children's Winnie the Pooh stories

Kevin Costner: American actor, director, producer, singer, musician

Al Capone: American gangster, led Prohibition-era crime syndicate

Edgar Allen Poe: American poet, author, playwright, editor, critic

29th Degree of Capricorn

If this is your sun sign, you can be dreamy, disenchanted, or just plain discouraged by what you see going on around you. Your perception of humanity can become easily skewed toward a surreal or satirical standpoint. Those who have this number-sign combination often strive for a very high standard and expect so much from others that anything less than near perfection can send them into a spiral of disillusionment or even despair. Those of you who can hold the high ground set a standard of achievement that can inspire and motivate the masses toward an improved way of living in harmony with universal design.

There is the karmic hint that in an earlier episode of the soul, you could have been a part of a religious or sacred sect that fanatically stressed virtue, purity, and a perfect state of holiness. Maybe you could not meet these standards and broke away from the group with a discrediting air of mockery and scorn. Perhaps you witnessed one of the leaders succumb to behind-the-scenes hypocrisy and unforgiving wickedness. You went through a rush of disillusionment and doubt within yourself and with those who preach the gospel of holiness. Now you are striving to get back on a progressive path of soul cleansing and alignment with the higher vibrations and teachings that are coming into the planet in your time.

You may not outwardly appear to be the ambitious leader, organizer, and stable source of accomplishment associated with your sign. Your exterior demeanor may appear less stable and more scattered by some methods of measurement. However, you can be just as capable and powerful in your influence, although you may take a somewhat less tested tack in the way you do it. At best, you are guided by the higher light of your intuition and are able to put hard-to-teach metaphysical and spiritual philosophies into a program of practice that results in real-world achievements and a transformation of the mundane tasks of daily human habitation.

AQUARIUS

0 Degree of Aquarius

If this is your sun sign, you will experience many unpredictable and unusual life moments. What you want may not come the way you expect, and what you don't want could come when you least expect it. The twists and turns of your life cycle might make for good daytime soap opera episodes. Well, maybe it's not all that dramatic. You most likely find it difficult to stay on course in your life pursuits. In fact, for many with this number-sign combination, it might be difficult just to set a course. You feel like there are too many options or none.

There is the karmic suggestion that in another life situation, you were blessed with wonderful personal assets but chose not to develop or utilize what you were given. Perhaps you were afraid. Maybe you found it easier to coast through life rather than try to accelerate your consciousness. You feel little motivation to get going while others around

NOTABLES WITH THIS DEGREE:

Carol Parrish: American mystic, author, founder of a self-growth community

Geena Davis: American actress, producer, athlete, model

Carolyn Dodson: American astrologer, author, metaphysician

Buzz Aldrin: American astronaut, pilot, second person to walk on the Moon

Christian Dior: French fashion designer

Bill Maher: American comedian, writer, TV host, political commentator

your seem to know exactly what they want and where to get it. You will very likely have to make a conscious effort to determine just what it is you want to accomplish. Once you are certain, you have the potential to zip right past those who had a head start.

People find you a trifle mysterious and unpredictable. In a world that grows increasingly socially correct, your refreshing gush of individuality is admired by most and irritating to those who do not have the gumption to do the same for themselves. You will find yourself in the position to devise something not previously done or invent something new. Your rich imagination gives you the insight to see a way to get something done from a completely different angle than conventional modes of thinking. You may be seen as ahead of your time or just missing the boat.

1st Degree of Aquarius

If this is your sun sign, you are an adventurer of thought and action, often speaking out against the oppressive and outworn. You are a bit of a visionary, and it is hard to hold the reality of what is going on in comparison to the realizations of what an evolved human consciousness can achieve. You miss the nobility and adherence to higher truths manifested by the enlightened. Deep within your soul is the memory of living in harmony with universal law and civilization. You long to see humanity reach a level of development in which the planet is once again in harmony with its higher purpose.

NOTABLES WITH THIS DEGREE:

Paul Allen: American billionaire, cofounder of Microsoft

Richie Havens: American singer-songwriter, guitarist

Sam Cooke: American singer-songwriter, entrepreneur

Gillian Chung: Chinese singer, actress

There is the karmic hint of having been part of an oppressive government or rulership that used power and force to silence the voices of those who tried to speak out about the injustices. You find yourself scathing in your attitude toward those who abuse power and cling to notions that no longer seem to be helpful in the advancement of human growth. Your inclination for change and progress will find you among some of the avant-garde of your era. Those who cling to conservatism might find you fanatical and extreme in your beliefs and behavior.

You have excellent skills of observation and take in much information about human nature. More often than not, you wish to contribute to human growth and potential. You may very well arrive at some very unusual and different solutions to improve individual and group awareness. This number-sign combination keeps you constantly active in thought and deed. You are restless and cannot sit still very long, as you become overburdened by boring and repetitive tasks. Your clever comments on human behavior often attract those who appreciate your wit and insight.

2nd Degree of Aquarius

If this is your sun sign, you can be an enigma both to others and to yourself. This number-sign combination can add to the already known tendency of the Aquarius to be aloof and at times not so easy to read. You may use this to your own ends by trying to appear mysterious and unwilling to yield information that might reveal your personal stance on things. This makes you a tough negotiator and gives the appearance that you are in charge. Your detached personality pattern may be interpreted as impersonal by some, and you may be drawn to machines and mechanisms more than people. You are no stranger to the far-out, and you will most likely participate in some kind of program or career that engages in uncovering mysteries of science and academia.

NOTABLES WITH THIS DEGREE:

Grigori Rasputin: Russian monk, mystic, healer

Lord Byron: British poet, leading figure in Romanticism

Rutger Hauer: Dutch actor, writer, environmentalist

Olivia d'Abo: English-American actress, singer-songwriter

Ann Sothern: American actress

There is a karmic hint that in other times and eras, you were willing to sell your soul to the highest bidder in your quest to get to the zenith of some new knowledge and power. There may be ambiguity about what you stand for and who you represent. Perhaps your quest was used to bring about some form of destruction or tragedy to humanity. Now you struggle with your inner soul to justify the things people do and the troubled fate of humanity. You are quick to see which way the wind blows and align yourself with those who have powerful positions and influence.

You can have an affable and entertaining nature. You may enjoy the restive state of music as a form of escape from the taxing mental drain of intellectual pursuits. Many of you are attracted to the combination of dexterity and physical discipline of sports and competition. You enjoy pondering the mysteries of the universe and the thought of opening the door to the higher realms of mind and soul.

3rd Degree of Aquarius

If this is your sun sign, you can come across as more open, pleasant, and approachable than many of your Aquarian contemporaries. You are somewhat more connected to your real feelings, and you are more comfortable with yourself than others of your sun sign. This number-sign combination adds potential luster to your already-recognized capacity for reaching unusual heights of brilliant thought and creative inspiration. You have the gift of explaining complex and difficult concepts with an ease that touches both the heart and the mind. Your sense of clarity can be refreshing in times of muddled communication and purposeful deception.

NOTABLES WITH THIS DEGREE:

Mary Lou Retton: American gymnast, Olympic gold medalist, spokesperson

Nastassja Kinski: German actress, model

Subhas Chandra Bose: Indian nationalist, leader of Indian Independence Movement

Santha Rama Rau: Indian diplomat, ambassador, travel writer

There is the karmic hint that you may have been observant or possessed insight and talent far ahead of your time. Perhaps you were castigated or considered a heretic for presenting something that threatened the collective thinking of your time. Your idea may have simply been too extreme for its time. You have come back at a time when your concepts can fit and the masses are ready to hear what you have to say. The combination of mental clarity and creative inspiration allow you to present your inspirations in a manner that appeals to the collective needs of mass consciousness.

This is a most creative combination, and many of you show a flair for unique and unexpected presentations that would not fit the norm for your area of expertise. At best, your conviction is contagious and your clarity is refreshing to those who have been misled time and again. This can be a wild and wonderful ride through the wheel of fate. Whether you find yourself in academics, science, commerce, or the arts, you bring a unique twist of innovation and development to the life you have chosen.

4th Degree of Aquarius

If this is your sun sign, you are tough and thorough, and you are determined to get to the bottom of mysteries that come into your life. Perhaps the nature of life itself is one of the biggest mysteries to catch your attention. Your independent and sometimes eccentric personality can go off exploring intellectual theories that defy the thought of the day and may not be substantiated. Even when disproved, you hold vigorously to your opinion. The flip side of this stubbornness is the ability to fend off criticism and come to an original breakthrough of thought or belief that can change the course of human thinking and planning.

NOTABLES WITH THIS DEGREE:

John Belushi: American actor, comedian, musician

Allison Dubois: American paranormal researcher, psychic investigator

Sharon Tate: American actress, murder victim of Charles Manson gang

Neil Diamond: American singer-songwriter, actor

There is a karmic hint that in another time and setting, your thinking and beliefs were ahead of their time and collided with the rules and regulations of the day. You may have been ridiculed or punished for going against the conventions of that period. You can be alternately afraid of public reaction and stubbornly arrogant in pressing your position or opinion on the platform of collective thought. You will encounter obstacles along the way as you strive to educate the masses about more modern and efficient ways of improving living.

This number-sign combination can push the stubbornness of the Aquarius personality to a fault. On the other hand, it can give you the strength and fortitude to stay with a belief long enough to push through resistance until you have demonstrated the proof positive of your proposal. You may prefer to get away from the crowd and work on your thoughts and ideas in a more secluded environment. You can be a deeply loyal friend, sharing your life with a few intimate associates. Those who are close to you benefit from your generosity and appreciation.

5ᵗʰ Degree of Aquarius

If this is your sun sign, you share a perspective of life that makes you adaptable and tolerant, as well as a fine student of human behavior. You enjoy studying the nuances of communication and human interaction. Although you may have very strong feelings about certain issues, you are also capable of respecting the strong feelings of other people who are also committed to what they think and do. This rare combination gives you an almost universal appeal. You will meet all kinds of people from the most diverse origins and behaviors. You may choose to follow a path of education or some form of communication about the art of being human.

There is a karmic hint that in another setting, you became distracted from your inner purpose by the glitter and hedonism of human indulgence. Exotic, erotic, and egoistic experiences seduced you and enticed you for many rounds. You are readily attracted to the unconventional and bizarre. You can be distracted from your course but seek to realign with your true self. You attract others whose course is to distract humanity from its upward spiritual spiral. There will be a time when you have to make a choice of which direction to take that will test the depths of your soul.

With this number-sign combination, you are likely an old soul who is wise in the ways of human nature. You can get along with people from a very wide range of cultural backgrounds and interests. This can be an asset as you progress toward your destiny. You may very well call on a most unusual and unconventional component of your personality to pull off your life's greatest accomplishment. At your best, you are funny, fickle, and full of fanciful aspirations that just might come true. Yours can be a rich and rewarding life with many tales to tell your grandchildren.

6th Degree of Aquarius

If this is your sun sign, you may be seen as anything from magnanimous to a manipulator and exploiter. There is an air of benevolence about this number-sign combination that makes many of you come off as real charmers, and you may use this attribute to scheme and plot. You have acquired very deep insights into the motives and intents of people. This can be used to exploit others, or it can be used to enlighten them. There is the karmic hint that you have previously used your insight to exploit others for personal gain. Now you are learning to value

NOTABLES WITH THIS DEGREE:

Douglas MacArthur: American military general, U.S. Army Chief of Staff

Paul Newman: American actor, humanitarian, director, entrepreneur

Ellen Degeneres: American talk show hostess, comedienne, actress

people for who they are and render assistance when you can. A deep sense of satisfaction surges through your soul when your efforts make others' paths a little easier.

Your growth comes through group learning. You are at your best when you are with the right team at the right time doing what that team does best. You are learning to trust your heart and the subtle feelings of the soul. That is not easy in the emotional clamor of the times in which you live.

When you take time to listen, you learn fast and garner information with acuity. Because of your sense of pride, it is not easy to acknowledge that others may know as much, but when you realize all souls have part of the truth, you can find that truth and put it together quickly and usefully. Your intuition is often reflected back to you through those with whom you associate. You are learning to trust that intuition, but you have conflicts with the rational mind. At times, it is easier to hear the truth through another than to trust your own connection to Source.

7th Degree of Aquarius

If this is your sun sign, you don't like to be bothered by the trivial and boring. Although you will make light conversation as a matter of social convention, you are much more at home pondering the more meaningful questions of life. This can include weighty speculation into metaphysical, existential, and humanitarian issues. This number-sign combination often yields a more deliberate and rational approach to matters than the oft reckless, and at times unreliable, members of the Aquarian family. Even so, you may tend toward the eccentric end of behavior.

NOTABLES WITH THIS DEGREE:

Wolfgang Mozart: German classical composer, musician

Brugh Joy: American author, spokesperson of occult and New Age thought

Mohamed Al-Fayed: Egyptian business mogul

Donna Reed: American actress

There is a karmic clue of influences carried over from previous trips to planet Earth. There is the suggestion of having taken things with a cavalier and even irresponsible attitude. Perhaps you were just having a good time and missed the whole point of what you were doing. Possibly you were given an opportunity and did not apply yourself in the way that you could have. Maybe you were not willing to apply the necessary effort to meet the rigors that were requested of you. There is the sense of having missed a deeper lesson and meaning to life. You seek to balance the good times with a good search for deeper wisdoms.

Your natural outgoing disposition and depth of perception can be a good combination for situations that require sleuthing and investigating. Many of you will pursue distinguished academic training and find yourself in positions to uncover some revealing nuggets. You are blessed with the ability to share deep insights in a straightforward and often entertaining manner. This could lead you to public prominence during your life. There will be a time when you want to teach what you've learned from your extraordinary life experiences.

8th Degree of Aquarius

If this is your sun sign, you are likely to be more driven to go higher and get there faster than many of the others in your Aquarian family. For a sun sign that's often cavalier and indifferent to power, you like this. Although this sun sign can readily detach from the material world and go headlong into mental and theoretical worlds of thinking and contemplation, you often attract material wealth. There is a paradoxical twist at work when these combinations mix. The choice is yours as to how much you want and how you are going to use it. There is often a dilemma of sorts with this number-sign combination. You may find yourself with a craving for power, but once you get it, you are uncertain just what you want to do with it. It is not that you disdain power necessarily. It's just that there are so many other aspects of life to pursue that this is not usually a priority for the Aquarius personality.

NOTABLES WITH THIS DEGREE:

Nicolas Sarkozy: president of France

Dorothy Malone: American actress

Carlos Slim Helú: Mexican billionaire investor, philanthropist

Lee Shau-kee: Chinese billionaire real-estate tycoon

There is a karmic clue suggesting that in another life setting, you may have been part of a near-utopian society in which you maintained a position of considerable abundance and influence. Maybe out of naiveté, the realm was undermined or overrun by sinister forces. Perhaps you bore some of the responsibility for allowing the kingdom to be torn apart. There is an urgency to take part in creating a perfect world. You will be called on to both discern potential abuse and recognize truly inspiring leaders and spokespersons for numerous causes and social movements.

You like to display the valuable things that you have earned along your path of life. This can be particularly true for those of you who overcame abuse and hardships to accrue the finer things in life. As is often the tendency with the Aquarian personality, there is a strong inclination to want to share these gifts with others. You are capable of being very generous in assisting the less fortunate.

9th Degree of Aquarius

If this is your sun sign, you will go through many ups and downs in your life but will likely come through it all with a generous, optimistic, and positive outlook on life. Your outward penchant for giving can hide a tough emotional interior. You sometimes let money be the spokesperson for feelings that you have trouble conveying. You might feel that it is easier to convey emotions through intellectual formats rather than address your true feeling directly to the public. Your optimism and eccentric ways win you a kind of cult following among those who know you and appreciate your efforts.

NOTABLES WITH THIS DEGREE:

Oprah Winfrey: American media proprietor, talk show hostess, actress, philanthropist

William McKinley: American president, military leader

Tom Selleck: American actor, producer

Emanuel Swedenborg: Swedish scientist, philosopher, mystic, theologian

Early childhood abuse can cause you to be compulsively idealistic toward the world in an unconscious attempt to hide from earlier experiences of misery and pain. The downside of this number-sign combination is that you can turn bitter and anarchistic toward the world. If it is not going to be a perfect world, then tear it down and start a new and better one. You can become a self-sacrificing philanthropist and compensatory do-gooder. This may be a karmic reaction to having contributed to the emotional abuse of others in another time and place. Whatever you experience, you will most likely be found supporting charities and self-help projects whose aim is to bring relief and hope to the less fortunate.

This combination can take you right to the front of the avant-garde, gifted, and unusual. Among the various mood swings that you will experience, there will be times of great public celebration and sharing. You support utopian and idealistic philosophies and can be attracted to the leaders of groups whose messages espouse humanitarian principles at the forefront. Your willingness to communicate and engage others opens doors in the field where communication is essential. You are likely to take on social issues such as global warming, civil rights, or ecological improvements.

10th Degree of Aquarius

If this is your sun sign, you see yourself as a visionary and spokesperson for the new world that is to come. There is a strong, idealistic force at work that motivates you to vigorously pursue your chosen cause. Oftentimes with this combination, the vision is clear but the manner of going about making it happen can be grossly impersonal. You can step on toes, overpowering those who disagree with or oppose you. Your detachment from emotional involvement can be a blessing in times of crisis when decisions must be made quickly and without prejudice. However, you can easily convince yourself that the only way to make decisions is with such dispassion. This can lead to an almost dictatorial rather than ennobled role.

NOTABLES WITH THIS DEGREE:

Baba Vanga: Bulgarian prophet, healer

Maureen Ambrose: American author, astrologer

Preity Zinta: Indian actress

Portia de Rossi: Australian-American actress, model, philanthropist

Gene Hackman: American actor, novelist

This number-sign combination indicates a lively personality and spirit of adventure that encourages others to become involved in the efforts of life that bring about change. You have a commanding presence when called on, and you are capable of being a powerful motivator. You are a compulsive doer, and the downside to this is that you can be so busy doing that you may not notice your actions cause negative impact on others. This hints at the karmic pattern of having destroyed or prevented others from having the chance to fulfill their own dreams and wishes in another time and place. The upside to this is your ability to push reform and change through staid bureaucracies and outdated infrastructures.

Many of you will be found at the forefront of technological, scientific, and social advancement. You think in terms of the things that people will be using dozens and even hundreds of years from now. You tend toward being optimistic and excited about what is just around the corner. Practicing humor, whimsy, and celebration allow you to enjoy the festivities and celebrations of humanity.

11ᵗʰ Degree of Aquarius

If this is your sun sign, you are intuitive, articulate, and creative. You know how to channel your Aquarian quest for independence with a touch of the unconventional in such a way as to make those around you believe that you fit into their traditional agenda. All the while, you may be exploring avenues of human experience from the realm of the ordinary. This may include your ventures into the heightened states of consciousness. Your sensitivity to the etheric dimensions brings you visions of events that most of the population would not receive or recognize. These might include troubling views of coming events that are not pleasant or would cause considerable discomfort among the masses. It might even be troubling to you.

NOTABLES WITH THIS DEGREE:

Clark Gable: American actor, entertainer

Franklin D. Roosevelt: American president

Marguerite Carter: American astrologer, columnist

Cheb Hasni: Algerian Raï musician

Boris Yeltsin: Russian politician

Fritjof Capra: Austrian-born American physicist, connected science to Eastern metaphysics

There is the karmic hint of having spoken out in previous times about information that was not accepted by those in control. You may have espoused idealistic views that threatened the elite. Perhaps you were envied and ridiculed for your insight. You are learning to trust your intuition and to develop discernment when choosing those with whom you will share vital and event-changing information.

Your enthusiasm and intuitive grasp makes you a sought-after source for advice and counseling. Your general Aquarian sense of concern for others adds to your popularity and recognition. Many with this degree are political advisors or consultants to commerce. You could well enter the public arena in some fashion during your lifetime. This might be on a grand scale or simply as a member the board of advisors at your local library. You see what is coming and are often the first to have new items. Some of you with this number-sign combination will get frustrated with what is out there and invent your own gadgets or gizmos.

12th Degree of Aquarius

If this is your sun sign, you often experience the feeling that there is much you have to learn about giving. It may seem to you that much of what you believe you deserve often manages to go to someone else. This does not make sense to your keen Aquarian intellect. Your detached manner and cool exterior can cause many to think that you are impersonal and insensitive. There is the suggestion of a karmic pattern in which you spent lifetimes focusing on the art of getting and taking. This may have been at the suffering and expense of others. There can be unconscious feelings of guilt that make you believe you are ordained to give without deserving to get.

NOTABLES WITH THIS DEGREE:

Ken Wilber: American author, meditator, proponent of the integral theory of consciousness

Michael C. Hall: American actor

Francis Bacon: English philosopher, statesman, advocate of scientific revolution

Tony Leung Ka-fai: Chinese actor

You might experience more than the usual hurdles as you tread the Aquarian path through life. That need not be discouraging, as it also suggests a chance to encounter a variety of experiences that would be envied by most. Well, they may not be Herculean, but they are certainly most challenging. You can slip easily into the victimized mode of martyred behavior. It is easy to blame fate and other people for your misfortunes. You have been given the mental tools and inquiring mind to sort through the issues and come out with some rather startling — and probably unorthodox — solutions.

Many of you with this number-sign combination will find that you are attracted to roles of service and enjoy helping others survive and recover from setbacks of trauma and suffering. You may be blessed with artistic skills that have become a part of your life's work, which serves as a source of catharsis as well. You move well through social occasions and mingle with a mixed bag of social types. Despite feigned indifference, you possess sensitivity and deep concern for the needs of others. You may be somewhat unconventional, however, in the way you go about showing it.

13th Degree of Aquarius

If this is your sun sign, you might find yourself lumped into the group of confounding Aquarians, which is not such a big deal since those with other sun signs usually find most Aquarians confounding. Your brethren are noted for being eccentric and sometimes for thinking outside the box, but you usually remain more staid and solid. When pushed, you just add to your reputation of being a fixed old fuddy-duddy. You may become more fearful of change than other members of the Aquarian clan.

There is the karmic hint that you may have previously witnessed the downside of rapid change during another sojourn through this planet. Perhaps rapid change was forced on a population and damage resulted to the collective psyche and soul because people simply could not easily let go of long-nurtured traditions. You struggle with the emotional pain of release that comes when something dies and rebirth has yet to begin. Such emotional grief may prevent you from taking the plunge to make a new effort successful. As mental as your sun sign personality may want to be, you are learning to integrate feelings with thoughts to reach balance and harmony in your life's work.

You can be dogged and determined to push through pet projects to your fullest capacity. It is even within the range of possibility that you could, on occasion, be confused with a Taurus! Huh? Those with this number-sign combination are often blessed with dexterous bodies and nimble wit. You maneuver well and make your way across the stage or athletic venue blessed with both prowess and empowerment. It's possible that you could set new standards for your profession or craft because of your innovative flair and tenacious patience.

NOTABLES WITH THIS DEGREE:

Shakira: Columbian singer-songwriter, producer, dancer, model

Carroll Righter: American astrologer, syndicated columnist

Jostein Saether: Norwegian artist, author, color consultant, spiritual spokesperson

Ayn Rand: American novelist, playwright, screenwriter, philosopher

14th Degree of Aquarius

If this is your sun sign, you will experience many moments that are mysterious and magical. You sometimes live in awe of the powers and possibilities of human potential. You seek to know more about your own potential and how to develop talents that have been given to you. The Aquarius personality tends toward the more unconventional and unique of the sun signs, and this number-sign combination adds a potential exotic element of intrigue to your personality type. There is an interest in the physical part of life, such as working with your hands or pursuing a vocation that requires precise execution and performance. A part of you seeks to improve how things get done with less wear and tear on the physical body. You enjoy the opportunity to elevate and improve human performance.

NOTABLES WITH THIS DEGREE:

Norman Rockwell:
American painter, illustrator

Charles Lindbergh:
American aviator, adventurer, author, inventor

There is the karmic hint that in another life setting, you could have neglected your God-given physical attributes. Perhaps you were envious of someone who seemed to have more power than you, causing you to do something to injure them or reduce their perceived advantage. With a little searching and honest assessment, you can begin to get back in touch with the rather extraordinary potential you possess.

You tend to be more independent, outspoken, and self-determined than many in your social environment. Life will find you around the curious, adventurous, and expanded-thinking groups of your community. You find exciting friends and adventurous things to do. In many cases, you like to press the limits of convention and flaunt the restrictions that socially correct advocates enjoy imposing on the masses. Because of your witty and entertaining manner, you are often the center of spinning yarns and passing on the most illuminating life experiences. You traverse many of the levels of human experience in this and perhaps other worlds of perception.

15th Degree of Aquarius

If this is your sun sign, you find yourself torn between an inclination to observe humanity from a view of compassion — desiring to witness the improvement of the human experience — and harboring an element of ill will, or even contempt, for its brash and destructive tendencies. Whoa, maybe it's not all that existentially dramatic! You struggle with impulses from your ego that compete with the inspirations coming in from your higher self. Do you serve humankind, or do you feed

NOTABLES WITH THIS DEGREE:

Hans Bender: German parapsychologist, pioneer of consciousness

Abhishek Bachchan: Indian actor

Alice Cooper: American songwriter, musician

the neurotic and out-of-control needs of the ego? This is an archetypal number-sign combination for this dilemma that we all deal with as humans.

There is a karmic hint of having previously been in the position to participate in an experiment to uplift the conditions of humanity or take advantage of your position to feed the ravages of your own personal needs. Possibly, you manipulated the spiritual ideals of the masses. Maybe you took the threads of their aspiring dreams and wove them into a nightmare for personal gain. You have the tools of enlightenment and will likely end up in positions where temptation lures you back toward the path of self-indulgence. The downside of this combination is that you might become attracted to drugs and stimulants as a substitute for the discipline of spiritually expanded consciousness.

You do care for people, although you may prefer not to wear your emotions on your sleeve, allowing the public to witness your personal emotional state. Your travels and variety of human experiences make you culturally aware of the many strata of social and cultural values and norms. You weave your way through diverse groups of socioeconomic cultures and come away with a better perception of the universality of the human creature. This allows you to touch the lives of others so that those with the same universal insights and all-encompassing approach to rallying the masses bring out their best efforts.

16th Degree of Aquarius

If this is your sun sign, you will experience your share of the unexpected and unusual. Your picture of the global view is permeated with concern about possible disasters and calamity. Alongside of such concerns, there is a deep-seated belief in human evolution and high expectations that humanity will soon emerge into a more golden age of harmonious existence with a more peaceful spirit of cooperation and goodwill among nations. Your personal life, on the other hand, may not reflect such peacefulness and stability. You seek experience that is outside of the norm and often find it in risky and unorthodox adventures.

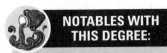

NOTABLES WITH THIS DEGREE:

Tom Brokaw: American journalist, newscaster

Ronald Reagan: American president, actor

Hank Aaron: American professional baseball player

François Truffaut: French actor, director, producer, screenwriter

There is the karmic hint that in another time and setting, you were a participant in the downfall and destruction of a society whose intent was to reach the heights of utopian bliss. In this time, you hear the words of those who speak of such dreams and hopes for humanity. However, you are urgently aware of the compromise and sordid corruption that has engulfed modern efforts to evolve. Institutions crumble around you once more, and you are confused and frustrated that this dream will not manifest. What you can do is make the necessary adjustments within yourself so that when the day for utopia does appear, you will be ready to truly be a utopian citizen.

Your complex and sometimes totally baffling behavior can be a turn-on to people who like the thrill of entering into unexpected adventures and personality exploration. Those with this number-sign combination see novelty in areas for which others express disdain. You find multiple uses for things that others have discarded. At times, your eccentric behavior helps you meet other people who reveal their unconventional sides to you without feeling threatened or judged. Great feats can come from meeting such people.

17th Degree of Aquarius

If this is your sun sign, you have an air of optimism and a beneficent view of the world that can cast doubt on the common belief that Aquarians are cold and indifferent. In a world of power plays and parasitic competition, you hold to the traditional beliefs of honor and justice in human discourse. You look for the best in others, and they respond to the best in you. When you do encounter injustice, you are prone to speak out and take action against such while others complain and do nothing.

There is an organizational quality associated with this number that helps you to carry through with ideas and get things accomplished. You would make a good president of

NOTABLES WITH THIS DEGREE:

Bob Marley: Jamaican singer-songwriter, guitarist, political activist

Charles Dickens: English author, social activist

Mamie van Doren: American actress, model, sex symbol

Natalie Cole: American singer-songwriter, performer

your local optimists' club. One great asset is your ability to grasp the greater vision of things and at the same time administer matters in such a way to make the vision become a reality. You have the conviction of thought and the will to get whatever you believe in accomplished. The karmic suggestion is that there have been other times where you were rigidly dogmatic and unyielding. That attitude does not work for you now, and you will find it a real joy to empower others and see them blossom into productivity and self-esteem as everyone contributes to the success of a given assignment.

This number-sign combination suggests a depth, thoroughness, and brilliance of mind that leaps over the boundaries of convention into realms of research and reverie. You are like a walking dictionary of possible science-fiction scenarios. Your personal manner is open and inquiring, yet you are not readily inclined to be emotionally available. You are more of a doer and thinker than a touchy-feely type. In a trusted relationship, you can open up to become a really fun and loyal partner. This is especially true when two minds meet along with two bodies.

18th Degree of Aquarius

If this is your sun sign, you are likely to be more guarded and skeptical than many of your Aquarius family. You share less of a utopian vision and more of a down-to-earth pragmatism that has gotten you through the many gnarls of life. Many of you take on an almost impersonal and detached persona as a means of protecting yourselves from the threat of human intimacy and close contact. You might choose a hard work ethic as one source of directing your personal energy and keeping busy from other, more personal threats. There is a very strong inclination for survival and overcoming limitations with this number-sign combination.

NOTABLES WITH THIS DEGREE:

Jules Verne: French novelist, poet, playwright

Alfred Adler: Austrian physician, psychoanalyst, founder of school of individual psychology

James Spader: American actor

Georgina Rinehart: Australian billionaire mining heiress

There is the karmic hint of having been emotionally scarred in prior lives because you were too open and almost naïve in trusting others. Maybe you were just gullible and inexperienced. Perhaps those with more sophistication and subtle hidden agendas seduced you. You seek to be outright and truthful but are wary and worried when caught up in group dynamics or intense, intimate confrontations. You are learning to know who and when to trust and where to focus your intentions to obtain the best results.

You will most likely find yourself caught in power struggles within your family or the groups in which you associate. You have an innate sense of caution around power figures and those who administrate authority. You could very well find yourself in a position of attaining financial prosperity and being offered a position of considerable influence. Then you will have to assess your own motives for being there. Once you have learned to deal with your dark side and center yourself within your highest consciousness, you can be a very influential source of motivation toward improvement among those who administrate and lead.

19ᵗʰ Degree of Aquarius

If this is your sun sign, you emit a positive air of radiance that can make you popular, profound, and sometimes prophetic. This number-sign combination adds to the already prominent Aquarius qualities of universality and humanitarianism. You are concerned with conflicts in the world and the passing of every-day events. This concern, although sincere, may lack the presence of empathy necessary to convince the detractors of your sincerity. You see a grander picture for the fate of human-ity and become frustrated when you witness waste and abuse of nature and of other human beings.

NOTABLES WITH THIS DEGREE:

Marc Robertson: American astrologer, speaker

Terry Melcher: American musician, producer

Lana Turner: American actress

Garner Ted Armstrong: American evangelist, author

Jack Lemmon: American actor, comedian, musician

Evangeline Adams: American astrologer

There is a karmic clue that during another sojourn, you may have become overly excited about the prospects for the improvement and transformation of the collective in which you resided. When the positive predictions did not materialize and things went bad, you lost favor and perhaps even suffered punishment. You may have trusted other sources rather than your own wisdom, or possibly you just missed the timing of events that you knew were going to happen. What had been given to you as a wonderful gift from spirit turned into a nightmare of misunderstanding and dismay. Now you seek to reconnect to your most sacred state of consciousness and awaken the power of the eternal gift that you have come to share with humankind.

You can be most paradoxical in your behavior, and those who are close to you will have to be flexible and nonjudgmental about your behavior. If not, you will fly off to a new coop of compatible compatriots. Since you are often unconventional and outspoken, there is a chance that people will miss the great significance of what you have to offer when it is truly valuable and full of possible advantages to those who listen. This combination enhances the natural charisma of Aquarius, and when you are fine-tuned to your highest consciousness, you may be regarded as saint-like by those who admire your presence.

20th Degree of Aquarius

If this is your sun sign, you seek balance, fairness, and cooperation between factions of social thought. There is somewhat of a paradox in that you can become controversial in your attempt to bring the factions of disagreement together. At one moment, you are an ardent supporter of some event or cause, and then in the next moment, you may engage in the most eccentric or unpopular behavior. You might speak conservatively about social issues while indulging in quite a different lifestyle behind the scenes. You are inclined to believe

NOTABLES WITH THIS DEGREE:

Mia Farrow: American actress, humanitarian, model

Joe Pesci: American actor, comedian, musician

Carole King: American songwriter, musician

Arthur Rubinstein: Polish-American concert pianist

in conspiracies and must be careful you do not become the source of one by your misconduct. You are never at a loss for trying out the new and untried.

There is the karmic hint that during other times and places, you were in the middle of fierce political power struggles. You were passionate in your beliefs and perhaps intolerant of those who opposed you. You may not have been above using deception and lies to undermine your enemies. While you seek fairness and openness in this lifeline, these old patterns can bleed through and undermine the impact of what you are trying to do. Your inquisitive nature will always find you near the place where new things are developing and ideas are being exchanged.

You move among the masses within the mixing pot of social activity. You seem to be more comfortable socializing within groups rather than dwelling on an intimate one-on-one relationship. This number-sign combination may mellow some of the extremely eccentric and unconventional behavior that is often associated with the Aquarius persona. You are likely to be among those who approach life with a softer touch, and even though you may appear tough, you are the kind of friend who will give whatever you can to assist someone in dire need.

21st Degree of Aquarius

If this is your sun sign, you may likely become a colorful artist or performer, but perhaps not in the professional sense. Whatever you do, it will have an unusual flair. You combine a curious mix of discipline and abandoned indulgence. If synergized in a constructive manner, this number-sign combination can lead to much success and accomplishment. This is a curious mix of mind, body, and emotion that may leave you feeling totally disjointed, or it may come together in a way that results in megaperformances of some manner. You are ever mindful of the out of the ordinary and often thrive in roles that are uncommon or less popular in society.

There is the karmic hint of having presented extremely contemporary manifestations of ideology, art, or performance that were perhaps way ahead of the times or too disturbing to those in charge. You were condemned or ridiculed and met with much grief. Now there is a part of you that wants to push the boundaries of creativity as far as possible. At the same time, there is a part of you that wants public approval and is tempted to sell out for the good review rather than stick to your creative convictions. It is time to follow that deep inner surge of pure universal expression.

You can be most engaging and entertaining to friends and relatives. Many of you voyage into a more bohemian lifestyle, getting back to the roots of your Earth connection and finding harmony with the planetary evolution. You like to push the limits, and you attract enterprising and unconventional souls who sense the cosmic flux of time and consciousness. You may be one who helps give humankind a peek into the realm of new colors, sounds, and blends of etheric energies that are just now coming into the human spectrum of perception.

22nd Degree of Aquarius

If this is your sun sign, you are blessed with a vision and knowledge of the heavens and humanity that transcends that of many mortals. You can use this expanded viewpoint in numerous ways to be of service to your fellow human beings. On the other hand, there can be such a feeling of responsibility to do so much that you become almost paralyzed about where you should start. There is the karmic hint of having been afraid to develop inspirations that would have benefited many people. Instead, there was upheaval and discomfort for many. This can lead you to retreat from social interaction and work behind the scenes.

NOTABLES WITH THIS DEGREE:

Franco Zeffirelli: Italian film and opera director, producer

Jack Van Impe: American author, televangelist

Harold MacMillan: UK prime minister, statesman

Those of you with this number-sign combination are very sensitive to what others think and feel. You do not wish to stir up the stew of confrontation. You possess an almost childlike charm in disarming others. Underneath this apparent innocence, however, you are driven to get things accomplished and can be very forceful about getting your way. The Aquarius personality is often known to be less than warm in personal matters. Although outwardly friendly, you can turn away from people coldly once you believe they no longer benefit you.

You believe you were born to do something important. The idea of having an important destiny rings loud in your bell chamber of priorities. You are attracted to organizations that are altruistic, humanitarian, and charitable in their purpose and plan. Your inclination is to think beyond conventional boundaries and into the unknown and unexplored. For many of you, there is a wish to know more about our place in the whole universal scheme of evolution. You ponder over the possibility of life elsewhere and contemplate the reaction to interaction with other life forms beyond our world. Although you may not be seen as an intellectual, your mind is active and fertile, exploring many mysteries. You prefer a mate who also has a rich and inquisitive mind. Mental rapport can be a great stimulant for intimacy and a rigorous sexual exchange. You seek to find an orderly universe and a rational explanation of the developments in humanity, finding joy in contemplating the possibilities.

23rd Degree of Aquarius

If this is your sun sign, you can be a bit starry-eyed and engaging. The tendency is toward optimism and ability to bounce right back from adversities. There is a youthful innocence about this number-sign combination that makes you exuberant and vital. At the same time, there is a beguiling and seductive quality that causes you to attract sexual attention. It is not easy to hold you down because of your enthusiastic approach to life and desire to experience so many things. Circumstances can rather easily slip out of control and into a pattern of overindulgence.

NOTABLES WITH THIS DEGREE:

Jennifer Aniston: American actress, director, producer

Charles Darwin: English naturalist, geologist author

Abraham Lincoln: American president, lawyer

Sarah Palin: American politician, governor of Alaska

Because of your zest for living, many people will want to tag onto your existential coattails and go for the vicarious ride with you. You will have to be careful about hangers-on and learn to be a better judge of character. The Aquarius personality is prone to want to take a ride on the wild side, and you have an inclination to take that even further. It will not be easy to learn restraint, particularly if you are given the means to afford an indulgent lifestyle. There is a hint of a previous karmic pattern of excess and extravagance. Some of you try to compensate for that tendency by putting on an austere and stoic countenance in an attempt to downplay your hidden desires. You are confronted with many temptations and hardships, and you will have to struggle to stay on the path of a noble and meaningful life.

You can be very popular because of your charm and multiple interests in life. This flexibility helps you to break through some of the usual inhibitions associated with the Aquarius personality and leaves you a little more vulnerable to interaction with others. You have a way of presenting far-out things to the masses in such a manner that encourages them to reach higher toward the stars rather than fear the new and unexplored.

24th Degree of Aquarius

If this is your sun sign, you are careful, caring, and cunning when the need arises. You are attuned to the social trends and moods of the times and might be found right in the middle of stirring up a storm of interest or even controversy. You will often do what is needed in order to get your point across to others. Most of you with this number-sign combination, however, prefer to take a more conservative approach in handling hot social topics of the day. Social image may have been important in your household, and putting on the right face was probably a requirement of being part of the pact.

NOTABLES WITH THIS DEGREE:

Robbie Williams: English singer-songwriter, actor

Jerry Springer: American television host, musician, actor, mayor of Cincinnati, Ohio

George Segal: American actor

There is a karmic hint that in another life setting, you were probably anti-social and may have been an outcast or outlaw. You rebelled against corrupt authority figures and justice that was carried out under the table or behind the scenes. Perhaps you were a more honest outlaw than those who administered the laws. Now you can be confused on where your stand with public issues and may take the devil's advocate route just to be contrary. You desperately seek righteousness in the marketplace and in governing. As you establish a point of integrity within, you will likely be called to take on an activist's role in your chosen community or country.

As a competitor, you often beat more talented opponents through guile and cleverness rather than by overpowering them. You can be urbane and conversational when called on, but you are more inclined to take a passive tack during social occasions. You are family-oriented and are a desirable mate once you settle down in a relationship. You are inclined to take work very seriously, which may take you away from your family for extended periods of time.

25ᵗʰ Degree of Aquarius

If this is your sun sign, you will find yourself experiencing a wide range of human experiences and events. You like the variety and spice of life and live hard and fast in an attempt to try out as much of it as you can. This can lead to much excess of diet, daring, and doing. A potential upside is that having figured out a lot of life, you have much to teach others about the art of living. When it comes to embellishment and flair, you are a master at providing the extra touch or special addition to the moment.

NOTABLES WITH THIS DEGREE:

Barbara Hand Clow: American astrologer, author

Raphaëlle Ricci: French talent coach, television personality

Renée Fleming: American opera singer

Jimmy Hoffa: American labor union leader

There is a lot of rebellion with this combination, and you will likely find yourself stepping outside of conventional social standards and, at the extreme, outside the law. There is the karmic hint of having gone too far to the extreme in other times and places. This may have led to instability and a breakdown of the social structure, resulting in much chaos and suffering for the population. You are always pushing the norms, but at the same time, you want the approval of others and wish to have your ideas accepted.

You wander through a myriad studies and searches, not always sure of just what you are looking for. However, that doesn't stop you from the ongoing quest. You are always interested in the nature of humanity, creation, and the universe. You'll ponder over how people relate to the grand scheme of things, and then just as soon go out for a beer or try bungee jumping to get away from the heaviness of such existential pondering. You get great pleasure from the sensual and sexual part of life. You will most likely get into such studies along the way.

26th Degree of Aquarius

If this is your sun sign, there is an element of nonconformity that can be both cute and contentious. You are torn between the desire for freedom of expression and the need to release your most exorbitant attributes while trying to fit into a world of ordinary and conforming values. It is not easy for you to find a comfortable circle of associates that you can both trust and enjoy being with. You are mentally observant and able to size up social situations adroitly and quickly. This instinct more often than not helps you to avoid getting into conflict even though you may not fit well into the conventions of the day.

NOTABLES WITH THIS DEGREE:

Reinhold Ebertin: German physician, astrologer

Jack Benny: American comedian, vaudevillian, actor, violinist

Carl Icahn: American billionaire financier, corporate raider

Jane Seymour: English actress, artist, author

This number-sign combination is born to lead, but you often wonder if it is worth the necessary effort amid this world of dissent and disdain. You struggle between being too harsh or too soft or maybe just not caring about the consequences of trying to organize the unruly. Many of you encounter a contemptuous world full of criticism and dissent. There is a karmic hint of having a previous conflict with the role of leadership and command. Perhaps you were part of overthrowing a country or government only to see an equally inept and repressive one spring up in its place. You have been on both sides of rebellion and have seen the futility of discovering neither really improves the conditions of humanity.

Your empathetic trait is not as easily identified as it is in most of your Aquarius contemporaries. You can be most disarming and charming when relaxed or with a group of compatible souls. You can be an inspirational leader and know how to find the best in those you inspire to accomplish great deeds. During times of stress, you are able to bring out these qualities in people and accomplish feats of heroic proportion.

27th Degree of Aquarius

If this is your sun sign, you are dreamy and daring, and you don't like to compromise perfection. You can be openly critical of a confused and compromised social fabric. There is an element of perfection that goads you to be your best and do as well as you can, and you expect the same from others. More often than not, others do not share your intensity or drive to be as good or do as well. Many of you with this number-sign combination harbor almost utopian aspirations for the future of society. Supposed leaders frustrate you with their delays and denials of progress. A touch of anarchy may run through your veins.

NOTABLES WITH THIS DEGREE:

William Miller: American religious leader

Kim Jong-il: North Korean leader, politician

James Ingram: American singer-songwriter, musician, producer

Baba Sitar: Indian guru, spiritual teacher

There is a karmic hint of having been part of a grand and prestigious society in another time and sequence of your soul. Possibly, you were an administrator or assistant to one who had considerable influence on the decisions of that culture. Perhaps you witnessed compromise and acceptance of lower standards in the administration of that time. Maybe you were exiled or severely rejected for speaking out about flaws within the system and shortcomings in leadership. You are determined to carry through on your beliefs, doing whatever necessary to encourage competency in leadership and integrity of the true vision that inspires the influential in your world.

You are poetic, polished, and proud of your progress with gifts God bestowed on you. There is an air of sensitivity and refinement that follows many of you and makes you stand out where mediocrity and the superficial prevail. Your mixture of intellectual perception and intuitive vision enables you to put hard-to-express, abstract concepts into day-to-day homilies and simple parables for all to appreciate. Much wisdom comes to you in quiet and contemplative moments of reverie.

28th Degree of Aquarius

If this is your sun sign, there is often a dilemma regarding your role in society. Underneath your desire to fit in and your survival strategies of performing up to someone else's standard, there is a rebellious and fierce sense of independence that cries out for the freedom to just be who you really are. As you resolve the underlying anger associated with this rebelliousness, you can turn that energy into the passion necessary to make your dreams and wishes come true.

There is the karmic hint of possibly having been a traitor or vehement dissident in another life cycle. Maybe you tried to make changes in an era when the leadership or majority did not wish to change. Possibly you spoke out in dissidence and lost your life or were severely admonished for such an outburst. You readily see the flaws in the system and within the people who run it. Deep down, you know you have answers to many of the issues and problems that plague the leadership of the times we are living in. Once you are clear within yourself, you will attract people around you who are clear in their intentions. As you meet and mingle with these people, you will mutually accomplish much in the nature of improving life on this planet.

Your uniqueness and sometimes eccentric ways may just turn out to be the most important personal traits that help you to get done what your heart and soul most desire to do. You just want to be careful not to go so far out that you can no longer stay engaged with those of more traditional and conventional values. People with this number-sign combination often have an almost encyclopedic knowledge of events and figures at their disposal. Such a wealth of information comes in handy when explaining issues or when you wish to attract others to assist you on your path toward higher awareness.

NOTABLES WITH THIS DEGREE:

Michael Jordan: American professional basketball player, entrepreneur

Paris Hilton: American socialite, heiress, model, actress

Matt Dillon: American actor, director

Lou Diamond Phillips: American actor, director

Hal Holbrook: American actor, Mark Twain impersonator

29th Degree of Aquarius

If this is your sun sign, you are likely to view the world on a large scale and go after things with an idealistic verve that amazes the cynics and delights the optimists. This being the combination of organizations and groups, you will most likely at some point in your life find yourself getting the attention of large numbers of people or being associated with institutions that reach out to the masses. It is easy for you to become engrossed in an ideological movement or utopian schemes. It is comforting to some to lose their identities by

NOTABLES WITH THIS DEGREE:

John Travolta: American actor, dancer, singer

Dr. Dre: American rapper, actor, producer

Cybill Sheppard: American actress, singer, model

Lee Marvin: American actor

becoming part of the greater structure. You desperately want to believe in the whole and look to institutions for social change.

There is the karmic suggestion of having been a part of devious and undermining plots to break down society in other times and places that involved misleading others and creating divisiveness and stress within the group structure. Now you might hide from that dark side of your own nature by overcompensating in your attempt to bring good to the mass consciousness. You may not realize the flaw is internal rather than external.

There is a drama and artistic flair that goes with this number-sign combination, and you will leave your personal stamp on whatever you choose to do. For the most part, you tend to get along with people and make it a point to try to find a midpoint of compromise to maintain cooperation and peace between parties. This high tolerance may diminish when people do not live up to the high expectations you have placed on them. Many practitioners of the intuitive arts can be found with this combination, as it lends itself to awareness of things taking place on the other side or in other dimensions.

PISCES

0 Degree of Pisces

If this is your sun sign, you will find yourself caught up in many unusual emotional entanglements and circumstances as you travel your path through life. You are placed in situations that may not be to your liking, and you might find yourself pressured to meet other's demands that are not always in your own best interest. You have an opportunity to experiment and lead with innovation and refreshing reforms that could improve the social climate in which you live. Your personality may be difficult for others to fathom. This can make you alluring and mysterious to some and apparently devious and questionable to others. You are complex and at times most unpredictable.

NOTABLES WITH THIS DEGREE:

Pierre Boulle: French novelist, engineer

Adolphe Menjou: American actor, political activist

Karl Albrecht: German entrepreneur, cofounded Aldi's supermarkets

Gordon Brown: UK prime minister, politician

You may find yourself frequently caught in complicated situations that require a delicate balance to maintain peace among your contemporaries. While you may aspire to bring about the best within yourself and others, you can find yourself placed in positions in which you are tempted with compromises and resignation to the demands of those who are inclined to exploit the opportunities of a flawed world. There is a karmic hint that in another life sequence, you were uncertain and unable to make decisions. This allowed you to be easily compromised and persuaded by people pushing their own agendas. You desire to be just and commanding, but you might buckle under the pressure of overt or hidden persuaders.

You may be offered so many choices in life that you take the position of making none or as few as possible. You believe that you are making your life simple but may be going nowhere. On the other hand, there are those with this number-sign combination who become immersed in so many projects and interests that those less diverse regard you as amazing. Paradox follows this combination and will pop up its quizzical head throughout your life.

1st Degree of Pisces

If this is your sun sign, you are inclined to take the first step with your emotions when many of your Pisces contemporaries may duck and cover. This can get you into some tight spots. However, with time, it will more likely bring you some truly magnificent life moments of emotional joy and depth of experience. Your refreshing openness and clarity of mood and motive make you a trusted companion and associate. This can be a favorable number-sign combination for the intuitive and artistically inclined since it allows easy attunement to both the collective consciousness and higher levels of awareness. You are often one step ahead of the game, receiving the pulse of the public or maybe new archetypes and images coming in from the universal mind.

NOTABLES WITH THIS DEGREE:

Kurt Cobain: American musician, songwriter, artist

Rihanna: Barbadian singer, actress, fashion designer

Cindy Crawford: American supermodel, actress, spokesperson

Sidney Poitier: American-born Bahamian actor, director, social activist, diplomat

It has not always been easy for you to trust your emotions and feelings. There is the karmic hint here that in other times and places, you may have been afraid of your intuitive and emotional sensitivity. Possibly you received information with negative consequences, making you feel as if you were responsible for some negative occurrences. Perhaps you were forced to use your knowledge for someone else whose motives were malicious and detrimental to the people you loved. Now you seek ways to become reconnected to your source and to trust the inspirations that come in from very high levels of your consciousness.

Your perky personality and quirky way of expressing yourself can endear you to many. For the creative and artistically inclined, this combination can be very favorable for getting ahead of the game. You are very likely to produce original and unique creations no matter what field of endeavor you find yourself pursuing. Your detective-like instincts lead you right to the forefront of emerging consciousness and new levels of archetypal information entering the planet at this time.

2ⁿᵈ Degree of Pisces

If this is your sun sign, you are a puzzling person of panache and persuasion. Your clever manner of maneuvering and innate sense of others' motives make you a shrewd negotiator and admired spokesperson. You possess a keen sense of taste and make a good impression on others. You may be chosen to represent a third party because you can present others equally well. For the most part, you are well liked because you are mild mannered and demonstrate interest in and sensitivity toward others. If you aren't winning awards, you likely pick up the congeniality trophy.

A downside to this number-sign combination is that, having no center point, you are easily susceptible to persuasion and in some cases corruption. With no center point of conscience or moral belief, you can be easily persuaded to go in any direction with the right reward. There is the karmic hint of scandals and skullduggery in other times and settings. Perhaps you sold yourself to the highest bidder or to the one you believed would ascend into power. You can behave impersonally and without remorse toward others when your reputation is on the line. You struggle to find a moral compass and to right your ship's course on the ocean of life.

You move among those who have an impact and enjoy being in the middle of a good debate. Your sense of public opinion is keen, and you know how to ride the tide of interest until the crest of the wave has passed. When that happens, you already have an alternative in mind and have started to shift the weight of your interest to another territory that will test your taste for stirring the stew of counterpoint. You have a crafty knack for finding the majority support just long enough to get what you want and then moving on to another objective.

NOTABLES WITH THIS DEGREE:

Sir John Mills: English actor

Ted Kennedy: U.S. senator, campaign organizer, diplomat

Nina Simone: American musician, songwriter, arranger, social activist

Laurent Petitguillaume: French television and radio show host

3rd Degree of Pisces

If this is your sun sign, your mood range is accentuated even more than the traditional Pisces personality. You swim to the mystical heights of euphoria and bliss, and then you delve down to the depths of depression and despair. Sometimes you take the emotional weight of the collective's angst on your Pisces shoulders, hoping to alleviate some of the suffering you see around you. It can be difficult for you to establish healthy boundaries in your relationships with others. This number-sign combination is clever, kind, and conscientious about life's little matters. You are appreciated as a trusted friend and mate.

There is a karmic suggestion that you have been in a previous position of influence in which you purposely inhibited the emotional evolution of others. Now you find yourself frustrated and blocked when opportunity appears. You feel resistance from others when you are ready to go. As you reconnect to your core inner feelings, you will find your direction and purpose of soul once again. You have the talent and tools to inspire and help reawaken many souls who have given up hope for the possibility of freedom of living and finding the joy of life itself.

At your best, you are witty, wacky, and wonderful. Your enthusiasm and zest for living are infectious, and you are an inspiration to those you meet. As you train your talents and fine-tune your repertoire of personal skills, you can be a force of influence in any community you live in. Group is the name, and dynamics is the game. Your soul lights up when you see an entire gathering of people come together in harmony and alignment with the collective good of the oversoul and with the music of the spheres ringing in their collective ears.

NOTABLES WITH THIS DEGREE:

George Washington: American president, military leader

Sybil Leek: English astrologer, psychic, occult author

Viktoras Kulvinskas: American holistic health practitioner

Julius Erving: American professional basketball player

Pedro Tornaghi: Brazilian astrologer, yogi

4ᵗʰ Degree of Pisces

If this is your sun sign, you demonstrate an ability to stay grounded and carry through with projects and interests with much greater efficiency than many of your Pisces brethren. This mixture of dreams, made in heaven but with its ideological boots placed firmly on the ground, can make you a mover and a shaker. This number-sign combination gives you the capacity to formulate and articulate your visions of betterment for all. Although you may be perceived by many as more serious than what is usually expected from a Pisces person, you are quite capable of demonstrating that famous disarming openness that comes so easily to Pisces.

NOTABLES WITH THIS DEGREE:

Patricia Sun: American New Age lecturer, author

Michael Dell: American billionaire business mogul, philanthropist, founder of Dell Inc.

Phil Knight: American billionaire business magnate, cofounder of Nike Inc.

There is the karmic suggestion of wasted time and unused opportunity left over from earlier journeys of your soul. Maybe you were afraid of taking a chance when opportunity knocked. Perhaps you were a dreamer but unable to put any of your visions into practical use or application. You may have been ahead of your time and tried to get people to believe in projects that the mass consciousness could not comprehend. You have something to get done, and have come back with the organizational skills to do just that.

Your folksy Pisces personality and entertaining ways help you to catch the attention and imagination of the populace once you are ready to get things going and, more importantly, are determined to get things done. You attract a colorful cast of characters as you put together the necessary ingredients for a concoction of growth and transformation of the collective awareness. Once you have things confidently under way, your playful and pleasant personality beams with joy and delight as you see the effects of awakening taking place in those close to you and strangers alike.

5th Degree of Pisces

If this is your sun sign, your life takes many twists and turns through exceptional and oftentimes atypical moments of life experience. There is a sleuthing quality about this number-sign combination that may find you exploring rare and unusual people and events. Even if you don't push any limits of extreme behavior, there is a strong likelihood that you will go through a variety of experiences beyond the average person's life experience. This can leave you with your cup running over with good fortune and a cornucopia of life memories.

NOTABLES WITH THIS DEGREE:

George Harrison: English musician, songwriter, actor

Steve Jobs: American computer entrepreneur, cofounder of Apple Inc.

Kristin Davis: American actress

Helen Shaver: Canadian actress, director

Billy Zane: American actor, producer

It might not always be this way and certainly wasn't always that way. There is the karmic suggestion that in another life cycle, your inhibited and repressive belief system caused you to react severely toward those who deviated from your prescribed course of human behavior. Perhaps you were in a role of religious, political, or social leadership and would not tolerate any display of perceived negative comments, criticism, or complaints about the implementation of your authority. Possibly, fear of potential excess of behavior put you in the position of trying to control everyone and everything happening around you. You are now learning to love life and allow others to do the same.

Your exposure to so much of life allows you to share experience in a most animated and enlivened manner. You are sought after for your fascinating way of communicating and the manner in which you encapsulate so much meaning into so few words. Your appearance, manners, and methods will often deviate from the expected social norms. When overdone, this can leave you eccentric and out of touch with almost everyone. However, for the most part, it just endears you to those who care because of your willingness to be refreshing and true to yourself.

NUMEROLOGY OF ASTROLOGY

6th Degree of Pisces

If this is your sun sign, you may have the opportunity to bring emotional freedom and alleviation of suffering to the masses. If you take the positive path, the potential comes to approach an enlightened stage that you strive to pass on to others. If you take the path of denial, it is more likely you will experience the feeling of confusion and being cut off from emotional connections to the real world. You can become easily manipulated and drawn under the spell of those who know how to assert emotional control over others. It is a common pattern to shut down much of your inner feelings, which can make much of your external emotional behavior affected rather than real.

NOTABLES WITH THIS DEGREE:

Chester Nimitz: American Navy admiral

Meher Baba: Indian yogi, spiritual leader

Johnny Cash: American singer-songwriter, actor, author, social activist

Jackie Gleason: American actor, comedian, musician, UFO researcher

There can be a karmic tendency toward frozen feelings, or this can be the result of abusive experiences in childhood. You try to say the things people are supposed to say. You try to act the "socially correct" way, but you suffer from lapses of your own repressed nature coming to the surface in sometimes awkward ways. You see yourself as one who renders assistance to others. There are many compulsive counselors associated with this number-sign combination. You are a caretaker at heart, and once you have dealt with your own demons, you may become a fine healer or counselor to many.

You are frequently found among the ranks of medical, educational, and social servants, as well as religious spokespeople. Your penchant for public service is strong, as there is a need to believe you are helping others. As you come out of your own darkness, you can be a powerful inspiration in the art of helping others to reclaim the joy and enthusiasm of life. You may well find that you have a gift for the fine arts, and this can be a great source of pleasure along with being a great avenue of catharsis. A bit stubborn in your ways, you can be slow to change. However, once you see the need for change, you can be imaginative and capable of coming up with novel ideas to advance human evolution.

7ᵗʰ Degree of Pisces

If this is your sun sign, you are ever cognizant of the social turmoil around you, which
seems to be a product of human behavior.
While moved deeply by what you see, it is not
easy for you to directly experience what you
are feeling inside. You are perhaps religious
or seek some psychological and philosophical
explanations as guidelines to understand why
people do what they do. You spend much
of your life searching for answers regarding human nature and how the condition of
humanity can be improved. This number-sign
combination can lead to having great faith in
the beyond, but it can often leave you with
despair about the condition of the world in which you live.

NOTABLES WITH THIS DEGREE:

Victor Hugo: French playwright, political leader, novelist, poet

Rudolf Steiner: Austrian philosopher, architect, author, scholar, esotericist

Elizabeth George: American mystery novelist

Elisabeth Welch: American singer, actress, entertainer

You are influenced by ideology in your approach to life matters. Contrary
to your Pisces personality, you can be unemotional and, to some, uncaring in
your decision making. It is not that you are necessarily inhuman; rather, you
are able to put policy ahead of heart, since it is what you believe that counts.
There is the karmic suggestion of having been responsible for much human
sacrifice and suffering in other times and places. One of the ways you defend
yourself against pain and memory is to philosophize about a condition rather
than admitting to your true feelings.

Underneath it all, you do care, and you experience a wide range of feelings common to all humans. Your search of faith and longing for connection
to experience may lead you to the stage or an art form as a platform to express
your inner emotions. You may have to cultivate humor or a more lighthearted
approach to living, since it is not natural to your personality makeup. Your
longing for the ideal can lead you to explore metaphysical and existential
philosophies.

8th Degree of Pisces

If this is your sun sign, your idealism and cherished dreams of utopia become quickly tempered in life by the reality of human endeavors that are so often overwhelmed with dysfunctional human behavior. You are too frustrated with the characteristics of this planet to be mired in such an amount of behavior. It is even more discouraging that most people do not seem to realize it, and if they do, choose to do little about it. You watch with hopeless angst as individual dysfunctional patterns permeate into the institutions

of society. Eventually, these institutions are governed by dysfunctional patterns and will do anything necessary to keep them in place in order to preserve the institution. There is a karmic hint that you have been highly responsible for emotional abuse and the perpetration of such behavior in a previous setting.

You want to be seen and heard. Unlike many Pisces who like to blame and complain, you will take the lead when your convictions are strong and your beliefs are confirmed. The conviction may result from the desperation of having seen your ideals and faith in others collapse under the strain of human weakness and the corruption of power. Your unusual drive may be unnerving to some who expect a more compliant personality. There can be a very detached compassion associated with this number-sign combination. You may have trouble defining exactly how you feel, so you put your frustration into action.

With unfavorable aspects, your assertiveness may just accentuate an already somewhat eccentric behavior pattern. Many of you will capitalize on your eccentricity and turn it into a plus, whereas the other Pisces hide theirs under a bushel. When favorably aspected, this combination has an effervescent element that dazzles and delights others with wisdom and well-thought-out treatises of life's many amazing metaphysical and existential complexities. You are attracted to legal issues, and many of you like to speculate about the nature of divine laws.

9th Degree of Pisces

If this is your sun sign, your experience is somewhat like being a double Pisces. You soar into the clouds of the sagacious, sanguine, saintly, and sublime. Alternatively, you also dive into the depths of depression, discouragement, and despair. You spend little time in the middle range of emotional moods. This ability to consciously render yourself on a regular basis to such a wide range of emotional variations can result in establishing a solid foundation of compassion and empathy for the plight of abuse, suffering, and stress that many humans experience. You are inclined to be idealistic and at times cling to utopian dreams of a perfectly loving and harmonious world.

NOTABLES WITH THIS DEGREE:

Irwin Shaw: American playwright, screenwriter, novelist

Linus Pauling: American chemist, peace activist, author, Nobel Prize laureate

Zero Mostel: American actor, comedian, political activist

There is a karmic suggestion that in another time sequence, you were involved in a philosophy that was of extremely high moral, ethical, and spiritual standards. Your participation and perception may have been so pure that you were unwilling or unable to recognize that there were members who espoused the ideals but exploited the naiveté and innocence of members for self-interest agendas and personal gain. By wanting to see the best in everyone, you may have been blind to their dark sides and exploitive practices. It is highly possible that someone with this number-sign combination was the first to look at the world through rose-colored glasses. Perhaps you ignored your own vulnerability to shades of shadow behavior lurking within yourself.

It is easy to lift yourself into expanded realms of consciousness, and each time you touch the stars, it can be more difficult to keep your feet planted solidly on the Earth plane. For some of you, there can be a kind of spiritual schizophrenia that you run away from the stress and ugly reality of the world by joining some reclusive order or way of life that does not confront the bad and ugly along with the good. You will have a broad range of human experience that enables you to better grasp the universal aspects of human nature. Out of empathy and concern, you could well be part of a group whose goal is to elevate the consciousness of the greater population.

10th Degree of Pisces

If this is your sun sign, the combination brings an upbeat and more optimistic quality to the sometimes-moody Pisces personality. Also, you are more inclined to be out front and take charge with more assertiveness than some of your Pisces brothers and sisters. You have that visionary trait and deep sense of connection to the collective angst and unconsciousness of humanity. Your sensitivity to social injustice can make you an ardent spokesperson for reformation and realignment of the power structure. There is the karmic suggestion that you have manipulated the emotions of others in another period of history. You have a particular pet peeve with the runaway egos that drive business, politics, and social programs.

NOTABLES WITH THIS DEGREE:

Marcello Borges: Brazilian engineer, astrologer, near-death survivor

Glenn Miller: American musician, composer, orchestra leader

Nicolaus Copernicus: Polish astronomer, mathematician, physician, scholar

Tony Robbins: American life coach, self-help guru, motivational speaker

This number-sign combination adds a flair of energy to the Pisces knack for drama and emotional display. It can leave you irritatingly melodramatic and hysterical. On the other hand, it can also represent the presence of an uncanny, almost performance-like sense of timing and elocution. When that occurs, you can have an enormous impact on those you are conveying your message or agenda to. You are able to take all of that stored wisdom and emotionally charged experience and put it together with a flash of brilliance. This is a good combination for people in advertising or motivational positions.

The Pisces personality tends to drift from one area of interest to another while experiencing difficulty when concentrating on a select focus. Unfortunately, with this combination, that tendency is perhaps even greater. Knowing this, you may want to place yourself in rapidly changing venues of work and interest that allow your adaptability and flair for change to be of benefit. Your depth of experience and capacity to travel in both this and other worlds give you an almost mystical touch to your poetic perception and altruistic aspirations for humanity. You can make the visions come true.

11ᵗʰ Degree of Pisces

If this is your sun sign, you are supple, swift, and clever in the ways of daily social give and take. You size things up and move ahead more deliberately than many of your Pisces contemporaries. Your competitiveness is cloaked in a disarming external persona that makes it more difficult to recognize just how determined you can be. You are sensitive to rules and regulations and believe everyone should follow them except when it suits your needs to transgress. You can be euphemistic about your own shortcomings while speaking critically about those who have the same.

There is the karmic hint of having been a bit of a prima donna in another time and setting. You enjoy the limelight and can be harsh with those who do not want to reflect in your glory. You are learning to be modest and sincere about both the extraordinary and ugly within your own human nature. You may find that working with the disadvantaged or sickly enables you to appreciate being healthy and perhaps gifted.

At some time, many of you will hobnob with the elite in your social circle. You have the power to persuade and may take up public speaking as an outlet for espousing your social views. Many of you find yourselves becoming politically active in hopes of bringing better change to the condition of life around you. Those with this number-sign combination tend toward the slender and may show proclivity toward physical activities. While this is not one of the most competitive combinations, once you set your goals for something, you can be determined and dogged in the pursuit of the trophy or prize. You enjoy status and place yourselves around people and situations in which there is an aura of confidence and getting things done. You look for good taste in your appearance but do like to make a statement.

NOTABLES WITH THIS DEGREE:

Desi Arnaz: Cuban-born American musician, actor, producer

Pope Leo XIII: Roman Catholic Pope, known as the Pope of the working man

Theodor Seuss Geisel: American author of Dr. Seuss books

Esther Cañadas: Spanish actress, supermodel

12th Degree of Pisces

If this is your sun sign, you are mystified by the unexpected demands and unusual requirements that are made of you by outside sources. You have honed excellent coping skills and handle things with pride and a sense of acquiescence. Many of you more than rise above the occasion and become very proficient at what you have chosen to do in life. You are inclined to be clever and original in the way that you do it. Many of you carry a chip on your shoulder, acting as if you must prove yourselves to society or a hidden someone.

NOTABLES WITH THIS DEGREE:

Hans Jurgen Eysenck: German psychologist, author

Julie Bowen: American actress

Jon Bon Jovi: American musician, singer-songwriter, actor

Sandra Reynolds: South African professional tennis player

There is a karmic hint of having been unable to get things done right in a previous life setting. Maybe you were embarrassed in front of a large number of people. Perhaps you failed to meet someone's expectations and were severely reprimanded. Possibly, the punishment was unfair or administered unjustly. There is the strong likelihood of repressed fear, anger, and very possibly elements of revenge running through your age-old memories. You feel driven, as if compelled, to prove yourself. One of many lessons to be learned from this number-sign combination is to be true to yourself; do what is closest to your heart and soul.

Your somewhat laid-back "aw, shucks" disposition can be cute and disarming to many people. You use it to open doors and set yourself up for future needs. You are intuitive and sense people's motives and worth in an instant. There is distrust inherent with this combination that can turn perception into paranoia when you get out of balance and let your negative, neurotic fears rule your emotions. For the most part, you get along easily with others and make your way through the social matrix with a low-key, off-the-radar subtly.

13th Degree of Pisces

If this is your sun sign, you are charming, cherished, and sometimes childish. There is a refreshing openness that goes with this number-sign combination. You seek life with verve and abandon, entering situations with an open heart and curious mind. For many of you, this can end with much disappointment and pain, especially in your early years. When you are up, your life is a dream and goes so well. When you are down, it is hard to pull yourself out of the tears and depression that come from being betrayed, abused, or simply used.

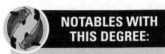

NOTABLES WITH THIS DEGREE:

Nicholas Campion: English historian, author, astrologer

Lucio Dalla: Italian songwriter, musician, actor

Carlos Surinach: Spanish composer, conductor

Many of you are inclined to have the "shoot yourself in the foot" syndrome. Just when things start to go well, you find a way to sabotage them. For example, you might end a good relationship or not go to an interview for a potentially good job. Maybe you are unwilling to audition for a part in the community choir, even though you have the best voice of anyone in the village. There is the karmic suggestion that in another time and setting, you did something so bad that you no longer believe you deserve to have anything good. Perhaps you were responsible for the loss of many lives, including those you loved. You punish yourself now by not allowing anything lovely to come into your life.

This combination blesses you with many unique talents and potential abilities. You may find it difficult to choose one in a pool of possibilities. Your charming appearance and gracious manner make you a social hit and welcomed guest wherever people gather. When you are at ease, you can be witty and fun while totally disarming people with your humor and compassion. Compassion is the name and service is the game. Just be sure you do not take care of others at the neglect of your own health, needs, and wants.

14th Degree of Pisces

If this is your sun sign, there is likely an element of transcendence about you that lifts you to hallowed heights of vision and artistry. From the stage of your sixth-grade class play to the writing of verse and rhythm for the world, you bring an extra dimension of wisdom and exhilaration to whatever you do. This number-sign combination embellishes the already inherent Pisces tendency toward intuitive wisdom and sensitivity to other worlds and realms of awareness. You are a seer and for some a healer. You see colors beyond the range of most people; you listen to the music of the spheres and revel in the riches of sacred geometry.

NOTABLES WITH THIS DEGREE:

P. D. Ouspensky: Russian philosopher, mathematician, metaphysician

Pope Paul II: Roman Catholic Pope, merchant

Bryan Cox: English physicist, scientific collaborator, musician

You strive to share your gifts with others and to encourage people to find their inner purpose and inherent talents. This can almost become an obsession. There is the karmic hint of having been given a special gift in another time and place. You may have taken it for granted, misused it, or perhaps failed to develop and honor it. Now you scramble to catch up with lost time and get it done right. Travel and intrigue come naturally, and you find yourself introduced to a wide variety of cultural and ethnic variety. Your knack for diversity makes it difficult to settle into one interest or routine.

There is a healing quality about you, whether it is through medicine, a kind voice, or maybe some form of alternative practice. You bring a new perspective into your science or study of the universe. Once you do find your heart's interest, this combination gives you the tools to knuckle down and get things done in the right way. This adds a more practical side of the Pisces tendency toward staying unfocused and far-out.

15ᵗʰ Degree of Pisces

If this is your sun sign, your life will include dramatic ups and downs and emotional tides. Your life fluctuates from overt sensual and intellectual overindulgence to periods of loneliness and social drought. You are interested in people but detached from real intimacy. You can use rather than be with the friends and associates who enter your life spectrum. It is characteristic of this number-sign combination to be less connected to your true feelings than many of your Pisces contemporaries. You are more curious about group dynamics than individual relationships. This does not deter you from some very intense personal encounters and relationships over the years.

NOTABLES WITH THIS DEGREE:

Larry W. Sonsini: American corporate lawyer, litigator

Bernard Arnault: French billionaire business mogul, art collector

Al-Waleed bin Talal: Saudi Arabian prince, billionaire investor

Élisabeth Badinter: French author, feminist, professor of philosophy

You wrestle with much subterranean angst and are riddled with unconscious tension. The karmic suggestion here is that you have at other times been a master manipulator of mass consciousness and have used knowledge to control rather than enlighten humankind. You are interested in entertainment and media and fascinated by the way they effect public reaction and social evolution. You see the potential for the use of media to enlighten or control mass consciousness. This is a combination of savvy, guts, and sometimes a lot of gall.

You are spirited, fun, and full of mischievous delight. It is difficult for friends and associates to guess what you will do next because you do not like to be put into a certain niche and become predictable. Your flair for change and inventiveness is recognized by contemporaries, and you may very well find yourself in places where invention, creativity, and innovation thrive. You enjoy the rush of risk and can be easily prone to gambling. You are often attracted to theoretical and alchemical research that leads to the transformation of the individual and the entire spectrum of human awareness.

16th Degree of Pisces

If this is your sun sign, your life will be filled with unaccountable undulations and enough twists of fate to make you want to write a novel — well, perhaps not for all of you. The aspects and houses play a big role in determining whether your kismet is to get kissed by the prince or kicked in the butt by the brash and daringly bold. Expect the unexpected, and then keep an eye out for the bizarre. This could mean many out-of-this-world experiences and a plate full of the improbable may come your way. The wonderful thing is that the universe provides you with what it takes to grow and benefit from your fabulous fate.

NOTABLES WITH THIS DEGREE:

Tammy Faye Bakker: American evangelist, gospel singer, television personality

Connie Britton: American actress, singer, producer

Anna Magnani: Italian actress

Moira Kelly: American violinist, actress

Franco Harris: American professional football player

There is a karmic hint of having been part of some major disappointment or perhaps severe adversity that put you into hot water with a lot of people. Maybe you were expected to give forewarning of a coming calamity but did not see it coming. Perhaps you spoke of a coming tragedy and people blamed you for causing it to happen. Possibly you forecasted the coming of some good news that did not take place as predicted. Now you find yourself second-guessing yourself and your intuition. You are compulsive in preparing yourself for being placed into a position of responsibility and worry about the outcome. You do not like to be wrong and become very uneasy and nervous about making mistakes.

Being around those with this number-sign combination can be quite an adventure. You are ahead of the curve and think outside of the box. Many of you live within subcultures on the fringe of conventional social discourse. Those of you who make an effort to fit into the routine of conventional thinking and living will often have a hidden unconventional interest or outlet.

17th Degree of Pisces

If this is your sun sign, you take on life with an underlying belief that things will work out well and the best of human nature will rise to the surface. You will most likely run into many setbacks with this outlook, especially in your early years. Your drive for success and desire to be on top of things can threaten others with less talent and motivation. You are often less moody and pessimistic than other members of the Pisces family. You may have a low tolerance for people who just can't seem to get a grip on things. Such a reaction can be surprising to those who expect your softhearted Pisces nature to bend and weep in sympathy.

NOTABLES WITH THIS DEGREE:

Luther Burbank: American botanist, horticulturalist

Bryan Cranston: American actor, screenwriter, director, producer

Mouloud Feraoun: French-Algerian writer

Gary Numan: English songwriter, musician, electro-pop pioneer

There is the karmic hint that in another life setting, you could have been rather heartless and insensitive to the emotional needs and suffering of those around you. Perhaps your desire to achieve some major accomplishment or attain a prominent goal was so important to you that it did not matter who you used or misused along the way. As long as you got your recognition, the human toll of despair was not of your concern. You are quite capable of going far and doing much. Along the way, you want to assist others to reach their dreams and realize their potential.

You are not averse to participating in the spoils of success, and you enjoy the trappings of luxury and prosperity. A little grandeur as you reach an elevated level of accomplishment just adds to the perks of being good at what you do. You display refinement of taste and a touch for choosing products of high caliber. It is always entertaining to be around notable people of achievement who have excelled in their chosen professions. You can be a little more cerebral than some of the other Pisces number-sign combinations and might find yourself around the academically elite if that is your chosen calling.

18th Degree of Pisces

If this is your sun sign, you ramble your way through a labyrinth and unusual collage of human experiences. Your natural Pisces intuition is fine-tuned to the undercurrents of consciousness in the mainstream of human endeavors. You search for the hidden and dance around the unknown. There is the constant concern of something lurking in the shadow spaces that is a threat and possible danger. It is not easy for those of you with this number-sign combination to trust other people — or your own emotions, for that matter. Your optimism is frequently subdued by the quiet concern that some intruding force will take away the good that is meant to be.

NOTABLES WITH THIS DEGREE:

David Wilcock: American author, filmmaker, futurist, consciousness consultant

Bobby Fischer: American chess grand master

Pope Paul III: Roman Catholic Pope, called for the Council of Trent

Ion Caramitru: Romanian actor, director, politician

There is the karmic hint of having had psychic access or premonitions in the past regarding what was to come. Maybe you were blamed for some calamity after having tried to warn others of impending danger. Perhaps you saw the potential negative impact in the intent of people in positions of power. You may have been punished or eliminated as a threat after speaking out. The gift of foreknowledge can be a mixed bag of blessings and back-aching despair. Such a gift can carry a load of responsibility with it. You seek the most appropriate way to develop and decipher this extended view into the cycles of time and travel.

Your natural flair for the ethereal and refined very frequently results in your introduction to very gifted and talented people who excel in their specialties of creativity and self-expression. You are poetic and profound, and you live pretty much on the precipice of advanced knowledge that can be inspirational to many. Many of you are found in the background influencing the transition and transformation of society. You may not be the frontrunner for change, but you will often have a heavy hand in positive social evolution.

19th Degree of Pisces

If this is your sun sign, you are idealistic, proud, inspirational, and deeply devoted to your vision of humankind. There are often strong religious or spiritual beliefs associated with this number-sign combination. Whatever denomination or creed you follow, you seek to find a way to live in harmony with your spiritual beliefs. For many of you, this will include opening the metaphysical door to delve into the origin and nature of humanity and the universe. You feel inspired and driven to fulfill some mission or destiny, and you will have a yearning within your heart until you feel you have discovered such.

NOTABLES WITH THIS DEGREE:

Chuck Norris: American actor, martial artist

Osama Bin Laden: Saudi Arabian militant, founder of Al-Qaeda

Camille Dalmais: French singer, songwriter, actress

Seiko Matsuda: Japanese pop singer-songwriter

The karmic suggestion here is that there have been previous lifetimes of blind faith and fanatical obedience to a creed or doctrine. You are learning to be more tolerant of others' beliefs. There can be much resistance to your spiritual progress if you attempt to impose your doctrine forcefully on others. There is a great attraction to rituals and routines that are designed to develop spiritual faith and strength. Many of you might quest into philosophy, physics, or other scientific pursuits that delve into the mysteries of creation and how things work on a universal level.

You enjoy relationships like anyone, but those who are with you will either have to share your zeal or be willing to give you a lot of space to pursue your dreams. You are generous and possess deep compassion for those near to you and humanity in general. You believe in the abundance of the giver and that under the right conditions of living, there is enough of what humanity really needs for everyone on the globe. This can also be a combination of those who seek abstinence and minimalist living conditions in the hopes that lack of material clutter will enhance spiritual receptivity.

20ᵗʰ Degree of Pisces

If this is your sun sign, you can be far beyond most of your Pisces family members and fine-tuned to the most subtle nature and needs within the collective unconscious of humanity. You are capable of stretching the already indecisive nature of the Pisces to its very limits. This could lead to both instability and major setbacks to your aspired growth. On the other hand, you may flux and flow amid the most divergent groups and collectives of souls with the utmost grace and finesse. You are capable of dancing delicately between the arbitrary duality constructs of humanity and piercing the veils of the many dimensions of the universe.

NOTABLES WITH THIS DEGREE:

Ralph Abernathy: American minister, civil rights activist

Olivia Wilde: American actress, accomplished journalist

Gianni Agnelli: Italian industrialist, principle Fiat shareholder

Douglas Adams: English author, humorist, dramatist

Quite a potential! The flipside is that your insecurities create doubt and the fear of plunging into the deeper dilemmas of spirit, mind, and the material world.

There is a karmic hint that you were blessed with similar spiritual potential and gifts in another soul setting of your evolution. Perhaps something went wrong, and your best of intentions were misinterpreted or contested and denied by a corrupt society. You might have been undermined by those in power and suffered for revealing your beautiful repository of wisdom and expanded awareness. You are now starting to remember the gifts, along with the karmic fear of the many things that went wrong in the evolution of your soul consciousness. You are starting to reconnect and develop your sensitivity to the higher vibrations of human awareness.

Those with this number-sign combination often exhibit a refined, aesthetic taste for the finer things in life. You seek harmony and encourage respectful interaction and dialogue among people. When out of sync, you can turn to artificial stimulants in an attempt to reach the other worlds that seem so near at hand. However, in the end, most of you find spiritual paths rather than artificial thrusts toward the light.

21st Degree of Pisces

If this is your sun sign, you carry a lyrical tune and walk a soulful walk wherever you go. It is pretty easy to read your moods, as you wear them right on your shoulder and make little attempt to be coy or complacent. You are colorful, quaint, and conversational. This number-sign combination can make you delight in having dialogues and discussions with one or many present. You are bursting with possibilities, and it can be difficult to focus on just one single interest. Most likely, whatever you find that moves your soul will very likely involve communications with a touch of entertainment thrown in to make your point more appealing.

NOTABLES WITH THIS DEGREE:

George Van Tassel: American author, paranormal researcher, UFO contactee

Liza Minnelli: American actress, singer, dancer

There is the karmic hint that in another life sequence, you may have been admonished or humiliated for being creative and outspoken. Possibly you spoke out against the prevailing leadership and elite of your time. Perhaps your ideas were just a little too advanced and ahead of the public's ability to grasp the meaning or see the truth that was contained within your message. You are learning to time yourself in such a way as to trust your inner conviction and soul guidance. At the same time, you are capable of keeping keenly attuned to the mood of the masses. You know when to reach out and how to get your message across with the greatest of ease and effectiveness.

You enjoy company and host social, and sometimes administrative, events with some regularity. An easygoing and gregarious nature allows you to solicit valuable information from those with whom you interact. You are skilled at networking and bring together people who have common goals and similar interests. This can be a valuable asset when working to bring about cooperation and the betterment of human conditions.

22nd Degree of Pisces

If this is your sun sign, you feel driven as if you have some cause or destiny to achieve. Your life's work and what you accomplish occupies much of your time and attention. You become enmeshed in human affairs and will likely find yourself at some time seeped in the life of institutional politics. This may be related to traditional politics, commerce, religion, or civil affairs. It is easy for you to find a cause and spend most of your life in the pursuit of bringing about right from wrong. There is the karmic hint that in another time, you did not follow through with the finishing touches of a project that would have saved many lives. This involved the loss of life and the loss of face.

NOTABLES WITH THIS DEGREE:

Alfred Abel: German actor, producer, director

Vaslav Nijinsky: Russian ballet dancer, choreographer

Yann Arthus-Bertrand: French photographer, journalist, environmentalist

William H. Macy Jr.: American actor, director, screenwriter

You can be almost too sensitive to the collective unconscious, which makes you want to pull in your intuitive antenna in order to have some privacy of mind and soul. Much emotional information goes into your inner being but less comes out. You are able to touch others through your oratory because you can talk about inner feelings in a collective manner. However, when it comes to addressing your own personal crises, you are inclined to follow the same behaviors that you help your constituency avoid.

Those with this number-sign combination are often called into public action. Although you crave spending more time thinking about things of heaven and the universe, you are called on to deal with very pragmatic matters of Earth. The pressure of keeping things in order in this physical reality takes its toll on your health and well-being. You give for the sake of others and can be negligent about nurturing your own body and mind. Those who share a relationship with you will have to understand that your destiny can take you unexpectedly from home and hearth to render aid to strangers. All that aside, you do make a good, sincere partner and family member.

23rd Degree of Pisces

If this is your sun sign, you do not like to be bound by the normal rules and restraints of convention. Many of you will choose a more rebellious stance toward the status quo of your time and place. Whatever your chosen attitude toward life, you are likely to be noticed. The upside of this number-sign combination is the possibility to become noted for advancement and discovery. The downside of this combination is a built-in tendency toward excess and self-destruction through the refusal to cooperate when it would be to your advantage to accept outside assistance. There is a kind of childlike, explorative attitude toward life, and you can get yourself into some rather cute mischief. However, sometimes this goes too far for social convention, and you could find yourself as the source of controversy and dubious behavior.

NOTABLES WITH THIS DEGREE:

Dana Delany: American actress, producer, health activist

Albert Einstein: German theoretical physicist, scientist, mathematician

Emile Hirsch: American actor

Jimmy Swaggart: American televangelist, pastor, musician

There is a karmic hint that in another time and setting, you may have had privy to valuable information that could have benefited the masses. Maybe you withheld or protected information that you thought might have led to the population getting out of control. Perhaps you represented an organization or institution that would be weakened by the release of such information. Possibly you were in a position to place unnecessary restraints on other people and their free pursuit of life's opportunities. It is a tough quandary attempting to determine when and how to give explosive new material to the mass consciousness.

You are one to question life and existence. You enjoy being around friends and associate with those who are able to live life to the fullest and take in the many pleasures this Earth provides. It is not easy for you to stay emotionally attached to any one person or position. Your quest for experience leads you into many sensual adventures and possible misadventures. It is simply difficult to put restraints on people with this combination because it is not so easy for you to keep yourselves contained.

NUMEROLOGY OF ASTROLOGY

24ᵗʰ Degree of Pisces

If this is your sun sign, you will find yourself working with people and for people in some form of service-oriented endeavor. Your caring nature and awareness of human frailty makes you a natural at rendering aid and assistance. You can carry the weight of too many people on your shoulders. Because of your sensitivity and concern for others, it is easy for you to get involved with other people's problems and concerns. Many of you will end up in a counseling or caregiving community of some type. Once you have learned to set the proper boundaries, you will be able to maintain your own priorities and purpose in proper perspective.

NOTABLES WITH THIS DEGREE:

Andrew Jackson: American president, lawyer, military commander

Judd Hirsch: American actor

Sylvie Noachovitch: French actress, consumer advocate

Victor Emmanuel II: first king of united Italy

There is the karmic suggestion that in another time, you were exploitive of human weakness for your own gain. There is still a part of you now that can easily do this. However, having become aware of that pattern, you strive to be of service rather than take advantage of others. You might be found among charitable or philanthropic organizations in which many serve to help others. This could be a number-sign combination of labor leaders and political activists oriented toward the working class and their rights. You are emotionally strong and driven to get things done right.

Your skills at mediation are prominent throughout your life, and you may be the center point of your vocation. You see the waste and misuse of human resources, and you strive to improve efficiency and productivity while keeping the needs of the working class in mind. On a personal note, you want to be cautious about becoming compulsive regarding simple daily routines of living. Too much control and rigidity can rob you of wonderful, spontaneous human experiences. You are appreciated for your flair for good timing and good taste in circles in which culture and refinement are given special attention.

25th Degree of Pisces

If this is your sun sign, you are a bit of a free spirit caught in a time when false values and social norms are thrust on you with almost hostile intent. You sometimes verge on the threshold of rebellion, as the social pressure seems intent on crushing the individual spirit within you and those around you. There is a karmic suggestion of having been caught up in the fanaticism of group thinking that led to much disruption and upheaval of social order. You have many issues with social injustice and are intent on finding the right group or organization where you can use your talents to be a part of social reformation.

NOTABLES WITH THIS DEGREE:

Jerry Lewis: American comedian, actor, singer, producer

J. Z. Knight: American channel, spiritual leader, author

Rudolf Nureyev: Russian dancer

Nat King Cole: American singer, musician

Those of you with this number-sign combination can possess a flair for drama, finding you actors and performers on the stage of life. Entertainment could well become one of the avenues you take to spread your message of transformation to humanity. You are sensitive to more subtle and harmonious ways that humanity can live together. You are attuned to the life principles of the spheres and suffer when you see chaos and abuse among humankind. When you dance with the angels, it is not so easy to stumble around the floor with a sleeping population.

Your colorful and dynamic personality can be a magnet to attract the right people and a place where you are a part of a team whose purpose is the transformation of human personality. Humor and the childlike play of a pure soul can be good medicine for those who are tainted by the corruption and dysfunction that monopolizes human consciousness at this time.

26th Degree of Pisces

If this is your sun sign, you can be crafty, cunning, and convivial as you go about getting things done. Those with this number-sign combination like power and being in charge. However, you may not be as direct or overbearing in your show of force as some of the other more aggressive signs. In fact for many of you, the power may be indirect, and you might use another as your spokesperson. This would be the proverbial "power behind the throne" syndrome. When in power, you may be known more for your diplomatic prowess. Much of your accomplishments might be done through good-old-boy practices and behind-closed-doors collaboration. You can be very concerned about public image, which could lead to some snags in your attempts to persuade and convince others of your intent.

There is the karmic hint of having been an inspirational leader or part of a popular and charismatic sociopolitical movement in another life setting. Maybe you were idealistic and outspoken, but you were undermined by more crafty and devious practitioners of power. Perhaps you took the fall for someone else's mishandling of the political processes of the time. You are quick to distrust dealing within groups and are more comfortable going one-on-one when it comes to hard negotiations. You sometimes become lost trying to meet the needs and demands of the many, and you are learning to follow your higher guidance in all of your affairs.

While quite agile in the theory of leadership, you may not be the best administrator when it comes to handling organizational matters and dealing with the details of administration. You may benefit by collaborating in such matters and employing skilled administrators to assist with daily functions. In your relaxed moments, you enjoy humor and lighthearted discussions with trusted associates. Your personal life and family matters are often more of a challenge than they are blissful, but there is a compassionate side that pays attention to the needs of those close to you.

27th Degree of Pisces

If this is your sun sign, you are refined, reflective, and ready to be a part of improving the planet. When it comes to being far-out, this number-sign combination of the Pisces family is quite capable of stepping way out there. You long for a world of substance and spiritual strength, and you can become easily annoyed or even depressed with the superficiality and lack of wisdom currently manifesting on this Earth. It is easy to be troubled by the waste of resources, both human and natural. You cling to high ideals and dreams of a possible paradise for all.

You may have gone through a similar dance in a previous life scenario. An idealistic streak runs deep in your blood. You

NOTABLES WITH THIS DEGREE:

Manly P. Hall: Canadian author, mystic

Mia Hamm: American Olympic soccer player, author

Grover Cleveland: American president, lawyer

Vanessa Williams: American singer, actress, producer, model

Nikolai Rimsky-Korsakov: Russian composer, sailor

have tried to bring paradise to the world before. Perhaps you were part of a belief or congregation of well-intended souls who held to high ideals, but you were short on emotional connection to the needs of humanity. You may have espoused a doctrine of purity and perfection but simply were not attuned to very basic human concerns about security, family ties, and the duties of daily living. You were woefully unprepared to deal with the gross, ugly, and particularly evil side of human nature. This is the time to integrate both the dark side and highest attributes of yourself. Suddenly you will find that it is much easier to touch the hearts of others.

Your poetic personality takes you on flights of love and laughter, and you experience many lively moments amid the squalor and dysfunctional corners of human neglect. It is not so easy for you to do hands-on work in the trenches of debauchery, as you are more comfortable up in the tower tossing roses and missives of hope and encouragement. Many of you have decidedly developed artistic and creative talents, and you put your talent to work by creating masterpieces that reach deep into the human psyche, inspiring the noble and pure to rise to the surface.

28th Degree of Pisces

If this is your sun sign, you long for an eternal mate and seek to find a means of trusting your emotions when dealing with matters of the heart. You delicately weave your way through relationships by trying to please others. Your insecurity can mask the strength of your will and tendency to want to be the top dog even when you may not have the top skills or best data. When you are at your best, you have the facts at hand, the drive to do, and the conviction to bring out the best in those who assist you. Together you can achieve much success.

NOTABLES WITH THIS DEGREE:

Edgar Cayce: American healer, intuitive, channel, theologian

Ursula Andress: Swiss-American actress, Bond girl

Glenn Close: American actress

Adolf Eichmann: German military officer

There is a karmic hint that in another soul setting, you might have been inspired by dreams and idealistic fervor. There is the suggestion that you took things on faith too many times and experienced too many failures. Maybe you went by faith and without facts. Perhaps you put all of your trust in someone else's dream without knowing their credentials or capability. As you become centered once more in your knowing, you will find the right people and acquire the proper training that prepares you for the challenging task in front of you.

This number-sign combination is often out in front of the masses when it comes to seeing clearly the signposts of what is to come. You can quickly rally enthusiasm among the crowd and get people doing things that need to be done. You may choose to use your flair for drama to emphasize the importance of the task at hand. Although it is not your favorite tactic, you are willing to enter into small talk as a way of slowly bringing your doubters and skeptics around to seeing your way. They may be caught off-guard when you burst into a commanding mode and take over the moment.

29th Degree of Pisces

If this is your sun sign, you can take ideal- ism to an extreme. There are many utopians and futurists among this group. The upside of this number-sign combination yields the visionaries and architects of future human evolution. The downside yields time-wasting dreamers, schemers, and unaccomplished wheeler-dealers. It is difficult for you to stay grounded in the here and now. You travel all over the realms of consciousness, often into unseen worlds and domains of other dimen-

NOTABLES WITH THIS DEGREE:

John Travolta: American actor, dancer, singer

Patrick McGoohan: American-Irish actor

William Jennings Bryan: American orator, politician, lawyer

sions. This combination can yield a delightful and slightly skewed sense of humor with an ironic grasp of human foibles. At your best, you can weave wondrous tales of drama and intrigue.

There is a karmic suggestion of previous misplaced idealism. You may have gotten involved with organizations that espoused lofty intentions but deteriorated into misleading and probably destructive results. You can become fanatical and extreme to a fault. On the other hand, your grasp of the future enables you to see things coming far in advance of the masses. It is essential that you deliberately take steps to keep yourself grounded and focused on the immediate reality in which you function.

If you are spooked by talk of realms and dimensions, just think of it as having a rich imagination. Many fantasy authors, poets, and artists have this combination. It can be difficult to keep your feet on the ground and attention focused on ordinary events of everyday living. You long to be spiritual and, at the extreme, loathe this material body. Drugs and alcohol can be a tempt- ing alternative to escape the monotony of existence. Once you decide to par- ticipate in the everyday work, you are likely to get involved in current social issues through which you can make the world a better place to live.

Afterthoughts

As I was finishing up this text, someone asked me to read the information about a popular personality from the past to see if the writing seemed to fit. I had previously checked the date of birth to determine that person's degree. The information given was most revealing regarding that person's character. However, on further observation, I noticed that I had mistakenly given the date of death rather than birth.

Perhaps this was one of those serendipitous moments that leads to a breakthrough of interpretative insight. Out of curiosity, I started to look up the death dates of some other notables of times past. Several times, it was like reading an epitaph — although not always flattering — summarizing key aspects of that person's life.

It only makes metaphysical sense that there could be additional revelation provided by this means. Since the date of birth is chosen by our higher self, it seems very likely that so too is our date of death. The stars and cycles of numbers may have a way of leaving a parting word for us as we pass on to yet another stage in the journey of the soul.

I invite the curious and inquisitive to further explore this phenomenon to see if it leads to repeated accuracy, opening the door to yet another way of assessing our progression of soul growth. My intuition tells me there is something to this procedure that merits greater consideration. Now, it does not seem to be my destiny to put in the time and effort to make that determination, as other opportunities appear to be calling. Perhaps you, the reader, will be the one who takes it a step further. For a couple examples, go to the Scorpio and Taurus chapters and read the following degrees for these historic figures:

John F. Kennedy: 29th Degree of Scorpio (at death)

J. Edgar Hoover: 12th Degree of Taurus (at death)

About the Author

Lynn Buess, MA, EdS, has been active in the self-awareness movement for over one half of a century. Forty years ago in 1973, his master's thesis was published as his first book, *The Tarot and Transformation*. This book was one of the first of its kind to look at tarot in a way other than as a set of static symbols. Rather, he approached the symbolism as it depicted the living challenges and tests of progression along the path from self consciousness to cosmic consciousness. The book was a popular seller, particularly through the active era of New Age awareness in the 1980s.

During the 1960s and 1970s, Lynn also became an ardent student and practitioner of numerology. In 1977, he introduced a vastly expanded perspective of the psychology, cosmology, and spirituality of numerology with the publication of his second book, *Numerology for the New Age*. That book is the published version of his research paper for his EdS degree from the psychological counseling department of a well-known southern university.

During the 1970s, Lynn also became active in numerous forms of alternative healing and therapy. As a result of this experience, he was the originator of an alternative psychospiritual therapy technique known as Synergy Session. In 1980, he published his third book of the very same name. That groundbreaking volume combined skills from psychotherapy, past-life regression, crystal healing, etheric meridian, and chakra and aura attunement. All of these tools of transformation are incorporated into an intense, life-altering session of release and revelation.

One of Lynn's greatest personal breakthroughs in self-understanding came in the early 1980s when he realized the effects of personality development in adult children of alcoholism. As a result of the immense recognition of the benefit of the Adult Children of Alcholoics (ACOA) modality, Lynn penned *Children of Light, Children of Darkness* in 1990. This volume was a revelation for droves of seekers in the consciousness movement who used many of the alternative schools of thought and practices as a means to avoid deeply hidden issues of dysfunction and abuse.

In 2012 came *The Heart of Numerology*, which he considers his *magnum opus* for students and practitioners of numerology. This volume is a summation of wisdom and learning acquired from his nearly fifty years of study and practice of numerology, including over 50,000 personal sessions.

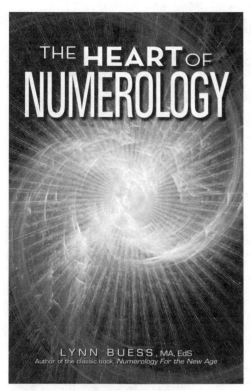

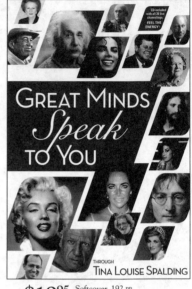

through Cheryl Gaer Barlow

Angels Explain Death and Prayer

ANGELS EXPLAIN
Death
AND
Prayer

through Cheryl Gaer Barlow

$16.95 • Softcover, 224 PP.
6 X 9 Perfect Bound
ISBN 978-1-62233-008-9

"We are the angels of the Mallbon. We are meant to tell those of Earth that the death of the body is never to be feared. We help in ways not understood by humanity. We can manifest anything we desire. We can live as humans on Earth. When we absorb the reality of Earth, we work God's wonders in ordinary ways.

"When the surroundings are not in focus or when you feel unable to cope with the people or circumstances around you, be still and ask God for help. God will respond to requests of help by mending emotions with aid from the angels. This is done by being aware of the angels. We surround you and bring you comfort.

"You must, as a human race, lift the quality of thought to the highest level. When the level of thought is low and miserable, it is generated through the entire world. When it is lifted to a level of joy, it lifts all minds. When you know the teachings of the angels, no ignorance will be left in the soul. You will no longer be afraid or in pain. Now is the time to stand with the angels of God and help humankind."
— The Mallbon Angels

Chapters Include:
- The Soul's Path
- The Death of Children
- Meeting God
- Dreams
- Birth on Earth
- Entering the Heavens
- The Joy That Awaits You
- Bonus: Prayer Guide!

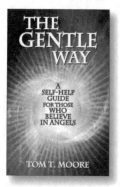

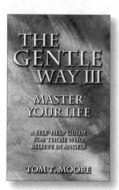

THE **ANCIENT SECRET**
OF THE **FLOWER** OF **LIFE**
VOLUME **2**

Chapters Include:

- The Unfolding of the Third Informational System
- Whispers from Our Ancient Heritage
- Unveiling the Mer-Ka-Ba Meditation
- Using Your Mer-Ka-Ba
- Connecting to the Levels of Self
- Two Cosmic Experiments
- What We May Expect in the Forthcoming Dimensional Shift

$25⁰⁰ Softcover, 252 PP.
ISBN 978-1-891824-21-0

The sacred Flower of Life pattern, the primary geometric generator of all physical form, is explored in even more depth in this volume, the second half of the famed Flower of Life workshop. The proportions of the human body; the nuances of human consciousness; the sizes and distances of the stars, planets, and moons; and even the creations of humankind are all shown to reflect their origins in this beautiful and divine image. Through an intricate and detailed geometrical mapping, Drunvalo Melchizedek shows how the seemingly simple design of the Flower of Life contains the genesis of our entire third-dimensional existence.

From the pyramids and mysteries of Egypt to the new race of Indigo children, Drunvalo presents the sacred geometries of the reality and the subtle energies that shape our world. We are led through a divinely inspired labyrinth of science and stories, logic and coincidence, on a path of remembering where we come from and the wonder and magic of who we are.

Finally, for the first time in print, Drunvalo shares the instructions for the Mer-Ka-Ba meditation, step-by-step techniques for the re-creation of the energy field of the evolved human, which is the key to ascension and the next dimensional world. If done from love, this ancient process of breathing prana opens up for us a world of tantalizing possibility in this dimension, from protective powers to the healing of oneself, of others, and even of the planet.

Phone: 928-526-1345 or 1-800-450-0985 • Fax: 928-714-1132

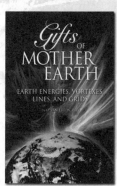

✦ Light Technology PUBLISHING

THE EXPLORER RACE SERIES

ZOOSH AND HIS FRIENDS THROUGH ROBERT SHAPIRO

The series: Humans — creators-in-training — have a purpose and destiny so heartwarmingly, profoundly glorious that it is almost unbelievable from our present dimensional perspective. Humans are great light-beings from beyond this creation, gaining experience in dense physicality. This truth about the great human genetic experiment of the Explorer Race and the mechanics of creation is being revealed for the first time by Zoosh and his friends through superchannel Robert Shapiro. These books read like adventure stories as we follow the clues from this creation that we live in out to the Council of Creators and beyond.

❶ THE EXPLORER RACE

Those of you reading this are truly a result of the genetic experiment on Earth. You are beings who uphold the principles of the Explorer Race. The key to empowerment in these days is to not know everything about your past but to know what will help you now. You are constantly being given responsibilities by the Creator that would normally be things that Creator would do. The responsibility and the destiny of the Explorer Race is not only to explore but to create. **574 PP. $25.00 ISBN 13: 978-0-929385-38-9**

❷ ETs and the EXPLORER RACE

In this book, Robert channels Joopah, a Zeta Reticulan now in the ninth dimension who continues the story of the great experiment—the Explorer Race—from the perspective of his civilization. The Zetas would have been humanity's future selves had humanity not re-created the past and changed the future. **237 PP. $14.95 ISBN 13: 978-0-929385-79-2**

❸ EXPLORER RACE: ORIGINS and the NEXT 50 YEARS

This volume has so much information about who we are and where we came from — the source of male and female beings, the war of the sexes, the beginning of the linear mind, feelings, the origin of souls — it is a treasure trove. In addition, there is a section that relates to our near future — how the rise of global corporations and politics affects our future, how to use benevolent magic as a force of creation, and how we will go out to the stars and affect other civilizations. Astounding information. **339 PP. $14.95 ISBN 13: 978-0-929385-95-2**

❹ EXPLORER RACE: CREATORS and FRIENDS, the MECHANICS of CREATION

Now that you have a greater understanding of who you are in the larger sense, it is necessary to remind you of where you came from, the true magnificence of your being. You must understand that you are creators-in-training, and yet you were once a portion of Creator. This book will allow you to understand the vaster qualities and help you remember the nature of the desires that drive any creator, the responsibilities to which a creator must answer, the reaction a creator must have to consequences, and the ultimate reward of any creator. **435 PP. $19.95 ISBN 13: 978-1-891824-01-2**

❺ EXPLORER RACE: PARTICLE PERSONALITIES

All around you in every moment you are surrounded by the most magical and mystical beings. They are too small for you to see individually, but in groups, you know them as the physical matter of your daily life. These particles might be considered either atoms or portions of atoms who consciously view the vast spectrum of reality yet also have a sense of personal memory like your own linear memory. Some of the particles we hear from are Gold, Mountain Lion, Liquid Light, Uranium, the Great Pyramid's Capstone, This Orb's Boundary, Ice, and Ninth-Dimensional Fire. **237 PP. $14.95 ISBN 13: 978-0-929385-97-6**

❻ EXPLORER RACE and BEYOND

With a better idea of how creation works, we go back to the Creator's advisers and receive deeper and more profound explanations of the roots of the Explorer Race. The liquid Domain and the Double Diamond portal share lessons given to the roots on their way to meet the Creator of this universe, and the roots speak of their origins and their incomprehensibly long journey here. **360 PP. $14.95 ISBN 13: 978-1-891824-06-7**

Zoosh and His Friends through Robert Shapiro

⑦ EXPLORER RACE: COUNCIL of CREATORS

The thirteen core members of the Council of Creators discuss their adventures in coming to awareness of themselves and their journeys on the way to the Council on this level. They discuss the advice and oversight they offer to all creators, including the Creator of this local universe. These beings are wise, witty, and joyous, and their stories of Love's Creation create an expansion of our concepts as we realize that we live in an expanded, multiple-level reality.
273 PP. $14.95 ISBN 13: 978-1-891824-13-5

⑧ EXPLORER RACE and ISIS

This is an amazing book! It has priestess training, shamanic training, Isis's adventures with Explorer Race beings — before Earth and on Earth — and an incredibly expanded explanation of the dynamics of the Explorer Race. Isis is the prototypal loving, nurturing, guiding feminine being, the focus of feminine energy. She has the ability to expand limited thinking without making people with limited beliefs feel uncomfortable. She is a fantastic storyteller, and all of her stories are teaching stories. If you care about who you are, why you are here, where you are going and what life is all about—pick up this book. You won't lay it down until you are through, and then you will want more.
304 PP. $14.95 ISBN 13: 978-1-891824-11-1

⑨ EXPLORER RACE and JESUS

The core personality of that being known on Earth as Jesus, along with his students and friends, describes with clarity and love his life and teaching 2,000 years ago. He states that his teaching is for all people of all races in all countries. Jesus announces here for the first time that he and two others, Buddha and Mohammed, will return to Earth from their place of being in the near future, and a fourth being, a child already born now on Earth, will become a teacher and prepare humanity for their return. So heartwarming and interesting, you won't want to put it down.
327 PP. $16.95 ISBN 13: 978-1-891824-14-2

⑩ EXPLORER RACE: EARTH HISTORY and LOST CIVILIZATIONS

Speaks of Many Truths and Zoosh, through Robert Shapiro, explain that planet Earth, the only water planet in this solar system, is on loan from Sirius as a home and school for humanity, the Explorer Race. Earth's recorded history goes back only a few thousand years, its archaeological history a few thousand more. Now this book opens up as if a light was on in the darkness, and we see the incredible panorama of brave souls coming from other planets to settle on different parts of Earth. We watch the origins of tribal groups and the rise and fall of civilizations, and we can begin to understand the source of the wondrous diversity of plants, animals, and humans that we enjoy here on beautiful Mother Earth.
310 PP $14.95 ISBN 13: 978-1-891824-20-3

⑪ EXPLORER RACE: ET VISITORS SPEAK

Even as you are searching the sky for extraterrestrials and their spaceships, ETs are here on planet Earth—they are stranded, visiting, exploring, studying the culture, healing Earth of trauma brought on by irresponsible mining, or researching the history of Christianity over the past 2,000 years. Some are in human guise, and some are in spirit form. Some look like what we call animals as they come from the species' home planet and interact with their fellow beings — those beings who we have labeled cats or cows or elephants. Some are brilliant cosmic mathematicians with a sense of humor; they are presently living here as penguins. Some are fledgling diplomats training for future postings on Earth when we have ET embassies here. In this book, these fascinating beings share their thoughts, origins, and purposes for being here. 340 PP. $14.95 ISBN 13: 978-1-891824-28-9

⑫ EXPLORER RACE: TECHNIQUES for GENERATING SAFETY

Wouldn't you like to generate safety so you could go wherever you need to go and do whatever you need to do in a benevolent, safe, and loving way for yourself? Learn safety as a radiated environment that will allow you to gently take the step into the new timeline, into a benevolent future, and away from a negative past. 177 PP. $9.95 ISBN 13: 978-1-891824-26-5